Make Memories All Year Long With Unforgettable Fare

HOLIDAYS are special moments to gather with family, catch up with close friends and appreciate the blessings in our lives. A special spread of home-cooked foods helps make the occasion more joyful and the memories more vivid.

That's why we're pleased to present *Taste of Home's Holiday & Celebrations 2005*. This photo-filled treasury features 264 mouth-watering recipes to make your Christmas, Thanksgiving, Easter and other celebrations throughout the year even more memorable. We've done the planning, offered menu options and provided timetables so entertaining is easy and enjoyable.

'Tis the Season. Take the worry out of what to make for every holiday happening with this chapter's 122 dazzling dishes, including Peppery Beef Roast, Sweet Potato Bake, Herb Potato Rolls and Cappuccino Torte. Check out the scrumptious selection of speedy sweet treats like Crispy Peanut Butter Truffles and Raspberry Cheesecake Pie. We also present three complete menus—a formal Yuletide dinner...a casual Christmas buffet...a merry mid-morning brunch.

Giving Thanks. Looking for ways to liven up your standard Thanksgiving meals? Guests will fall for Fruit-Glazed Turkey when paired with an assortment of sides, including Asparagus Pea Medley, Cheesy Corn Casserole and Savory Orange Dressing. Cranberries—a staple in fall cooking—are featured in delightful dishes like Cranberry Spinach Salad and Mallow Cranberry Cheesecake. Warm up with steaming bowls of soups such as Potato Clam Chowder and Hearty Vegetable Soup.

Easter Gatherings. The party of six at your Easter table will have a spring in their step after sampling Cilantro-Lime Pork Chops and Easter Nest Torte. Or tuck homemade confections like Chocolate Popcorn Balls, Caramel Cashew Clusters and Marbled Orange Fudge into the kids' colorful Easter baskets.

Special Celebrations. Occasions throughout the year also call for special celebrations. Get the year going by hosting an elegant surf-and-turf New Year's Eve party. As spring approaches, plan a special meal for Passover. Celebrate two special people—mom and the graduate—with gatherings in their honor. In the heat of the summer, enjoy a refreshing July Fourth ice cream social or a tropical Hawaiian luau. Then bewitch family and friends with a "spook-tacular" Halloween bash!

Can-Do Decorating Ideas. There are dozens of ideas for stunning centerpieces (turn to page 23 for a Blooming Gift Boxes display), fun food crafts (like the Gingerbread Candle Holders on page 111) and eye-catching napkin folds (see page 163 for Rose Napkin Blossoms).

With flavorful fare, easy decorating ideas and perfect party menus, *Taste of Home's Holiday & Celebrations Cookbook 2005* will help you make entertaining fun for you...and unforgettable for your family!

WOULD YOU like to see one of your family-favorite recipes featured in a future edition of this timeless treasury? See page 256 for details!

Taste of Home's HOLIDAY *&* Celebrations COOKBOOK 2005

Senior Editor: Julie Schnittka
Senior Art Director: Linda Dzik
Assistant Food Editor: Karen Scales
Craft Editor: Jane Craig
Executive Editor, Books: Heidi Reuter Lloyd
Food Editor: Janaan Cunningham
Associate Editor: Jean Steiner
Proofreader: Julie Blume
Editorial Assistant: Barb Czysz
Graphic Art Associates: Ellen Lloyd, Catherine Fletcher
Associate Food Editors: Coleen Martin, Diane Werner
Senior Recipe Editor: Sue A. Jurack
Recipe Editors: Janet Briggs, Mary King
Test Kitchen Director: Mark Morgan
Test Kitchen Home Economists: Peggy Fleming, Nancy Fridirici, Tina Johnson, Ann Liebergen, Annie Rose, Pat Schmeling, Wendy Stenman, Amy Welk-Thieding
Test Kitchen Assistants: Suzanne Kern, Rita Krajcir, Kris Lehman, Sue Megonigle, Megan Taylor
Food Photographers: Rob Hagen, Dan Roberts
Set Stylists: Julie Ferron, Stephanie Marchese, Sue Myers, Jennifer Bradley Vent
Food Stylists: Kristin Arnett, Sarah Thompson, Joylyn Trickel
Photographers Assistant: Lori Foy
Senior Vice President, Editor in Chief: Catherine Cassidy
President: Barbara Newton
Chairman and Founder: Roy Reiman

Taste of Home Books
©2005 Reiman Media Group, Inc.
5400 S. 60th St., Greendale WI 53129
International Standard Book Number: 0-89821-456-4
International Standard Serial Number: 1535-2781
All rights reserved.
Printed in U.S.A.

For additional copies of this book, write *Taste of Home* Books, P.O. Box 908, Greendale WI 53129. Or to order by credit card, call toll-free 1-800/344-2560 or visit our Web site at **www.reimanpub.com**.

PICTURED ON THE COVER: Stuffed Crown Roast of Pork (p. 18) and Green Beans with Cashews (p. 21).

'TIS THE
Season

From formal dinners, casual meals and mid-morning
brunches to planning appetizers for a card-writing
party, baking breads and making an assortment of sweet
treats, the Christmas season is bustling with a slew of
activities. Take the worry out of what to make for
all of your holiday happenings by turning to this
chapter's appealing assortment of appetizers, side dishes,
breads, entrees and desserts. There's even a special
section devoted to just gingerbread!

'TIS THE Season

A Merry Christmas Morning

ON CHRISTMAS MORNING, it's hard to know what folks will anticipate more...opening presents or sitting down to the breath-taking breakfast pictured at right!

An early-day Yuletide gathering is easy when you make Fruit Salad with Citrus Yogurt Sauce and Mini Cherry Muffins. That's because both of these dishes can be prepared the night before.

And with the flurry of the day's activity, folks won't have to scramble to prepare Cheese and Sausage Strudels. See the make-ahead features for this recipe on page 9.

So make mugs of your favorite hot chocolate and call your hungry clan to the table on Christmas morning with this bright-eyed brunch!

EARLY-DAY DINING

Cheese and Sausage
Strudels (p. 9)

Mini Cherry Muffins (p. 8)

Fruit Salad with Citrus
Yogurt Sauce (p. 8)

Fruit Salad with Citrus Yogurt Sauce

(Pictured at right and on page 7)

*Making this fruit salad the night before gives me one less thing to think about
during the rush of gift opening on Christmas morning.*
— *Wanda Peterson, Lindsay, Ontario*

3/4 cup water
1/2 cup sugar
1/2 cup orange juice
1/4 cup lemon juice
　1 teaspoon grated orange peel
　2 tablespoons orange liqueur,
　　optional
　2 medium kiwifruit, peeled,
　　sliced and halved
　2 medium ripe pears, peeled
　　and chopped
　2 medium Red Delicious
　　apples, chopped
　2 medium navel oranges, peeled
　　and sectioned
　2 cups seedless red grapes,
　　halved

　1 medium pink grapefruit, peeled and sectioned
CITRUS YOGURT SAUCE:
　1 cup plain yogurt
　2 tablespoons brown sugar
　2 tablespoons sour cream
　1 teaspoon grated orange peel
1/2 teaspoon vanilla extract

For syrup, combine the first five ingredients in a large saucepan; bring to a boil. Reduce heat; simmer, uncovered, for 10 minutes. Cool; stir in orange liqueur if desired.

In a large bowl, combine the kiwi, pears, apples, oranges, grapes and grapefruit; add syrup and gently toss. Cover and refrigerate overnight. In a small bowl, combine sauce ingredients. Cover and refrigerate overnight.

Serve fruit salad with a slotted spoon; drizzle with yogurt sauce. **Yield:** 8-10 servings.

Mini Cherry Muffins

(Pictured above right and on page 6)

*These pretty muffins from our Test Kitchen are perfect for Christmas morning.
Make them the night before and keep on the counter in an airtight container.*

3/4 cup butter, softened
3/4 cup sugar
　1 egg
1/2 cup plain yogurt
1/2 teaspoon almond extract
　1 cup all-purpose flour
1/4 teaspoon baking soda
1/4 teaspoon salt
1/2 cup red candied cherries,
　　chopped

In a small mixing bowl, cream butter and sugar. Beat in the egg, yogurt and extract. Combine the flour, baking soda and salt; stir into creamed mixture just until moistened. Fold in cherries.

Fill greased or paper-lined miniature muffin cups two-thirds full. Bake at 350° for 15-17 minutes or until a toothpick comes out clean. Cool for 5 minutes before removing from pans to wire racks. **Yield:** about 2 dozen.

Cheese and Sausage Strudels

(Pictured at right and on page 6)

Instead of a typical egg bake, our Test Kitchen home economists came up with this elegant entree. Each phyllo dough strudel features a flavorful cheese sauce and hearty pork sausage.

1/4 cup butter
1/4 cup all-purpose flour
  2 cups milk
2/3 cup shredded Swiss cheese
1/4 cup grated Parmesan cheese
  1 teaspoon salt
1/4 teaspoon ground nutmeg
Dash pepper
1/2 pound bulk pork sausage
 10 eggs, well beaten
  1 teaspoon dried thyme
  2 teaspoons dried parsley flakes
PASTRY:
 20 sheets phyllo dough (14
    inches x 9 inches)
  1 cup butter, melted
1/2 cup dry bread crumbs
TOPPING:
1/4 cup grated Parmesan cheese
Minced fresh parsley

In a large saucepan, melt butter. Stir in flour until smooth; gradually add milk. Bring to a boil; cook and stir for 2 minutes or until thickened. Stir in the cheeses, salt, nutmeg and pepper. Cook and stir until cheese is melted; set aside.

Crumble sausage into a skillet; cook over medium heat until no longer pink. Drain. Add eggs and thyme; cook and stir gently until eggs are completely set. Stir into cheese sauce; add parsley. Cool completely.

Carefully unroll phyllo dough. Place one sheet of phyllo on a sheet of waxed paper (keep remaining dough covered with plastic wrap to avoid drying out). Brush with butter; sprinkle lightly with bread crumbs. Top with a second sheet of phyllo; brush with butter. Spread 1/2 cup egg mixture along the short side of dough to within 1 in. of edges. Beginning from the filled end, fold short side over filling. Fold in sides and roll up. Place seam side down on an ungreased baking sheet. Repeat nine times.

For topping, combine Parmesan cheese and parsley. Brush each roll with remaining butter; sprinkle with topping. Bake at 350° for 15-20 minutes or until crisp and lightly browned. Serve immediately. **Yield:** 10 servings.

SECRETS TO SPEEDY STRUDELS

CHEESE and Sausage Strudels have several make-ahead features.

The night before, prepare the cheese sauce as directed; cool, cover and refrigerate. Reheat in a saucepan over low heat before combining with the sausage mixture.

Early in the morning, finish assembling the strudels. Cover with plastic wrap; refrigerate for up to 2 hours before baking as directed.

Egg 'n' Pepperoni Bundles

My family calls these "one more gift to open" because it's the last present they unwrap on Christmas morning. Everyone's mouth waters when they break open these delicious bundles.
—Helen Meadows, Trout Creek, Montana

1 package (16 ounces) frozen phyllo dough (18 inches x 14 inches), thawed
1/2 cup butter, melted
1/4 cup dry bread crumbs
1 package (3 ounces) cream cheese, cut into 12 cubes
6 eggs
32 slices pepperoni, quartered *or* 2 ounces Canadian bacon, diced
1/2 cup shredded provolone cheese
1 tablespoon minced chives

Place one sheet of phyllo dough on a work surface; brush with butter. Top with another sheet of phyllo; brush with butter. Repeat three times. (Save remaining phyllo dough for another use.) Cut phyllo in half lengthwise, then cut widthwise into thirds.

Carefully place stacks in six greased jumbo muffin cups. Brush edges of dough with butter. Sprinkle 2 teaspoons of bread crumbs onto the bottom of each cup. Top each with two cubes of cream cheese.

Break each egg separately into a custard cup; gently pour egg over cream cheese. Sprinkle with pepperoni, provolone cheese and chives. Pinch corners of phyllo together to seal. Bake at 400° for 13-17 minutes or until golden brown. Serve warm. **Yield:** 6 servings.

Fluffy French Toast

My family can't wait for golden slices of this French toast to come off the griddle. We prefer the homemade Molasses Syrup to any store-bought variety.
—Julie Sterchi, Flora, Illinois

1-1/2 cups all-purpose flour
2 teaspoons baking powder
1 teaspoon salt
3 eggs
1-1/2 cups milk
10 slices day-old bread, halved
MOLASSES SYRUP:
3 cups sugar
3/4 cup water
3 tablespoons molasses
1 teaspoon vanilla extract
1 teaspoon maple flavoring

In a shallow bowl, combine the flour, baking powder and salt. Combine eggs and milk; add to dry ingredients and mix well. Dip bread into batter, coating both sides; cook on a greased hot griddle until golden brown on both sides and cooked through.

Meanwhile, for syrup, in a large saucepan, combine the sugar, water and molasses. Bring to a boil; boil for 1 minute. Stir in vanilla and maple flavoring. Serve with French toast. **Yield:** 5 servings.

Asparagus Cheese Quiche

(Pictured at right)

The fluffy texture of this quiche practically melts in your mouth! The green asparagus and red tomatoes on top make this a natural for the holidays.
—Sheryl Long
Lincolnton, North Carolina

1/2 **pound fresh asparagus, trimmed and halved lengthwise**
1 **cup (8 ounces) sour cream**
1 **cup (8 ounces) small-curd cottage cheese**
2 **egg whites**
1 **egg**
2 **tablespoons butter, melted**
5 **tablespoons grated Parmesan cheese, *divided***
1/4 **cup all-purpose flour**
1/2 **teaspoon baking powder**
1/4 **teaspoon salt**
1 **plum tomato, sliced**

In a large saucepan, bring 4 cups water to a boil. Add asparagus; cover and boil for 3 minutes. Drain and immediately place asparagus in ice water. Drain and pat dry. Arrange half of the spears in a spoke pattern in a greased 9-in. pie plate.

In a blender, combine the sour cream, cottage cheese, egg whites, egg and butter; cover and process until smooth. Add 3 tablespoons Parmesan cheese, flour, baking powder and salt; cover and process until smooth. Carefully pour over asparagus. Arrange remaining asparagus in a spoke pattern over the top. Sprinkle with remaining Parmesan cheese.

Bake at 350° for 25-30 minutes or until a knife inserted near the center comes out clean. Garnish with tomato slices. Let stand for 10 minutes before slicing. **Yield:** 6 servings.

Bacon Popovers

This recipe proves that simple ingredients oftentimes result in the best-tasting dishes.
These popovers are a nice change from ordinary toast or muffins.
—Donna Gaston, Coplay, Pennsylvania

3 bacon strips, diced
1 cup all-purpose flour
2 tablespoons grated Parmesan
  cheese
1/4 teaspoon salt
2 eggs
1 cup milk

In a skillet, cook bacon over medium heat until crisp; remove to paper towels to drain. Grease cups of popover pan with bacon drippings.

In a mixing bowl, combine the flour, Parmesan cheese and salt. Add eggs and milk; beat just until smooth and blended (do not overbeat). Stir in bacon. Place prepared popover pan in a 450° oven for 3 minutes. Carefully remove and fill cups half full with batter. Bake for 20 minutes.

Reduce heat to 350° (do not open oven door). Bake 20 minutes longer or until very firm and golden brown (do not underbake). Cut a slit in each popover to allow steam to escape. Serve immediately. **Yield:** 6 servings.

POPOVER POINTERS

SUCCESS with popovers is easy with these tips:
- In order for popovers to reach the maximum height while baking, all ingredients should be brought to room temperature before mixing.
- Place the oven rack in the lowest position.
- Generously grease the popover pan cups.
- Don't open the oven door while baking or the popovers will fall.
- After removing popovers from the oven, prick the tops with the point of a sharp knife, allowing steam to escape.

Warm Spiced Citrus Punch

I serve this drink every year during the holidays. It's one of my most requested recipes.
It can be doubled if you're entertaining an even larger group.
—Edie DeSpain, Logan, Utah

2-1/2 quarts water, *divided*
1-1/2 cups sugar
1 can (6 ounces) frozen orange
  juice concentrate, thawed
3/4 cup lemon juice
1 teaspoon almond extract
1 teaspoon vanilla extract
1/8 teaspoon *each* ground
  allspice, cinnamon and cloves

In a large kettle, bring 1 qt. of water and sugar to a boil; stir until sugar is dissolved. Stir in the remaining water. Add the orange juice concentrate, lemon juice, extracts and spices; cook and stir over medium heat until hot (do not boil). Serve warm. Refrigerate leftovers. **Yield:** 16 servings (3 quarts).

Coffee Ripple Coffee Cake

(Pictured at right)

I love presenting oven-fresh coffee cakes to the guests in our bed and breakfast. This moist coffee cake recipe really has coffee in it!
—Sandy Znetko, Flagstaff, Arizona

    1 cup chopped walnuts
  1/4 cup sugar
  1/4 cup packed brown sugar
    2 teaspoons instant coffee
      granules
    2 teaspoons ground cinnamon
CAKE:
    4 teaspoons instant coffee
      granules
    2 teaspoons hot water
  1/2 cup butter, softened
1-1/2 cups packed brown sugar
    3 eggs
    1 cup (8 ounces) sour cream
  1/2 cup unsweetened applesauce
  1/4 cup buttermilk
    1 teaspoon vanilla extract
    3 cups all-purpose flour
1-1/2 teaspoons baking powder
    1 teaspoon baking soda

GLAZE:
  2/3 cup confectioners' sugar
    3 to 4 teaspoons brewed coffee
    1 teaspoon butter, melted

In a small bowl, combine the walnuts, sugars, coffee granules and cinnamon; set aside. For cake, in a small bowl, dissolve coffee granules in water; set aside. In a large mixing bowl, cream the butter and brown sugar. Add eggs, one at a time, beating well after each addition. Combine the sour cream, applesauce, buttermilk, vanilla and coffee. Combine the flour, baking powder and baking soda; gradually add to creamed mixture alternately with sour cream mixture.

Pour half of the batter into a greased and floured 10-in. fluted tube pan. Sprinkle with walnut mixture. Top with remaining batter.

Bake at 350° for 45-50 minutes or until a toothpick inserted near the center comes out clean. Cool for 10 minutes before removing from pan to a wire rack to cool completely. Combine glaze ingredients until smooth; drizzle over cake. **Yield:** 12 servings.

Artichoke Tartlets

Refrigerated pie pastry gives me a head start in this wonderful recipe.
You can also serve these bite-size quiches as a special appetizer.
—Kelly Thornberry, La Porte, Indiana

2 packages (15 ounces *each*)
   refrigerated pie pastry
3 eggs
1-1/2 cups heavy whipping cream
1/2 teaspoon salt
12 pitted ripe olives
2 jars (6-1/2 ounces *each*)
   marinated artichoke hearts,
   drained and chopped
1 cup (4 ounces) shredded
   Swiss cheese
Coarsely ground pepper

Roll each pastry sheet into a 10-in. x 8-in. rectangle. Using a 2-1/2-in. round cookie cutter, cut out 12 circles from each rectangle. Press pastry rounds into the bottom and up the sides of ungreased miniature muffin cups; set aside.

In a small bowl, whisk the eggs, cream and salt. Cut each olive into four slices. Place 1 heaping teaspoonful of artichokes in each prepared cup; top with an olive slice and 1 teaspoon of cheese. Pour egg mixture into cups to within 1/4 in. of the top.

Sprinkle with pepper. Bake at 375° for 22-26 minutes or until a knife inserted near the center comes out clean. Serve warm. **Yield:** 4 dozen.

Spinach Egg Bake

This potluck pleaser showcases mouth-watering Wisconsin cheddar cheese.
I first made this egg bake for an after-church breakfast.
The big pan disappeared in a hurry!
—Genny Derer, Madison, Wisconsin

4 bunches green onions, finely
   chopped
1/4 cup butter
1 pound fresh spinach, trimmed
6 tablespoons minced fresh
   parsley
12 eggs
1/2 cup sour cream
1/2 teaspoon salt
1-1/2 cups (6 ounces) shredded
   cheddar cheese
1/2 cup grated Parmesan cheese

In a large skillet, saute onions in butter for 2 minutes. Add spinach and parsley; saute 3 minutes longer. Remove from the heat. In a large mixing bowl, beat the eggs, sour cream and salt. Stir in the spinach mixture and cheddar cheese. Pour into a greased 15-in. x 10-in. x 1-in. baking pan. Sprinkle with Parmesan cheese.

Bake, uncovered, at 350° for 25-30 minutes or until a knife inserted near the center comes out clean. Cut into squares. **Yield:** 15 servings.

A Bright Brunch Table

(Pictured at right)

ON A CRISP and snowy Christmas morning, the bold color of red is stunning against a wintry white table.

For the vibrant floral arrangement pictured at right, we purchased an assortment of red and white flowers (such as daisies, carnations, roses and tulips) as well as some vibrant greens. (We first filled the vase with hydrated water polymer crystals to give an icy effect. See the tip box below.)

We then tied a sheer red ribbon around the vase and tucked in a large candy cane. (We carried this cute candy cane theme onto individual mugs of hot chocolate. These small candy canes make sweet stirrers!)

If you're serving a brunch buffet, consider making some handy cutlery bundles by tying a knife, fork and spoon together with the same sheer red ribbon as used on the vase and mugs.

WHAT ARE WATER POLYMER CRYSTALS?

YOU CAN FIND water polymer crystals at any large craft store. The crystals will look like hard pellets (see photo, left). But when you hydrate them as instructed on the package, they soften and take on the look of crystal (see photo, right).

Place the hydrated crystals in a vase and arrange flowers as desired. Water polymer crystals can be dried and hydrated over and over again.

Regal Christmas Dinner

ON CHRISTMAS DAY, the house is decked out in your most festive decorations...everyone is dressed in their finest fashions ...the table is adorned with sparkling china and crystal.

On this holy holiday, the meal should match the importance of the occasion.

Treat your family like royalty and prepare Stuffed Crown Roast of Pork. It's an impressive entree when served alongside the simply delicious Green Beans with Cashews and Herb Potato Rolls.

Dinner guests will sing your praises when pretty Poached Pears in Raspberry Sauce appear on the table. (All of these recipes are shown at right.)

FARE FIT FOR A KING
(Clockwise from left)

Stuffed Crown Roast of Pork (p. 18)

Green Beans with Cashews (p. 21)

Herb Potato Rolls (p. 19)

Poached Pears in Raspberry Sauce (p. 22)

Stuffed Crown Roast of Pork

(Pictured on page 16 and on cover)

Folks may be intimidated to prepare an elegant crown roast of pork, but it's actually an easy entree. Our four grown sons and their families expect this every Christmas.
—*Mary Ann Balam, Tujunga, California*

1 pork crown roast (16 ribs and about 10 pounds)
2 garlic cloves, slivered
2 tablespoons olive oil
Salt and pepper to taste
2 cups apple juice *or* cider
APPLE RAISIN STUFFING:
1 cup raisins
1 cup boiling water
1 cup chopped onion
1 cup chopped celery
1 garlic clove, minced
3/4 cup butter
5 cups soft bread crumbs
3 cups chopped peeled tart apples
1/4 cup minced fresh parsley
1 teaspoon salt
1/4 teaspoon paprika

Cut slits in the bottom of each rib; insert garlic slivers. Rub oil over entire roast; sprinkle with salt and pepper. Place in a shallow roasting pan. Cover rib ends with foil. Pour apple juice into pan. Bake, uncovered, at 350° for 1 hour, basting occasionally.

Meanwhile, for stuffing, place the raisins in a small bowl; pour boiling water over raisins. Let stand for 2 minutes; drain and set aside. In a skillet, saute the onion, celery and garlic in butter until tender. Add the bread crumbs, apples, parsley, salt, paprika and raisins; mix well.

Carefully spoon stuffing into center of roast. Bake 1 to 1-1/2 hours more or until a meat thermometer reads 160°-170° and juices run clear. Let stand for 10 minutes. Remove foil and stuffing. Cut between ribs. **Yield:** 12-16 servings.

Sweet Potato Bake

This sweet and savory casserole is part of our traditional Christmas dinner. It goes great with any meaty entree.
—*Lynn McAllister, Mt. Ulla, North Carolina*

2-1/2 pounds sweet potatoes
1/2 cup sugar
1/2 cup milk
1/2 cup butter, melted, *divided*
2 eggs, beaten
1/4 cup all-purpose flour
1/2 teaspoon salt
1/2 teaspoon vanilla extract
3/4 cup chopped pecan *or* walnuts
3/4 cup packed brown sugar
1 teaspoon ground cinnamon

Place unpeeled sweet potatoes in a large kettle; cover with water. Cover and bring to a gentle boil; cook for 30-40 minutes or until potatoes can easily be pierced with a sharp knife. Drain and cool slightly; peel and cube.

In a large bowl, mash the sweet potatoes. Add sugar, milk, 1/4 cup butter, eggs, flour, salt and vanilla. Pour into a greased 1-1/2-qt. baking dish. Combine the nuts, brown sugar, cinnamon and remaining butter; sprinkle over the top. Bake, uncovered, at 350° for 40-45 minutes or until golden brown. **Yield:** 8 servings.

Herb Potato Rolls

(Pictured at right and on page 17)

My grandma always made these rolls.
She herself enjoyed them as a child in
Germany. I practiced for years before
I finally perfected the recipe!
—Lonna Smith, Woodruff, Wisconsin

5 to 5-1/2 cups all-purpose flour
1 cup mashed potato flakes
2 packages (1/4 ounce *each*)
   active dry yeast
1 tablespoon sugar
1 tablespoon minced chives
2 teaspoons salt
2 teaspoons minced fresh
   parsley
2 cups milk
1/2 cup sour cream
2 eggs

In a large mixing bowl, combine 3 cups flour, potato flakes, yeast, sugar, chives, salt and parsley. In a saucepan, heat milk and sour cream to 120°-130°. Add to dry ingredients; beat just until moistened. Add the eggs; beat until smooth. Stir in enough remaining flour to form a soft dough.

Turn onto a floured surface; knead until smooth and elastic, about 6-8 minutes. Place in a greased bowl, turning once to grease top. Cover and let rise in a warm place until doubled, about 45 minutes.

Punch dough down. Turn onto a lightly floured surface; divide into 24 pieces. Shape each into a roll. Place in a greased 13-in. x 9-in. x 2-in. baking pan. Cover and let rise until doubled, about 35 minutes. Bake at 375° for 30-35 minutes or until golden brown. Remove to wire racks. **Yield:** 2 dozen.

CHRISTMAS DAY TIMELINE

A Few Weeks Before:

- Prepare two grocery lists—one for non-perishable items to purchase now and one for perishable items to purchase a few days before Christmas Day.
- From your butcher, order a pork crown roast (16 ribs and about 10 pounds).
- Bake Herb Potato Rolls; cool. Freeze in a single layer in heavy-duty resealable plastic bags.
- Gather boxes for the Blooming Gift Boxes (page 23). Wrap and decorate with ribbon as desired.

Two Days Before:

- Buy your remaining grocery items, including the crown roast you ordered. Also pick up flowers for the centerpiece.
- Set the table.
- Finish assembling the Blooming Gift Boxes.

Christmas Eve:

- Assemble Sweet Potato Bake; cover and refrigerate.
- Clean and trim the 2 pounds of fresh green beans for the Green Beans with Cashews. Store in a plastic bag in your refrigerator's crisper drawer.
- Prepare Marinated Cauliflower Salad; cover and chill.

Christmas Day:

- In the morning, poach pears; cool. Place pears in a large serving dish or in individual dishes. Cover with plastic wrap and chill. Make the raspberry sauce; cool. Cover and refrigerate.
- Thaw the Herb Potato Rolls at room temperature.
- Bake the Stuffed Crown Roast of Pork as directed.
- Remove Sweet Potato Bake from the refrigerator 30 minutes before baking. (Please note if you refrigerate this casserole overnight, you may need to bake it a little longer than the recipe specifies.)
- If desired, wrap the rolls in foil and reheat in a 350° oven for 15-20 minutes.
- While the roast is standing, make Green Beans with Cashews.
- Set out rolls with butter and the Marinated Cauliflower Salad.
- For dessert, reheat raspberry sauce in a saucepan over low heat if desired. Serve Poached Pears in Raspberry Sauce.

Marinated Cauliflower Salad

(Pictured at right)

I often serve this as an appetizer alongside a meat and cheese tray. But it can also be a side dish.
—Stephanie Hase, Lyons, Colorado

1/4 cup red wine vinegar
1/4 cup olive oil
2 tablespoons water
1 bay leaf
1 garlic clove, minced
1/4 teaspoon salt
1/4 teaspoon coarsely ground pepper
5 cups fresh cauliflowerets
1/2 cup shredded carrot
1/4 cup chopped red onion

1/4 cup minced fresh parsley
1/4 teaspoon dried basil

In a small saucepan, bring the vinegar, oil and water just to a boil. Meanwhile, place the bay leaf, garlic, salt, pepper and cauliflower in a large heat-proof bowl. Add hot oil mixture; toss to combine. Cover and refrigerate for at least 6 hours or overnight, stirring occasionally.

Add the carrot, onion, parsley and basil; toss to coat. Cover and refrigerate for 2 hours. Discard bay leaf. Serve with a slotted spoon. **Yield:** 12-16 servings.

Green Beans with Cashews

(Pictured on page 17 and on cover)

This nice, simple side dish is dressed up with salted whole cashews. Frozen whole green beans can be used instead of fresh beans. Just cook according to package directions.
—Cathleen Bushman, Geneva, Illinois

2 pounds fresh green beans, trimmed
1/4 cup butter, cubed
1 tablespoon dried parsley flakes
3/4 teaspoon salt
1/2 teaspoon pepper
3/4 cup salted whole cashews

Place the beans in a large saucepan and cover with water. Bring to a boil. Reduce heat; simmer, uncovered, for 8-10 minutes or until crisp-tender. Drain and return beans to the pan. Add the butter, parsley, salt and pepper. Cook, uncovered, over medium heat until heated through. Sprinkle with cashews. **Yield:** 8 servings.

Poached Pears in Raspberry Sauce

(Pictured at right and on page 17)

This fruity recipe is just right for anyone who loves elegant desserts, but not the extra pounds associated with so many of them.
—Clara Coulston
Washington Court House, Ohio

8 medium Bosc pears
2 cups pear juice
1 cinnamon stick (3 inches)
1-1/2 teaspoons minced fresh gingerroot
1 teaspoon whole cloves
1/4 teaspoon ground nutmeg
1 tablespoon cornstarch
1/2 cup cranberry juice
2 cups fresh raspberries *or* 1 package (12 ounces) frozen unsweetened raspberries, thawed
2 tablespoons maple syrup

Core pears from the bottom, leaving stems intact. Peel pears. If necessary, cut 1/4 in. from bottom so pears will sit flat. Place in a Dutch oven. Add the pear juice, cinnamon stick, ginger, cloves and nutmeg. Cover and bring to a boil. Reduce heat; simmer for 25-30 minutes or until pears are tender.

Remove the pears and place in serving dishes. Discard cinnamon stick and cloves from poaching liquid. In a small bowl, combine cornstarch and cranberry juice until smooth; stir into liquid. Bring to a boil; cook and stir for 2 minutes or until thickened. Add raspberries and syrup. Remove from the heat; cool slightly.

In a blender or food processor, puree raspberry sauce in batches until smooth. Strain and discard seeds. Pour sauce over pears. Serve warm, at room temperature or chilled. **Yield:** 8 servings.

CORING PEARS LIKE A PRO

TO CORE a fresh pear, insert an apple corer into the bottom of the pear to within 1 in. of its top. Twist the corer to cut around the core, then slowly pull the corer out of the pear to remove the core.

If you don't have an apple corer, use a sharp knife or vegetable peeler to cut the core from the bottom of the pear.

Blooming Gift Boxes

(Pictured above)

BY DINNERTIME on Christmas Day, all of the packages under the tree have been opened and the pretty wrappings have been discarded.

Enjoy the sight of pretty packages a while longer by creating this lovely arrangement.

First, chose a color theme for the wrapping paper, ribbons and flowers, making sure the colors work with your dishes and table linens.

For an elegant look, we chose green and gold wrapping paper and ribbons. Then we selected pretty paperwhites to pop out of the packages.

Next, look for boxes in varying sizes. We made three stacks with two boxes each. The largest boxes were used in the center of the display.

Then find narrow glasses or vases that are roughly the same height as each stack of boxes.

For each stack of boxes, wrap the top and bottom of the largest box separately. Then wrap the bottom only of the next largest box. Set the smaller boxes on top of the larger boxes.

With tape or a stapler, secure ribbons at the top and bottom on each side of the stacks.

With a utility knife, cut a large "X" in the bottom of the top box and through the lid of the bottom box.

Carefully fill each glass or vase with floral marbles if desired and water. Insert the glass or vase into each stack of boxes, making sure it's resting within the bottom box. Add flowers.

In the top box of each stack, fill in with tissue paper and gold angel hair or raffia, covering the glass or vase as much as possible.

To continue with the gift box theme, we set smaller decorated boxes at each place setting. The boxes could be empty or filled with a party favor, such as an ornament or candy.

Seasonal Home-Style Spread

INSTEAD of an elegant sit-down Christmas dinner, branch out and host a casual buffet featuring more informal fare.

Begin this down-home dinner by having everyone nibble Bean Spread on Pita Crackers.

Both young and old guests will be game for succulent Duck Breasts with Apricot Chutney. (This chapter also includes a recipe for more traditional Holiday Pork Loin Roast.)

Warm Mushroom Salad and Roasted Root Vegetables are fitting sides for this rustic supper.

Then watch appealing Caramelized Apple Tarts disappear from the dessert tray!

HEARTY HELPINGS
(Clockwise from top right)

Roasted Root Vegetables (p. 26)

Warm Mushroom Salad (p. 28)

Caramelized Apple Tarts (p. 28)

Bean Spread on Pita Crackers (p. 32)

Duck Breasts with Apricot Chutney (p. 27)

Roasted Root Vegetables

(Pictured on page 25)

Even finicky folks will eat their vegetables when they're tossed with seasonings and olive oil, then roasted. To save time, our home economists suggest you peel and cut the squash, rutabagas and turnips earlier in the day. Place in resealable plastic bags and chill until ready to use.

3 pounds butternut squash, peeled, seeded and cut into 1-inch pieces
2 large rutabagas, peeled and cut into 1/2-inch pieces
2 large fennel bulbs, cut into 1/2-inch pieces
2 small turnips, peeled and cut into 1/2-inch pieces
1/4 cup olive oil
1/4 cup lemon juice
2 tablespoons minced fresh thyme *or* 2 teaspoons dried thyme
1 teaspoon salt
1/2 teaspoon pepper

Place the squash, rutabagas, fennel and turnips in two 15-in. x 10-in. x 1-in. baking pans. Combine the remaining ingredients; drizzle over vegetables and toss to coat. Bake, uncovered, at 450° for 55-60 minutes or until tender, stirring twice. **Yield:** 12 servings.

RUTABAGA AND TURNIP TIPS

WHEN shopping for rutabagas and turnips, select those that are smooth-skinned, unblemished, heavy, firm and not spongy. Look for rutabagas no larger than 4 inches in diameter and turnips no larger than 2 inches in diameter.

Keep unwashed rutabagas and turnips in a plastic bag in your refrigerator's crisper drawer for up to 1 week. Just before using, wash, trim ends and peel.

Cranberry-Nut Wild Rice

It's amazing that just a few ingredients can result in such a great-tasting dish.
This recipe is a real bonus on busy holidays.
—Jauneen Hosking, Wind Lake, Wisconsin

2 cups uncooked wild rice
8 green onions, thinly sliced
3 tablespoons olive oil, *divided*
1 cup dried cranberries
2/3 cup pine nuts, toasted
Salt and pepper to taste

Cook wild rice according to package directions; drain if necessary. In a large skillet, saute onions in 1 tablespoon oil until tender. Stir in the rice, cranberries, nuts and remaining oil; heat through. Season with salt and pepper. **Yield:** 12 servings.

Duck Breasts With Apricot Chutney

(Pictured at right and on page 25)

When serving this entree as part of a buffet, our Test Kitchen suggests using a chafing dish to keep it warm.

1-1/2 cups orange juice
  2/3 cup sugar
    2 packages (6 ounces *each*) dried apricots, chopped
  1/2 cup dried cherries
  1/2 cup golden raisins
    2 teaspoons minced fresh gingerroot
  3/4 teaspoon ground coriander
  3/4 teaspoon ground cumin
  1/4 teaspoon salt
  1/4 teaspoon pepper
  1/8 teaspoon ground cloves
    2 teaspoons lemon juice

DUCK:
  12 duck breasts with skin (5 ounces *each*)
1-1/2 teaspoons salt
  1/4 teaspoon pepper
    2 tablespoons olive oil

ORANGE SAUCE:
  1/4 teaspoon minced garlic
  1/2 cup Marsala wine
  1/2 teaspoon cornstarch
  1/2 cup orange juice
  1/3 cup chicken broth
    2 tablespoons grated orange peel
    3 tablespoons cold butter
    1 tablespoon minced fresh basil

For chutney, in a saucepan, combine orange juice and sugar. Cook and stir over medium heat for 3 minutes or until sugar is dissolved. Add the apricots, cherries, raisins, ginger, coriander, cumin, salt, pepper and cloves. Bring to a boil. Reduce heat to low; cook for 10 minutes or until apricots are tender. Transfer to a bowl; stir in lemon juice. Let stand at room temperature for at least 2 hours.

Season both sides of duck with salt and pepper. In a large skillet, saute duck, skin side down, in oil until skin is browned; turn and cook for 1 minute. Set aside 1 tablespoon drippings. Place duck on a greased rack in a shallow roasting pan. Bake at 350° for 30-35 minutes or until juices run clear and a meat thermometer reads 180°.

For orange sauce, saute garlic in reserved drippings for 1 minute. Add wine; bring to a boil. Cook and stir until reduced by half. In a bowl, combine the cornstarch, orange juice, broth and orange peel until blended. Stir into wine mixture. Bring to a boil. Reduce heat; simmer, uncovered, for 5 minutes. Remove from the heat. Add butter and basil; whisk until smooth. Remove skin from duck if desired before slicing. Serve with orange sauce and chutney. **Yield:** 12 servings.

Caramelized Apple Tarts

(Pictured on page 24)

This recipe from our Test Kitchen cleverly dresses up frozen puff pastry and a no-bake cheesecake mix. Guests will be delighted to be offered their own individual tarts!

1 package (17.3 ounces) frozen puff pastry, thawed
1 package (11.1 ounces) no-bake cheesecake mix
1/2 cup butter, cubed
1 cup packed dark brown sugar
1/2 teaspoon ground cinnamon
5 medium apples, peeled and thinly sliced
3 tablespoons heavy whipping cream

Unfold pastry sheets on a lightly floured surface. Cut into eight 4-in. circles. Place on greased baking sheets. Bake at 400° for 15-18 minutes or until lightly browned. Remove to wire racks to cool.

Prepare cheesecake filling according to package directions; set aside. (Save packet of crust crumbs for another use.) In a large skillet, melt butter and brown sugar over medium heat; stir in cinnamon. Add half of the apples; cook and stir for 10 minutes or until tender. Remove with a slotted spoon to a bowl. Repeat with remaining apples. Drain cooking juices, reserving 1/3 cup in the skillet; discard remaining juices. Add cream to skillet; cook and stir for 2 minutes.

Split each pastry in half horizontally. Top each with 2 heaping tablespoons of cheesecake filling. Top with apple slices and drizzle with caramel sauce. Refrigerate leftovers. **Yield:** 16 servings.

Warm Mushroom Salad

(Pictured on page 25)

A blend of mushrooms, sun-dried tomatoes and salad greens make for a pretty presentation on a platter. The recipe comes from our home economists.

1 jar (7 ounces) oil-packed sun-dried tomatoes
1 package (8 ounces) sliced fresh mushrooms
1 package (5 ounces) sliced fresh shiitake mushrooms
1 small red onion, sliced
3 tablespoons butter
1 tablespoon olive oil
2 tablespoons balsamic vinegar
2 packages (10 ounces *each*) spring mix salad greens

1 package (4 ounces) crumbled goat cheese *or* feta cheese

Drain tomatoes, reserving oil mixture. Cut tomatoes into thin strips; set aside. In a large skillet, saute mushrooms and onion in butter and olive oil for 5 minutes or until mushrooms are browned. Stir in the vinegar, and reserved tomatoes and oil mixture. Bring to a boil. Reduce heat to low; cook for 10 minutes.

Arrange salad greens on a platter; top with mushroom mixture and cheese. Serve warm. **Yield:** 12 servings.

Walnut-Crusted Wheat Loaves

(Pictured at right)

This moist, flavorful round bread from our Test Kitchen has a wonderful balance of both white and wheat flours. Pass a basket of wedges with creamy butter.

    3 cups whole wheat flour
2-3/4 to 3 cups all-purpose flour
    3/4 cup toasted wheat germ
    2 packages (1/4 ounce *each*)
        active dry yeast
    2 teaspoons salt
    2 cups water
    1/2 cup honey
    1/3 cup shortening
    2 eggs
    1 cup chopped walnuts
GLAZE:
    1/4 cup sugar
    1/4 cup water
    1/4 cup chopped walnuts

In a large mixing bowl, combine the whole wheat flour, 2-1/2 cups all-purpose flour, wheat germ, yeast and salt. In a small saucepan, heat the water, honey and shortening to 120°-130°. Add to dry ingredients; beat just until moistened. Add eggs; beat until smooth. Stir in walnuts and enough remaining all-purpose flour to form a soft dough.

Turn onto a floured surface; knead until smooth and elastic, about 5-6 minutes. Place in a greased bowl, turning once to grease top. Cover and let rise in a warm place until doubled, about 1 hour.

Punch dough down. Turn onto a lightly floured surface; divide in half. Shape each portion into a ball; flatten slightly. Place on two greased baking sheets. Cover and let rise in a warm place until doubled, about 35 minutes.

For glaze, in a saucepan, bring sugar and water to a boil. Cook for 2 minutes or until thickened. Brush over top of loaves. With a sharp knife, make several shallow slashes across the top of loaves. Sprinkle with walnuts. Bake at 375° for 30-35 minutes or until golden brown. Remove from pans to wire racks to cool. **Yield:** 2 loaves.

Holiday Pork Loin Roast

This is the only way my family will let me prepare pork roast.
A flavorful currant sauce complements each mouth-watering bite.
—Karen Ellinwood, Liberty Center, Ohio

1 cup soy sauce
1 cup dry sherry *or* chicken
   broth
2 tablespoons ground mustard
2 teaspoons ground ginger
2 teaspoons dried thyme
4 garlic cloves, minced
1 boneless rolled pork loin
   roast (4 to 5 pounds)
CURRANT SAUCE:
1 jar (12 ounces) red currant
   jelly
2 tablespoons dry sherry *or*
   chicken broth
1 tablespoon soy sauce

In a bowl, combine the soy sauce, sherry or broth, mustard, ginger, thyme and garlic; mix well. Pour 1 cup marinade into a large resealable plastic bag; add the roast. Seal bag and turn to coat. Refrigerate for 3 hours or overnight, turning occasionally. Cover and refrigerate the remaining marinade for basting.

Drain and discard marinade from bag. Place the roast on a rack in a roasting pan. Bake at 325° for 1-3/4 to 2-1/4 hours or until a meat thermometer reads 160°, pouring the reserved marinade over meat during the last hour of baking. Baste occasionally. Let stand for 10 minutes before slicing.

Meanwhile, in a small saucepan, combine the sauce ingredients. Cook and stir for 4-5 minutes or until the jelly is melted. Serve with pork. **Yield:** 12-15 servings.

Cranberry Cherry Punch

This crimson-colored beverage is wonderful for Christmas and looks festive in a glass punch bowl.
—Lori Daniels, Beverly, West Virginia

1/3 cup fresh *or* frozen cranberries
2 slices lemon, cut into 6
   wedges *each*
1 package (3 ounces) cherry
   gelatin
1 cup boiling water
3 cups cold water
6 cups cranberry juice, chilled
3/4 cup lemonade concentrate
1 liter ginger ale, chilled

Place several cranberries and a piece of lemon in each compartment of an ice cube tray; fill with water and freeze. In a punch bowl or large container, dissolve gelatin in boiling water. Stir in the cold water, cranberry juice and lemonade concentrate. Just before serving, stir in ginger ale. Serve over cranberry-lemon ice cubes. **Yield:** 3-1/2 quarts.

Creamy Leek Soup with Brie

(Pictured at right)

Bits of brie add something special to this soup from our home economists. Soup is a satisfying addition to a buffet table. Use a slow cooker to keep it warm.

   5 cups chopped leeks (white
     portion only)
 1/4 cup butter
   5 cups chicken broth
4-1/2 cups half-and-half cream,
     divided
 1/2 cup all-purpose flour
   1 teaspoon salt
 1/4 teaspoon white pepper
   3 packages (8 ounces *each*) Brie
     cheese, rind removed
   3 tablespoons snipped chives

In a Dutch oven, saute leeks in butter until tender. Add broth; bring to a boil. Reduce heat; cover and simmer for 25 minutes. Strain, reserving broth in pan. Place leeks in a blender with 1/2 cup of the broth; cover and process until smooth. Return to the pan. Stir in 3 cups cream. Combine flour, salt, pepper and remaining cream until smooth; stir into soup. Bring to a boil; cook and stir for 2 minutes.

Reduce heat to medium. Cut Brie into small pieces; add to soup in batches, stirring until most of the cheese is melted. Garnish with chives. **Yield:** 12 servings (2-1/2 quarts).

LEARN ABOUT LEEKS

A MEMBER of the onion family, leeks resemble oversize green onions, with wide green leaves, a fat white stalk and roots at the bulb end. Yet, the flavor of leeks is very subtle.

Buy leeks with crisp, brightly colored leaves and an unblemished white stalk. Leeks that are larger than 1-1/2 inches in diameter will be less tender.

Refrigerate leeks in a plastic bag for up to 5 days. Before using, cut off the roots. Trim the tough leaf ends. Slit the leek from end to end and wash thoroughly under cold water to remove dirt trapped between the leaf layers. Chop or slice the white portion to use in a variety of recipes.

Bean Spread on Pita Crackers

(Pictured on page 24)

For extra ease, our Test Kitchen says to bake the pita crackers the night before.
Cool and store in an airtight container at room temperature. You can also prepare
and chill the spread overnight; remove from the refrigerator 30 minutes before serving.

1 cup chopped onion
1 garlic clove, minced
3 tablespoons olive oil
2 cans (15-1/2 ounces *each*)
    great northern beans, rinsed
    and drained
3/4 cup chicken broth
1 teaspoon minced fresh
    rosemary
1/2 teaspoon salt
1/4 teaspoon pepper
PITA CRACKERS:
4 pita breads (6 inches)
1/4 cup olive oil
1 tablespoon sesame seeds,
    toasted
2 teaspoons onion powder
1-1/2 teaspoons poppy seeds
1 teaspoon dried thyme
1/2 teaspoon kosher salt

In a large skillet, saute onion and garlic in oil for 3 minutes or until tender. Add the beans, broth, rosemary, salt and pepper. Bring to a boil. Reduce heat; simmer for 20 minutes. Cool slightly. Place half of the mixture in a blender or food processor; cover and process until smooth. Transfer to a bowl. Repeat with remaining mixture. Cool to room temperature.

For crackers, split each pita bread in half horizontally into two rounds; brush with oil. Combine the sesame seeds, onion powder, poppy seeds, thyme and salt; sprinkle over pitas. Broil 3-4 in. from the heat for 2 minutes or until lightly browned and crisp. Cool on wire racks. Break into large pieces. Serve with spread. **Yield:** 3 cups.

Family Traditions

EACH YEAR, my mom hides small framed pictures of each of her grandchildren on her Christmas tree.

On Christmas Day, the kids have such a good time searching for their picture-perfect gift. And we all get a kick out of seeing how much they've grown over the past year!
        —Bryan Czysz
Waukesha, Wisconsin

Tree Boughs 'n' Tapers

(Pictured above)

BRING a bit of the outdoors inside for your home-style buffet by making this table topper featuring tree branch candle holders.

First, head outside and collect an assortment of tree branches. Cut them into various lengths so they will stand on end. On one end of each branch, drill a hole in the center to serve as a holder for each candle. (We used a 3/4-inch bit for standard-sized taper candles.)

To protect your table surface, stand the branches on end on a large tray. Place candles in the drilled holes. Arrange Christmas greens, red berries, dogwood branches and pinecones around candle holders as desired.

'TIS THE *Season*

Christmas Card– Writing Party

DURING the height of the holiday season, sending out Christmas cards can seem like just another chore on your list of things to do.

This year, address this sometimes daunting task by turning it into a card-writing party!

Invite a few close companions to your home one evening and have them bring along their cards, envelopes, address books, pens and postage stamps.

While writing out the cards at the dining room table, nibble on simple, special appetizers such as Pesto Crostini, Shrimp Napoleons and Antipasto Kabobs. (All recipes shown at right.)

EATING & GREETING
(Top to bottom)

Pesto Crostini (p. 37)

Shrimp Napoleons (p. 36)

Antipasto Kabobs (p. 37)

Shrimp Napoleons

(Pictured on page 35)

Flaky and tender frozen puff pastry serves as the bread for these cold shrimp sandwiches.
Bake the pastry and prepare the filling a day ahead; assemble before guests arrive.
—Mary Lou Wayman, Salt Lake City, Utah

1 package (17.3 ounces) frozen puff pastry, thawed
2 packages (3 ounces *each*) cream cheese, softened
1 tablespoon thinly sliced green onion
1 tablespoon Dijon mustard
1 teaspoon Worcestershire sauce
2-1/2 cups chopped cooked peeled shrimp
1/3 cup finely shredded carrot
4 bacon strips, cooked and crumbled

Line two baking sheets with parchment paper. Unfold one puff pastry sheet on a lightly floured surface. Cut sheet into nine squares, about 3 in. Cut each square in half, forming 18 rectangles. Place on one prepared baking sheet. Repeat with remaining puff pastry. Bake at 425° for 12-15 minutes or until puffed and golden brown. Remove to a wire rack to cool.

In a small mixing bowl, beat the cream cheese, onion, mustard and Worcestershire sauce until well blended. Stir in the shrimp, carrot and bacon.

To assemble, use a fork to split each pastry in half horizontally. Spread a rounded tablespoonful of cream cheese mixture over the bottom halves; replace tops. Refrigerate until serving. **Yield:** 3 dozen.

Artichoke Ranch Squares

I love to cook but don't have much free time. So I appreciate fast and easy recipes
that are big on taste...like these savory snack squares.
—Joanne VanderSchaaf, Fond du Lac, Wisconsin

2 tubes (8 ounces *each*) refrigerated crescent rolls
1 can (14 ounces) water-packed artichoke hearts, rinsed, drained and chopped
1 cup (4 ounces) shredded mozzarella cheese
3/4 cup shredded Parmesan cheese
3/4 cup ranch salad dressing
1 jar (4 ounces) diced pimientos, drained

Unroll both tubes of crescent dough and pat into an ungreased 15-in. x 10-in. x 1-in. baking pan; seal seams and perforations. Bake at 375° for 8-10 minutes or until lightly browned.

Meanwhile, in a bowl, combine the remaining ingredients; spread over crust. Bake for 12-15 minutes or until cheese is melted and crust is golden brown. Cut into squares; serve warm. **Yield:** about 2-1/2 dozen.

Antipasto Kabobs

(Pictured at right and on page 35)

My husband and I met at a cooking class and have loved creating menus and entertaining ever since. These do-ahead appetizers are always a hit.
—Denise Hazen, Cincinnati, Ohio

1 package (9 ounces)
    refrigerated cheese tortellini
40 large stuffed olives
40 large pitted ripe olives
3/4 cup Italian salad dressing
40 thin slices pepperoni
20 thin slices hard salami, halved

Cook tortellini according to package directions; drain and rinse in cold water. In a resealable plastic bag, combine the tortellini, olives and salad dressing. Seal and refrigerate for 4 hours or overnight.

Drain and discard dressing. For each appetizer, thread a stuffed olive, folded pepperoni slice, tortellini, folded salami piece and ripe olive on a toothpick or short skewer. **Yield:** 40 appetizers.

Pesto Crostini

(Pictured on page 34)

Look no further when you're searching for an elegant appetizer that's easy to put together. A platter of these crostini will disappear quickly!
—Diane Kaplan, Riverdale, New Jersey

1 loaf (1 pound) French bread,
    cut into 1-inch slices
2 tablespoons butter, softened
1 tablespoon minced garlic
1 cup prepared pesto
3 small tomatoes, thinly sliced
1/2 pound fresh mozzarella
    cheese, thinly sliced

Place the bread slices on an ungreased baking sheet. Combine butter and garlic; spread over bread. Broil 3-4 in. from the heat or until lightly browned. Cool slightly. Spread pesto over butter mixture; top with tomatoes and cheese. Broil 3-5 minutes longer or until cheese is melted. **Yield:** 20 appetizers.

Editor's Note: Fresh mozzarella can be found in the deli section of most grocery stores.

Creamy Buffalo Chicken Dip

This slightly spicy dip cleverly captures the flavor of buffalo chicken wings.
Using canned chicken adds to the convenience.
—Allyson DiLascio, Saltsburg, Pennsylvania

1 package (8 ounces) cream
  cheese, softened
1 cup hot pepper sauce
1 cup ranch salad dressing
3 cans (4-1/2 ounces *each*)
  chunk white chicken, drained
  and shredded
1 cup (4 ounces) shredded
  cheddar cheese
Corn *or* tortilla chips

In a small mixing bowl, combine the cream cheese, hot pepper sauce and salad dressing. Stir in chicken. Spread into an ungreased 11-in. x 7-in. x 2-in. baking dish. Sprinkle with cheddar cheese. Bake, uncovered, at 350° for 20-22 minutes or until heated through. Serve with chips. **Yield:** 5 cups.

Editor's Note: This recipe was tested with Frank's Cayenne Pepper Sauce.

USE YOUR SLOW COOKER!

CREAMY Buffalo Chicken Dip can be prepared, then heated in a slow cooker instead of baked. This will also keep the dip warm during a party.

Bacon Cheese Fondue

When I'm looking for an appetizer with mass appeal but want a change from the usual
cheese spread, this is the recipe I make. Everyone enjoys the rich flavor.
—Bernice Morris, Marshfield, Missouri

4 to 5 bacon strips, diced
1/4 cup chopped onion
2 tablespoons all-purpose flour
1 pound process cheese
  (Velveeta), cubed
2 cups (16 ounces) sour cream
1 jalapeno pepper, seeded and
  chopped, optional
1 loaf (1 pound) French bread,
  cubed

In a large skillet, cook bacon over medium heat until crisp. Using a slotted spoon, remove to paper towels. In the drippings, saute onion until tender. Stir in flour until blended; cook and stir until thickened.

Reduce heat to low. Add cheese cubes; cook and stir until melted. Stir in sour cream, jalapeno if desired and bacon; cook and stir just until heated through. Transfer to a fondue pot and keep warm. Serve with bread cubes. **Yield:** 3-3/4 cups.

Editor's Note: When cutting or seeding hot peppers, use rubber or plastic gloves to protect your hands. Avoid touching your face.

Pear Pizza Wedges

(Pictured at right)

You won't be able to stop eating this sweet and savory appetizer. The recipe makes just the right amount for a smaller gathering.
—Mimi Merta, Dunedin, Florida

2 whole pita breads
2 teaspoons olive oil
1/2 cup crumbled Gorgonzola cheese
1 medium ripe pear, thinly sliced
1/4 cup coarsely chopped walnuts
1 tablespoon honey
1 teaspoon balsamic vinegar

Place pita breads on an ungreased baking sheet. Brush with oil; sprinkle with Gorgonzola cheese. Top with pear slices and walnuts. Bake at 400° for 12-15 minutes or until bread is crisp and cheese is melted. Combine honey and vinegar; drizzle over pitas. Cut each into four wedges. **Yield:** 8 appetizers.

Chutney Cheddar Spread

This is a quick appetizer to make with ingredients I have on hand in the kitchen.
—Regina Costlow, East Brady, Pennsylvania

4 ounces cheddar cheese, cubed
1/4 cup chutney
2 tablespoons butter, softened
1 tablespoon finely chopped onion
1/4 teaspoon Worcestershire sauce
Dash hot pepper sauce
Assorted crackers

In a food processor, combine the first six ingredients; cover and process until mixture achieves spreading consistency. Refrigerate until serving. Serve with crackers. **Yield:** about 1 cup.

Roasted Goat Cheese with Garlic

Now that we have kids, my husband and I don't entertain much. But when we do, I serve this savory spread. The combination of goat cheese, garlic and onions always earns rave reviews.
—*Carol Barlow, Berwyn, Illinois*

6 to 8 garlic cloves, peeled
1 tablespoon vegetable oil
1 medium red onion, thinly sliced
2 tablespoons butter
1 tablespoon brown sugar
8 ounces crumbled goat *or* feta cheese
1 tablespoon balsamic vinegar
Salt and pepper to taste
1/4 cup thinly sliced fresh basil
Thinly sliced French bread *or* crackers

Place garlic and oil in a pie plate. Cover and bake at 350° for 30 minutes. Meanwhile, in a skillet, saute onion in butter until tender and lightly browned. Add brown sugar; cook and stir until sugar is dissolved. Remove from the heat.

Remove garlic from pie plate. Spread onion in pie plate; top with cheese. Place garlic over cheese. Bake, uncovered, for 15-20 minutes or until cheese is melted. Mash garlic with a fork. Stir vinegar, salt and pepper into garlic, onion and cheese mixture. Transfer to a serving bowl; sprinkle with basil. Serve warm with French bread or crackers. **Yield:** about 1-1/4 cups.

Apple-Stuffed Mushroom Caps

These are no ordinary stuffed mushrooms! Blue cheese blends well with the more mild flavors of mushrooms and apples. The recipe can be doubled if needed.
—*Allen Mann, Warrior, Alabama*

18 large fresh mushrooms
3 tablespoons finely chopped celery
1 tablespoon butter
1/2 cup finely chopped apple
2 tablespoons dry bread crumbs
2 tablespoons finely chopped walnuts
1 tablespoon crumbled blue cheese
1 tablespoon minced fresh parsley
2 teaspoons lemon juice

Remove stems from mushrooms; set caps aside. Chop stems, reserving 1/3 cup (discard remaining stems or save for another use). In a small skillet, saute chopped mushrooms and celery in butter. In a small bowl, combine the mushroom mixture and the remaining ingredients.

Place mushroom caps on a greased baking sheet; stuff with apple mixture. Bake at 375° for 15-20 minutes or until mushrooms are tender. Serve warm. **Yield:** 1-1/2 dozen.

TIPS FOR STUFFING MUSHROOMS

WHEN making stuffed mushrooms, remove the stems, then scoop out some of the inside with a small round teaspoon (1/8 or 1/4 teaspoon). Use the teaspoon to easily stuff the mixture into the caps.

Baked Spinach Dip In Bread

(Pictured at right)

This is the only way my kids will eat spinach! The dip can be made ahead and chilled. Place in the bread shell and bake just before company arrives.
—Shauna Dittrick, Leduc, Alberta

2 packages (8 ounces *each*)
   cream cheese, softened
1 cup mayonnaise
1 package (10 ounces) frozen
   chopped spinach, thawed and
   squeezed dry
1 cup (4 ounces) shredded
   cheddar cheese
1 pound sliced bacon, cooked
   and crumbled
1/4 cup chopped onion
1 tablespoon dill weed
1 to 2 garlic cloves, minced
1 unsliced round loaf (1 pound)
   sourdough bread
Assorted fresh vegetables

In a large mixing bowl, beat cream cheese and mayonnaise until blended. Stir in the spinach, cheese, bacon, onion, dill and garlic; set aside.

Cut a 1-1/2-in. slice off top of bread; set aside. Carefully hollow out bottom, leaving a 1/2-in. shell. Cube removed bread and place on a baking sheet. Broil 3-4 in. from the heat for 1-2 minutes or until golden brown; set aside.

Fill bread shell with spinach dip; replace top. Place any dip that doesn't fit in shell in a greased baking dish. Wrap bread in heavy-duty foil; place on a baking sheet. Bake at 350° for 1 hour or until dip is heated through. Cover and bake additional dip for 40-45 minutes or until heated through. Open foil carefully. Serve dip warm with vegetables and reserved bread cubes. **Yield:** 4 cups.

Editor's Note: Fat-free cream cheese and mayonnaise are not recommended for this recipe.

Stuffed Banana Peppers

I received this recipe from a customer while working at my sister's produce market.
The peppers can be made a day in advance, making them great for get-togethers.
—*Cathy Kidd, Medora, Indiana*

2 packages (8 ounces *each*)
  cream cheese, softened
1 envelope ranch salad dressing
  mix
1 cup (4 ounces) finely
  shredded cheddar cheese
5 bacon strips, cooked and
  crumbled
8 mild banana peppers (6
  inches long), halved
  lengthwise and seeded

In a small mixing bowl, combine the cream cheese, salad dressing mix, cheese and bacon until blended. Pipe or stuff into pepper halves. Cover and refrigerate until serving. Cut into 1-1/4-in. pieces. **Yield:** 8-10 servings.

Editor's Note: When cutting or seeding banana peppers, use rubber or plastic gloves to protect your hands. Avoid touching your face.

BANANA PEPPER POINTERS

THE FLAVOR of banana peppers is sweet and mild. Look for peppers with evenly colored skins that are free of blemishes. They stay fresh in a plastic bag in the refrigerator for about 1 week.

TV Munching Mix

We keep this snack mix on hand for anytime munching.
At Christmas, we make it and add it to gift baskets for friends and family.
—*Becky Neuhart, Beaver Falls, Pennsylvania*

6 cups Crispix cereal
3-1/2 cups miniature pretzels
2 cups salted mixed nuts
6 tablespoons butter, melted
4 teaspoons lemon juice
1 tablespoon Worcestershire
  sauce
2 teaspoons Cajun seasoning
1-1/2 teaspoons soy sauce
1-1/2 teaspoons hot pepper sauce
1/2 teaspoon garlic powder
1/2 teaspoon ground mustard

In a very large bowl, combine the cereal, pretzels and nuts. In a small bowl, combine the remaining ingredients; pour over cereal mixture and toss to coat. Transfer to two greased 15-in. x 10-in. x 1-in. baking pans. Bake at 250° for 1 hour, stirring every 15 minutes. Spread on paper towels to cool. Store in an airtight container. **Yield:** about 3 quarts.

Crunchy Onion Sticks

(Pictured at right)

Although I've been collecting recipes for more than 50 years, I never tire of tried-and-true ones like this.
—Leora Muellerleile
Turtle Lake, Wisconsin

2 eggs, lightly beaten
2 tablespoons butter, melted
1 teaspoon all-purpose flour
1/2 teaspoon garlic salt
1/2 teaspoon dried parsley flakes
1/4 teaspoon onion salt
2 cans (2.8 ounces *each*) french-fried onions, crushed
1 tube (8 ounces) refrigerated crescent rolls

In a shallow bowl, combine the first six ingredients. Place the onions in another shallow bowl. Separate crescent dough into four rectangles; seal perforations. Cut each rectangle into eight strips. Dip each strip in egg mixture, then roll in onions.

Place 2 in. apart on ungreased baking sheets. Bake at 375° for 10-12 minutes or until golden brown. Immediately remove from baking sheets. Serve warm. **Yield:** 32 appetizers.

Corned Beef Spread

This recipe comes from a friend, who loves to cook...just like me!
The spread is always well received at parties when served alongside wedges of onion bagels.
—Pam Reul, Owatonna, Minnesota

2 cups mayonnaise
2 cups (16 ounces) sour cream
1 medium onion, finely chopped
2 tablespoons dill weed
1 teaspoon seasoned salt
2 cups diced cooked corned beef
Onion bagels, split and cut into wedges

In a large bowl, combine the mayonnaise, sour cream, onion, dill, seasoned salt and corned beef. Cover and refrigerate until serving. Serve with bagel wedges. **Yield:** 4 cups.

Clam Dip

Although you can serve this dip right away, the flavors blend better after chilling a few hours.
—*Frances Councill, Crawford, Florida*

2 packages (8 ounces *each*)
   cream cheese, softened
2 cans (6-1/2 ounces *each*)
   minced clams, drained
2 tablespoons mayonnaise
1 tablespoon chili sauce
1/2 teaspoon minced garlic
1/8 teaspoon Worcestershire
   sauce
Assorted crackers

In a small mixing bowl, combine the first six ingredients. Transfer to a serving dish. Cover and refrigerate for at least 4 hours. Serve with crackers. **Yield:** 2-3/4 cups.

EASY-TO-ADJUST RECIPE

THE RECIPE for Clam Dip yields a generous 2-3/4 cups. If you don't need that much, the recipe can easily be cut in half.

Bacon Roll-Ups with Mustard Sauce

When I invite friends over for an evening, they ask that I make a selection of appetizers instead of a meal. They're great sports who willingly try anything I serve.
—*Geneva Jorgenson, Buffalo, Minnesota*

1/2 cup water
1/4 cup butter, cubed
1-1/2 cups herb stuffing mix
1/4 pound uncooked bulk pork
   sausage
1 egg, lightly beaten
16 bacon strips, halved
MUSTARD SAUCE:
1 cup mayonnaise
3 tablespoons sour cream
1 tablespoon ground mustard
1 tablespoon white wine
   vinegar
1 tablespoon Dijon mustard
2 drops hot pepper sauce

In a large saucepan, bring water and butter to a boil. Remove from the heat. Stir in stuffing; cool. Transfer to a bowl; stir in pork sausage and egg. Refrigerate for 1 hour.

Shape stuffing mixture into 1-in. balls; wrap each with a bacon strip half and secure with a toothpick. Place in a 15-in. x 10-in. x 1-in. baking pan. Bake at 375° for 25-30 minutes or until bacon is crisp.

Meanwhile, in a small bowl, combine the sauce ingredients; cover and refrigerate until serving. Serve with warm roll-ups. **Yield:** 3 dozen.

Taco Pinwheels

(Pictured at right)

The colorful tomatoes, lettuce and chilies make these bite-size snacks a perfect addition to a holiday buffet.
— Beverly Matthews, Pasco, Washington

1 package (8 ounces) cream cheese, softened
1 tablespoon taco seasoning
1 can (16 ounces) refried beans
8 flour tortillas (10 inches)
3 cups shredded lettuce
2 large tomatoes, seeded and finely chopped
2 cans (4 ounces *each*) chopped green chilies
1 cup finely chopped ripe olives
Salsa

In a small mixing bowl, beat cream cheese and taco seasoning until blended. Stir in the refried beans. Spread 3-4 tablespoons over each tortilla. Layer lettuce, tomatoes, chilies and olives down the center of each tortilla; roll up tightly to 2-in. diameter. Wrap in plastic wrap and refrigerate for at least 1 hour. Cut into 1-in. slices. Serve with salsa. **Yield:** about 5 dozen.

Pizza Fingers

I assemble these homemade pizza rolls ahead of time, refrigerate and brush with butter just before baking. Experiment with filling ingredients if you like.
— Nancy Foust, Stoneboro, Pennsylvania

1/2 pound hard salami, cubed
1/2 pound process cheese (Velveeta), cubed
1 medium green pepper, cubed
1 can (6 ounces) tomato paste
1 tablespoon dried basil
1 tablespoon dried oregano
2 loaves (20 ounces *each*) sliced sandwich bread, crusts removed
1/2 cup butter, melted

In a food processor, combine the salami, cheese and green pepper; cover and process until finely chopped. Stir in the tomato paste, basil and oregano.

Flatten bread with a rolling pin. Spread 1 tablespoon salami mixture over one side of each slice of bread. Roll up tightly; cut in half. Place seam side down on a greased baking sheet. Brush with butter. Bake at 375° for 15-18 minutes or until lightly browned. Serve warm. **Yield:** about 6 dozen.

Beef-Stuffed Crescents

My family loves these hearty appetizers year-round...not just during the Christmas season.
—Alene Knesel, Northome, Minnesota

3/4 pound ground beef
1/4 cup chopped onion
1 tablespoon sweet pickle relish
2 garlic cloves, minced
1/2 teaspoon salt
1/2 teaspoon chili powder
1/4 teaspoon pepper
Dash sugar
1 cup (4 ounces) shredded
   cheddar cheese
2 tubes (8 ounces *each*)
   refrigerated crescent rolls

In a large skillet, cook beef and onion over medium heat until meat is no longer pink; drain. Stir in the next seven ingredients; set aside.

Unroll crescent dough and separate into triangles. Cut each in half lengthwise, forming two triangles. Place 1 tablespoon beef mixture along the wide end of each triangle; carefully roll up. Place point side down 2 in. apart on ungreased baking sheets. Bake at 375° for 11-15 minutes or until golden brown. Serve warm. **Yield:** 32 appetizers.

Cheddar Onion Squares

When I was a child, my parents always served these appetizers before holiday meals.
I like to use sharp cheddar cheese for more intense flavor.
—Debi Burrell-Thiem, Omaha, Nebraska

3/4 cup all-purpose flour
3/4 cup cornmeal
1/4 teaspoon salt
1/4 cup shortening
1/3 cup shredded cheddar cheese
1/4 cup water
TOPPING:
3 cups coarsely chopped onions
3 tablespoons butter
1/4 cup diced pimientos
1 egg, lightly beaten
1/2 cup sour cream
1/2 teaspoon salt
1/4 teaspoon paprika
1/4 teaspoon pepper
1 cup (4 ounces) shredded
   cheddar cheese

In a large bowl, combine the flour, cornmeal and salt. Cut in shortening until mixture resembles coarse crumbs. Stir in the cheese and water just until moistened. Press into a greased 13-in. x 9-in. x 2-in. baking pan. Bake at 400° for 5 minutes. Place pan on a wire rack. Reduce heat to 350°.

In a large skillet, saute onions in butter until tender. Stir in the pimientos. Spread over crust. Combine the egg, sour cream, salt, paprika and pepper; spread over onion layer. Bake for 20 minutes. Sprinkle with cheese. Bake 5 minutes longer or until cheese is melted. Cut into 1-1/2-in. squares. Serve warm. **Yield:** 4 dozen.

Ways to Reuse Christmas Cards

(Pictured above)

AS YOU PACK AWAY the holiday decorations after the new year, it's tempting to simply toss all the Christmas cards you received into the recycling bin.

Instead, read through those greeting cards one more time and put them in a box. Over the summer or in fall, pull out the cards and use them in the following creative ways:

Merry Markers. For beautiful bookmarks or gift tags, reach for the scissors and cut out images or words. Use a hole punch, then tie on a tassel. These homemade bookmarks make special stocking stuffers.

Pretty as a Picture. Framed photos of holiday scenes are a great way to liven up your decor at Christmastime, but they often can be costly. An easy and inexpensive alternative is to frame images from greetings cards. Use a traditional photo frame as a tabletop display. For an eye-catching wall hanging, purchase a larger matted frame.

Seasonal Stationery. The front, inside and even back of Christmas cards can have pretty images that would work well as postcards, note cards and recipe cards. (Be sure to check with your local post office regarding postcard size restrictions.)

'TIS THE *Season*

A Host of Holiday Breads

ARE YOU LOOKING for a way to awaken the sleepyheads in the household over the holidays? Try baking bread!

As the wonderful aroma of fresh-from-the oven favorites wafts through the house, your clan will rise from their slumber and come clamoring to the kitchen for a delightful taste.

This chapter features an assortment of both sweet and savory baked goods.

Buttermilk Drop Scones (paired with Mock Devonshire Cream), Maple Pecan Coffee Twist and Mini Swiss Cheese Loaves are just a taste of the tempting treats you'll find on the following pages.

OVEN-FRESH FAVORITES
(Clockwise from top)

Buttermilk Drop Scones (p. 50)

Mock Devonshire Cream (p. 50)

Maple Pecan Coffee Twist (p. 52)

Mini Swiss Cheese Loaves (p. 51)

Buttermilk Drop Scones

(Pictured on page 49)

*I came up with this recipe in an attempt to copy some terrific buttermilk scones I had at
a restaurant in northern Wisconsin. These easy drop scones are the delicious result!*
—Ellyn Graebert, Tillamook, Ontario

3 cups all-purpose flour
1-1/4 cups old-fashioned oats
2 tablespoons sugar
4 teaspoons baking powder
1/2 teaspoon salt
1/4 teaspoon baking soda
1 egg
1-1/2 cups buttermilk
2/3 cup vegetable oil
1/4 cup dried cranberries
1/4 cup chopped dried apricots
1/4 cup chopped pecans

TOPPING:
2 tablespoons sugar
1/2 teaspoon ground cinnamon
Mock Devonshire Cream (recipe below), optional

In a large bowl, combine the first six ingredients. Combine the egg, buttermilk and oil; stir into dry ingredients just until moistened. Fold in the cranberries, apricots and pecans.

Drop by 1/4 cupfuls 2 in. apart onto greased baking sheets. Combine sugar and cinnamon; sprinkle over dough. Bake at 400° for 12-15 minutes or until lightly browned. Remove to wire racks. Serve warm with Mock Devonshire Cream if desired. **Yield:** 20 scones.

Mock Devonshire Cream

(Pictured on page 49)

*I made this recipe often when I worked in the food service area of a local university.
The cream pairs well with scones and muffins.*
—Carol Allen, Emporia, Kansas

1/2 cup heavy whipping cream
2 tablespoons confectioners' sugar
1/2 cup sour cream

In a small mixing bowl, beat whipping cream for 2 minutes. Add confectioners' sugar and continue beating until stiff. Place the sour cream in a bowl; stir in a small amount of whipped cream. Fold in remaining whipped cream. Cover and refrigerate until serving. **Yield:** about 1 cup.

Mini Swiss Cheese Loaves

(Pictured at right and on page 48)

I usually make these little loaves in the morning, so they're ready for my husband, Hal, at lunchtime. There's nothing better than a sandwich prepared with homemade bread.
—Helen Wanamaker Vail
Glenside, Pennsylvania

1 package (1/4 ounce) active
   dry yeast
1/2 cup warm water (110°
   to 115°)
1 cup (8 ounces) sour cream
2 tablespoons sugar
1 teaspoon salt
1/4 teaspoon baking soda
1 egg
2-1/3 cups all-purpose flour
1 cup (4 ounces) shredded
   Swiss cheese
2 teaspoons sesame seeds

In a large mixing bowl, dissolve yeast in warm water. Add the sour cream, sugar, salt, baking soda, egg and 1-1/3 cups flour. Beat on low speed for 30 seconds; beat on medium for 2 minutes. Stir in Swiss cheese and remaining flour. Do not knead.

Spread batter into four greased 5-3/4-in. x 3-in. x 2-in. loaf pans. Sprinkle with sesame seeds. Cover and let rise in a warm place until doubled, about 45 minutes. Bake at 350° for 25-30 minutes or until golden brown. Remove from pans to wire racks to cool. **Yield:** 4 mini loaves.

Maple Pecan Coffee Twist

(Pictured on page 48)

Making sweet breads has been a hobby of mine since I was a teenager.
The addition of maple flavoring gives this coffee cake a tasty twist.
—Carolyn Strube, Garden City, Texas

  1 **package (1/4 ounce) active**
    dry yeast
1/4 **cup warm water (110°**
    to 115°)
3/4 **cup warm milk (110° to 115°)**
1/2 **cup mashed potatoes**
1/2 **cup shortening**
1/4 **cup sugar**
  2 **eggs**
  1 **teaspoon maple flavoring**
1/2 **teaspoon salt**
  4 **to 5 cups all-purpose flour**
FILLING:
1/2 **cup sugar**
1/2 **cup finely chopped pecans**
  1 **teaspoon ground cinnamon**
  1 **teaspoon maple flavoring**
  6 **tablespoons butter, softened**
GLAZE:
1-1/2 **cups confectioners' sugar**
  2 **to 3 tablespoons milk**
1/4 **teaspoon maple flavoring**

In a large mixing bowl, dissolve yeast in warm water. Add the milk, potatoes, shortening, sugar, eggs, maple flavoring and salt; mix well. Add 2 cups flour; beat until smooth. Stir in enough remaining flour to form a soft dough.

Turn onto a floured surface; knead until smooth and elastic, about 6-8 minutes. Place in a greased bowl, turning once to grease top. Cover and let rise in a warm place until doubled, about 1 hour.

For filling, combine the sugar, pecans, cinnamon and maple flavoring; set aside. Punch dough down. Turn onto a lightly floured surface; divide into thirds. Roll each portion into a 14-in. circle; place one circle on a greased baking sheet or 14-in. pizza pan. Spread with a third of the butter; sprinkle with a third of the filling. Top with a second circle of dough; spread with butter and top with filling. Repeat with remaining dough, butter and filling; pinch to seal.

Carefully place a glass in the center of the circle. With scissors, cut from outside edge just to the glass, forming 16 wedges. Remove glass; twist each wedge five to six times. Pinch ends to seal and tuck under. Cover and let rise until doubled, about 30 minutes. Bake at 375° for 25-30 minutes or until golden brown.

In a small bowl, combine glaze ingredients; set aside. Carefully remove bread from pan by running a metal spatula under it to loosen; transfer to a wire rack. Drizzle with glaze. Serve slightly warm or cool completely. **Yield:** 16 servings.

Grandma's Christmas Bread

(Pictured at right)

For as long as I can remember, this bread has been a part of my family's traditional Christmas morning breakfast. I modified the recipe so I could make it in a bread machine.
— Barb and Ray Schmeling
Rhinelander, Wisconsin

1-1/4 cups warm milk (70° to 80°)
  1/2 teaspoon lemon juice
    2 tablespoons butter, softened
    2 tablespoons sugar
1-1/2 teaspoons salt
    3 cups bread flour
    2 teaspoons active dry yeast
  3/4 cup golden raisins
  3/4 cup raisins
  1/2 cup dried currants
1-1/2 teaspoons grated lemon peel

GLAZE:
  1/2 cup confectioners' sugar
1-1/2 teaspoons milk
    1 teaspoon butter, melted
  1/4 teaspoon vanilla extract

In bread machine pan, place the first seven ingredients in order suggested by manufacturer. Select basic bread setting. Choose crust color and loaf size if available. Bake according to bread machine directions (check dough after 5 minutes of mixing; add 1 to 2 tablespoons of water or flour if needed).

Just before the final kneading (your bread machine may audibly signal this), add the raisins, currants and lemon peel. In a small bowl, combine glaze ingredients; drizzle over cooled bread. **Yield:** 1 loaf (about 2 pounds).

BREAD MACHINE BASICS

BREAD MACHINES are a boon for busy bakers. For the best result, follow these tips.
- Before beginning, carefully read your bread machine owner's manual.
- All liquid ingredients (water, milk, eggs, juice, etc.) should be at room temperature (70° to 80°) before adding to the machine.
- Measure ingredients accurately, then add to the machine in the order suggested by your bread machine manufacturer.

- For the best results, use bread flour.
- Check dough after 5 minutes of mixing. The dough should feel smooth, soft and slightly tacky. If it's moist or sticky, add 1 tablespoon of flour. If it's dry and crumbly, add 1 tablespoon of liquid.
- Recipes containing eggs, milk, sour cream and other dairy or perishable products should be baked immediately and not placed on a "time-bake" cycle.

Apricot Bubble Ring

Both of our daughters received ribbons for this recipe at the 4-H fair.
This bubble ring is perfect for serving a crowd at breakfast.
—Lois Schlickau, Haven, Kansas

1 package (1/4 ounce) active
   dry yeast
1/4 cup warm water (110°
   to 115°)
1/2 cup warm milk (110° to 115°)
1/3 cup butter, melted
1/3 cup sugar
2 eggs
1 teaspoon salt
3-3/4 to 4 cups all-purpose flour
FILLING:
3/4 cup sugar
1 teaspoon ground cinnamon
1/4 cup butter, melted and cooled
2/3 cup apricot preserves
3/4 cup finely chopped walnuts

In a large mixing bowl, dissolve yeast in warm water. Add the milk, butter, sugar, eggs and salt; mix well. Add 2 cups flour; beat until smooth. Stir in enough remaining flour to form a soft dough.

Turn onto a floured surface; knead until smooth and elastic, about 6-8 minutes. Place in a greased bowl, turning once to grease top. Cover and let rise in a warm place until doubled, about 1 hour.

For filling, combine the sugar and cinnamon in a shallow bowl; set aside. Punch dough down; cover and let rest for 10 minutes. On a lightly floured surface, divide dough into 20 pieces and form into balls. Dip each ball into melted butter, then roll in cinnamon-sugar. Place 10 balls in a greased 10-in. fluted tube pan. Spoon half of the apricot preserves between the balls; sprinkle with half of the walnuts. Repeat. Cover and let rise until doubled, about 45 minutes.

Bake at 350° for 30-35 minutes or until browned. Cool for 5 minutes before inverting onto a serving plate. Serve warm. **Yield:** 20 servings.

Oregano Quick Bread

At Christmas, I deliver dozens of these oven-fresh loaves to friends and neighbors.
—Paula Marchesi, Lenhartsville, Pennsylvania

5 tablespoons butter, softened
1 cup sugar
2 eggs
1-1/2 cups all-purpose flour
1-1/2 teaspoons baking powder
1 teaspoon ground cinnamon
1/2 teaspoon salt
1/2 teaspoon ground nutmeg
3/4 cup milk
1/2 cup chopped pecans
1/3 cup minced fresh oregano

In a large mixing bowl, cream butter and sugar. Add eggs, one at a time, beating well after each addition. Combine the flour, baking powder, cinnamon, salt and nutmeg; add to creamed mixture alternately with milk. Stir in the pecans and oregano.

Pour into a greased 9-in. x 5-in. x 3-in. loaf pan. Bake at 350° for 50-60 minutes or until a toothpick inserted near the center comes out clean. Cool for 10 minutes before removing from pan to a wire rack. Serve warm. **Yield:** 1 loaf.

Chocolate Chip Caramel Rolls

(Pictured at right)

As a teenager, I keep active with sports and friends. But baking is my favorite hobby. My five older brothers eat these delicious breakfast rolls right out of the oven!
—Julia Holm, Northfield, Minnesota

1 package (1/4 ounce) active
  dry yeast
3/4 cup warm water (110°
  to 115°)
3/4 cup warm milk (110° to 115°)
3 tablespoons vegetable oil
1/4 cup sugar
1-1/2 teaspoons salt
3-3/4 to 4-1/2 cups all-purpose flour
3/4 cup miniature semisweet
  chocolate chips
FILLING:
1/4 cup butter, softened
1/3 cup sugar
2 tablespoons ground cinnamon
1 cup miniature semisweet
  chocolate chips
SYRUP:
1 cup packed brown sugar
3/4 cup heavy whipping cream

In a large mixing bowl, dissolve yeast in warm water. Add the milk, oil, sugar, salt and 3 cups flour; beat on medium speed for 3 minutes. Stir in enough remaining flour to form a firm dough.

Turn onto a floured surface; knead in chocolate chips until dough is smooth and elastic, about 6-8 minutes. Place in a greased bowl, turning once to grease top. Cover and let rise in a warm place until doubled, about 1 hour.

Punch dough down. Turn onto a lightly floured surface. Roll into an 18-in. x 12-in. rectangle. For filling, spread butter over dough to within 1/2 in. of edges. Combine sugar and cinnamon; sprinkle over butter. Sprinkle with chocolate chips; gently press into dough. Roll up jelly-roll style, starting with a long side; pinch seam to seal. Cut into 12 slices.

Combine brown sugar and cream; pour into a greased 13-in. x 9-in. x 2-in. baking dish. Arrange rolls cut side down over syrup. Cover and let rise until doubled, about 50 minutes. Bake at 375° for 30-35 minutes or until golden brown. Cool for 10 minutes before removing to a serving platter. Serve warm. **Yield:** 1 dozen.

Cranberry Coffee Cake

A delightful cranberry filling is tucked inside every slice of this moist coffee cake.
The toasted almonds on top add pleasant crunch.
—*Karen Dietert, New Braunfels, Texas*

1/2 cup butter, softened
1 cup sugar
2 eggs
1/2 teaspoon almond extract
2 cups all-purpose flour
1 teaspoon baking powder
1 teaspoon baking soda
1/2 teaspoon salt
1 cup (8 ounces) sour cream
1 can (16 ounces) whole-berry cranberry sauce, *divided*
1/2 cup sliced almonds
GLAZE:
3/4 cup confectioners' sugar
2 tablespoons water
1/2 teaspoon almond extract

In a large mixing bowl, cream butter and sugar. Add eggs, one at a time, beating well after each addition. Stir in almond extract. Combine the flour, baking powder, baking soda and salt; add to creamed mixture alternately with sour cream. Spread half of the batter into a greased 10-in. tube pan; top with half of the cranberry sauce. Repeat layers. Sprinkle with almonds.

Bake at 350° for 50-55 minutes or until a toothpick inserted near the center comes out clean. Cool for 10 minutes before removing from pan to a wire rack to cool completely. In a small bowl, combine the glaze ingredients until smooth; drizzle over coffee cake. **Yield:** 10-12 servings.

Orange Zucchini Bread

These moist mini loaves have pretty flecks of green from the zucchini.
I won first place at the Ohio State Fair with this recipe!
—*Pat Woolley, Jackson Center, Ohio*

3 eggs
3/4 cup vegetable oil
1-1/2 cups sugar
2 teaspoons grated lemon peel
2 teaspoons grated orange peel
1/2 teaspoon orange extract
1/4 teaspoon vanilla extract
2 cups shredded unpeeled zucchini
2-1/2 cups all-purpose flour
2 teaspoons baking powder
3/4 teaspoon salt
1/2 teaspoon ground ginger

1/4 teaspoon baking soda
1/2 cup chopped walnuts

In a large mixing bowl, combine the eggs and oil. Add sugar; mix well. Stir in the lemon peel, orange peel and extracts. Add zucchini; mix well. Combine the flour, baking powder, salt, ginger and baking soda; stir into zucchini mixture just until moistened. Fold in walnuts.

Transfer to four greased 5-3/4-in. x 3-in. x 2-in. loaf pans. Bake at 350° for 35-40 minutes or until golden brown and a toothpick inserted near the center comes out clean. Cool for 10 minutes before removing from pans to wire racks to cool completely. **Yield:** 4 mini loaves.

Cherry Walnut Yeast Bread

(Pictured at right)

I created this delicious bread as a way to showcase the tart cherries that grow in abundance here in Door County. Slices topped with butter or jam make a great breakfast or midday snack.
—Max Sample, Baileys Harbor, Wisconsin

1/2 cup dried cherries *or* cranberries
1/2 cup hot water
2 to 2-1/4 cups bread flour
1 cup whole wheat flour
1 package (1/4 ounce) active dry yeast
1-1/2 teaspoons salt
1/2 cup milk
3 tablespoons maple syrup
2 tablespoons butter
1 egg
1/2 cup chopped walnuts

SLICING A ROUND LOAF OF BREAD

TO SLICE a round loaf of bread, first cut the loaf in half vertically. Place the cut side down and slice. Or you can simply cut the loaf into pie-shaped wedges.

Combine cherries and water in a bowl; let stand for 10 minutes. Drain, reserving juice; set cherries aside. In a large mixing bowl, combine 1 cup bread flour, whole wheat flour, yeast and salt. In a small saucepan, combine the milk, syrup, butter and reserved cherry liquid; heat to 120°-130°. Add to dry ingredients; beat just until moistened.

Add egg; beat until smooth. Add enough remaining bread flour to form a soft dough (dough will be slightly sticky). Beat for 2 minutes. Stir in walnuts and cherries. Turn onto a lightly floured surface; knead until smooth and elastic, about 6-8 minutes. Place in a greased bowl, turning once to grease top. Cover and let rise in a warm place until doubled, about 1 hour.

Punch dough down; turn onto a lightly floured surface. Shape into a 7-in. round loaf. Place on a greased baking sheet. Cover and let rise until doubled, about 40 minutes. Bake at 350° for 30-35 minutes or until browned. Remove from pan to a wire rack to cool. **Yield:** 1 loaf.

Sesame Cloverleaf Rolls

I modified this recipe from one I found a few years ago. The rolls have a nice light texture.
—Geri Barr, Calgary, Alberta

2-1/2 cups warm water (110°
    to 115°), *divided*
  2 packages (1/4 ounce *each*)
    active dry yeast
1/2 teaspoon plus 1/2 cup sugar,
    divided
1/2 cup butter, softened
  2 eggs
  7 to 7-1/2 cups all-purpose flour
  2 teaspoons salt
  1 egg yolk
  2 tablespoons cold water
  2 tablespoons sesame seeds

In a small bowl, combine 1/2 cup warm water, yeast and 1/2 teaspoon sugar; let stand for 5 minutes. In a large mixing bowl, cream butter and remaining sugar. Beat in eggs. Add 4 cups flour, salt and remaining warm water; beat until smooth. Beat in yeast mixture. Stir in enough remaining flour to form a soft dough.

Turn onto a floured surface; knead until smooth and elastic, about 6-8 minutes. Place in a greased bowl, turning once to grease top. Cover and let rise in a warm place until doubled, about 1 hour.

Punch dough down. Turn onto a lightly floured surface; divide into six portions. Divide each portion into five pieces. Divide each piece into three balls. Place three balls in each greased muffin cup. Cover and let rise until doubled, about 1 hour.

Beat egg yolk and cold water; brush over dough. Sprinkle with sesame seeds. Bake at 350° for 15-20 minutes or until golden brown. Remove to wire racks. **Yield:** 2-1/2 dozen.

Pineapple Nut Bread

My family loves this bread for snacks or with our meals as dessert. At Christmas,
I use mini loaf pans and give them as gifts.
—Betty Barker, Portland, Michigan

  1 can (8 ounces) crushed
    pineapple
  2 cups all-purpose flour
3/4 cup sugar
1/2 teaspoon baking powder
1/2 teaspoon baking soda
1/2 teaspoon salt
  1 egg
1/2 cup milk
1/4 cup butter, melted
  1 cup chopped walnuts

Drain pineapple, reserving 1/4 cup juice; set aside. In a bowl, combine the flour, sugar, baking powder, baking soda and salt. In a small mixing bowl, combine the pineapple, reserved juice, egg, milk and butter; mix well. Stir into the dry ingredients just until moistened. Stir in walnuts.

Pour into a greased 8-in. x 4-in. x 2-in. loaf pan. Bake at 350° for 55-60 minutes or until a toothpick inserted near the center comes out clean. Cool for 10 minutes before removing from pan to a wire rack to cool completely. **Yield:** 1 loaf.

Strawberry Cheesecake Muffins

(Pictured at right)

My mother-in-law has been a great inspiration to me in the kitchen. These fruity muffins are often part of our Sunday dinner menu.
—Iris Linkletter
Summerside, Prince Edward Island

1 package (3 ounces) cream cheese, softened
1/4 cup confectioners' sugar
2-1/2 cups all-purpose flour
3 teaspoons baking powder
1/2 teaspoon salt
1 egg
1-1/4 cups milk
1/2 cup packed brown sugar
1/3 cup butter, melted
1 teaspoon grated lemon peel
1/4 teaspoon almond extract
1/4 cup strawberry jam

In a small mixing bowl, beat the cream cheese and confectioners' sugar until smooth; set aside. In a large bowl, combine the flour, baking powder and salt. In another small mixing bowl, beat the egg, milk, brown sugar, butter, lemon peel and almond extract. Stir into the dry ingredients just until moistened.

Spoon half of the batter into greased muffin cups. Top each with 1 tablespoon cream cheese mixture and 1 teaspoon jam. Top with remaining batter.

Bake at 375° for 18-20 minutes or until a toothpick comes out clean and tops are golden brown. Cool for 5 minutes before removing from pan to a wire rack. **Yield:** 1 dozen.

'TIS THE *Season*

Dazzling Main Dishes

A SUCCESSFUL dinner on a special occasion like Christmas starts with the selection of just the right main course.

Whether you need something elegant (like Beef Tenderloin with Roasted Vegetables, shown at right) or something a little more casual (such as Seafood Lasagna Alfredo on page 65), you'll be pleased with the merry array of main dishes featured in this chapter.

From beef and seafood to pork and poultry, the following pages offer inviting entrees to suit any occasion!

ELEGANT
ENTREE

Beef Tenderloin
With Roasted
Vegetables (p. 62)

Beef Tenderloin with Roasted Vegetables

(Pictured on page 60)

I appreciate this recipe because it includes a side dish of roasted potatoes, brussels sprouts and carrots, giving me one less dish to think about!
—*Janet Tucker, Bellevue, Ohio*

1 beef tenderloin (3 pounds), trimmed
3/4 cup dry white wine *or* beef broth
3/4 cup reduced-sodium soy sauce
4 teaspoons minced fresh rosemary
4 teaspoons Dijon mustard
1-1/2 teaspoons ground mustard
3 garlic cloves, peeled and sliced
1 pound Yukon gold potatoes, cut into 1-inch wedges
1 pound brussels sprouts, halved
1 package (16 ounces) fresh baby carrots

Place tenderloin in a large resealable plastic bag. In a bowl, combine the wine or broth, soy sauce, rosemary, Dijon mustard, ground mustard and garlic. Pour half of the marinade over tenderloin; seal bag and turn to coat. Refrigerate for 4-12 hours, turning several times. Cover and refrigerate remaining marinade.

Place the potatoes, brussels sprouts and carrots in a greased 13-in. x 9-in. x 2-in. baking dish; add reserved marinade and toss to coat. Cover and bake at 425° for 30 minutes; stir.

Drain and discard marinade from tenderloin. Place tenderloin over vegetables. Bake, uncovered, for 30-45 minutes or until meat reaches desired doneness (for medium-rare, a meat thermometer should read 145°; medium, 160°; well-done, 170°).

Remove beef and let stand for 15 minutes. Check vegetables for doneness. If additional roasting is needed, cover with foil and bake for 10-15 minutes or until tender. Slice beef and serve with vegetables. **Yield:** 8-10 servings.

YUKON GOLD POINTERS

ALTHOUGH available in Europe and South America for centuries, Yukon gold potatoes are now becoming popular in North America.

Yukon gold potatoes have a golden flesh and a buttery, almost nutty flavor. It's a versatile potato that's excellent baked, boiled, fried or mashed.

Chicken Rolls with Pesto Pasta

(Pictured at right)

Fresh basil (which is available in grocery stores year-round) lends terrific flavor to these tasty chicken rolls. As the fantastic finishing touch, toss the pasta with purchased or homemade pesto just before serving.
—*Pat Stevens, Granbury, Texas*

4 boneless skinless chicken
    breast halves (6 ounces *each*)
Salt and pepper
1/4 cup chopped fresh basil
1/4 cup crumbled feta cheese
  2 garlic cloves, peeled and
    halved
  3 tablespoons olive oil, *divided*
1/2 pound sliced fresh
    mushrooms
  2 green onions, thinly sliced
  2 tablespoons chopped red
    onion
  1 tablespoon chicken broth
  8 ounces uncooked angel hair
    pasta
3/4 cup prepared pesto sauce

Flatten chicken to 1/4-in. thickness; sprinkle with salt and pepper. Down the center of each chicken breast half, place 1 tablespoon basil, 1 tablespoon feta cheese and a garlic clove half. Roll up and secure with toothpicks.

In a large skillet, brown roll-ups in 2 tablespoons oil on all sides. Place in an 8-in. square baking dish. In the same skillet, saute mushrooms and onions in remaining oil until tender. Add broth; cook and stir until bubbly. Pour over chicken. Cover and bake at 325° for 20-30 minutes or until juices run clear.

Cook pasta according to package directions; drain. Toss with pesto sauce. Discard toothpicks from roll-ups; serve over pasta. Top with mushroom mixture. **Yield:** 4 servings.

Baked Halibut with Onions

We once lived near Homer, Alaska, the Halibut Capital of the World.
We fondly recall Alaska's Kenai Peninsula every time we enjoy this dish.
—Rebecca McLaughlin, Pismo Beach, California

1 cup butter, melted
2 large onions, thinly sliced
1-1/4 cups mayonnaise
6 halibut steaks (8 ounces *each*)
1 cup finely crushed cornflakes

Place the butter in a 13-in. x 9-in. x 2-in. baking dish; top with onions. Bake, uncovered, at 400° for 8 minutes or until tender. Spread mayonnaise over both sides of halibut; coat with cornflake crumbs. Place over onions. Bake, uncovered, for 20-22 minutes or until fish flakes easily with a fork. **Yield:** 6 servings.

Editor's Note: Reduced-fat or fat-free mayonnaise is not recommended for this recipe.

Peppery Beef Roast

As a stay-at-home mom, slow cooker recipes are a lifesaver for me...especially on holidays!
—Kelly Lindsay, Longmont, Colorado

1 boneless beef rump roast
  (3-1/2 to 4 pounds)
1/2 cup ketchup
3 tablespoons brown sugar
1 tablespoon ground mustard
1 tablespoon lemon juice
2 teaspoons celery salt
2 teaspoons pepper
2 teaspoons Worcestershire
  sauce
1 teaspoon garlic powder
1 teaspoon onion powder
1 teaspoon Liquid Smoke,
  optional
1/2 to 1 teaspoon salt
1/8 teaspoon hot pepper sauce

Cut roast in half; place in a 5-qt. slow cooker. Combine the remaining ingredients; pour over roast. Cover and cook on low for 8-9 hours or until meat is tender. Thicken cooking juices if desired. **Yield:** 10-12 servings.

SLOW COOKER TIPS

- The slow cooker should be filled at least half full, but never more than three-fourths full.
- Unless the recipe instructs you to stir in or add ingredients, refrain from lifting the lid while the slow cooker is cooking. The loss of steam can mean an additional 15 to 30 minutes of cooking each time you lift the lid.
- Be sure the lid is sealed properly—not tilted or askew. The steam creates a seal.
- Remove food from the slow cooker within 1 hour after it's finished cooking. Promptly refrigerate leftovers.

Seafood Lasagna Alfredo

(Pictured at right)

Once when expecting a visit from a college friend, I wanted to serve something a little different. So I came up with this lasagna. It's perfect for company because it can be assembled in advance.
— *Dolores Jensen, Arnold, Missouri*

2 cans (6 ounces *each*) lump crabmeat, drained
1 package (5 ounces) frozen cooked salad shrimp, thawed and patted dry
1 carton (15 ounces) ricotta cheese
2 eggs, lightly beaten
1 tablespoon Italian seasoning
1 pound sliced fresh mushrooms
1 large onion, chopped
2 garlic cloves, minced
6 tablespoons butter
1/2 cup all-purpose flour
2 cans (12 ounces *each*) evaporated milk
1 cup milk
1 cup grated Parmesan cheese, *divided*
Salt and pepper to taste
9 lasagna noodles, cooked and drained
1 package (10 ounces) frozen chopped spinach, thawed and squeezed dry
4 cups (16 ounces) shredded mozzarella cheese
1 package (10 ounces) frozen chopped broccoli, thawed

In a small bowl, combine crab and shrimp; set aside. In another bowl, combine the ricotta cheese, eggs and Italian seasoning until smooth; set aside.

In a large skillet, saute the mushrooms, onion and garlic in butter until tender. Stir in flour until blended. Gradually add evaporated milk and milk. Bring to a boil; cook and stir for 2 minutes or until thickened. Reduce heat; stir in 1/2 cup Parmesan cheese, salt and pepper until cheese is melted.

In a greased shallow 4-qt. baking dish, layer three noodles, spinach, a third of the ricotta mixture, 1-1/3 cups mozzarella cheese and a third of the mushroom sauce. Top with three noodles, crab mixture, a third of the ricotta mixture, 1-1/3 cups mozzarella cheese, a third of the mushroom sauce and remaining noodles. Top with broccoli and the remaining ricotta mixture, mozzarella and mushroom sauce. Sprinkle with remaining Parmesan.

Bake, uncovered, at 350° for 45-55 minutes or until heated through. Let stand for 10 minutes before cutting. **Yield:** 12 servings.

Flavorful Grilled Flank Steak

*This grilled flank steak can be served with a side dish for a more elegant entree
or used to make fajitas at a casual gathering.*
—Lana Tabb, Lakeland, Florida

1 can (10-1/2 ounces)
  condensed beef consomme,
  undiluted
1 cup dry red wine *or* beef
  broth
2/3 cup soy sauce
1/2 cup sliced green onions
2 garlic cloves, minced
2 tablespoons brown sugar
2 tablespoons lime juice
1 beef flank steak (1-1/2
  pounds)

In a bowl, combine the first seven ingredients. Cover and refrigerate 1/2 cup for basting. Pour the remaining marinade into a large resealable plastic bag; add flank steak. Seal bag and turn to coat; refrigerate for 8 hours or overnight, turning once. Drain and discard marinade from steak.

Grill, uncovered, over medium heat for 6-10 minutes on each side or until meat reaches desired doneness (for medium-rare, a meat thermometer should read 145°; medium, 160°; well-done, 170°), basting occasionally with reserved marinade. Thinly slice meat across the grain. **Yield:** 4 servings.

Breaded Swiss Chicken

*Our four kids keep us hopping. So for special occasions, I appreciate recipes like
this that require few ingredients but are impressive to serve guests.*
—Susie Ecker, Richmond, Indiana

6 boneless skinless chicken
  breast halves (6 ounces *each*)
1 teaspoon salt, *divided*
2 eggs
1 cup seasoned bread crumbs
1/2 cup olive oil
1 cup (4 ounces) shredded
  Swiss cheese
2 tablespoons butter
3 tablespoons all-purpose flour
1/8 teaspoon pepper
2 cups milk
3 tablespoons white wine *or*
  chicken broth

Flatten chicken to 1/4-in. thickness. Sprinkle with 1/2 teaspoon salt. In a shallow bowl, beat the eggs. Place bread crumbs in another shallow bowl. Dip chicken in eggs, then roll in crumbs. Let stand for 5 minutes.

In a large skillet over medium heat, cook chicken in oil in batches for 6-8 minutes on each side or until juices run clear; drain. Place chicken in a greased 15-in. x 10-in. x 1-in. baking pan; sprinkle with cheese. Bake at 350° for 2-3 minutes or until cheese is melted.

Meanwhile, in a large saucepan, melt the butter. Stir in flour, pepper and remaining salt until smooth; gradually add milk. Bring to a boil over medium heat; cook and stir for 1-2 minutes or until thickened. Remove from the heat; stir in wine or broth. Serve with chicken. **Yield:** 6 servings.

Wild Rice-Stuffed Pork Loin

(Pictured at right)

This recipe features wild rice and apricot stuffing tucked inside a tender pork roast.
—*Kim Rubner, Worthington, Iowa*

1 whole boneless pork loin
  roast (4 pounds), trimmed
1 teaspoon salt
1/2 teaspoon garlic powder
1/4 teaspoon pepper
2 cups wild rice, cooked and
  drained
1-1/2 cups coarsely chopped dried
  apricots
1 cup chopped onion
3/4 cup finely chopped celery
3/4 cup minced fresh parsley
1/2 teaspoon rubbed sage
1/2 teaspoon dried thyme
1/2 cup chicken broth
5 bacon strips, cut in half

Cut roast down the center lengthwise to within 1/2 in. of bottom. Open roast so it lies flat. On each half, make a lengthwise slit down the center to within 1/2 in. of bottom. Sprinkle with salt, garlic powder and pepper.

In a large bowl, combine the rice, apricots, onion, celery, parsley, sage, thyme and broth. Divide half of the stuffing among the three slits. Roll up roast from a long side; tie with kitchen string at 2-in. intervals. Place the remaining stuffing in a greased shallow 2-qt. baking dish; set aside.

Bake roast, uncovered, at 350° for 1-1/2 to 2 hours. Carefully remove string. Place bacon strips over top. Bake 30-45 minutes longer or until a meat thermometer reads 160°. Cover and bake reserved stuffing for 30 minutes or until heated through. Let roast stand for 10 minutes before slicing. **Yield:** 8-10 servings.

BUTTERFLY A PORK ROAST

1. Lay the roast on a flat surface. With a sharp knife, make a lengthwise slit down the center to within 1/2 in. of bottom.

2. Open the roast to lay flat. On one half, make a lengthwise cut down the center, making sure not to cut all the way through.

3. Cut a lengthwise slit down the center of the other half.

Veal Cutlets Supreme

This dish has been in the family for years and is still one of our favorites.
Guests love it and usually ask for the recipe.
—Irene Bruntz, Grand Rapids, Michigan

6 veal cutlets (1/2 inch thick)
2 garlic cloves, minced
1 teaspoon salt, *divided*
1/4 teaspoon pepper
4 tablespoons butter, *divided*
2 medium onions, chopped
3/4 pound sliced fresh
   mushrooms
3 tablespoons crushed butter-
   flavored crackers
1 cup heavy whipping cream
3/4 cup dry white wine *or* chicken
   broth

2 tablespoons minced fresh parsley
3/4 cup shredded cheddar cheese

Sprinkle veal with garlic, 1/2 teaspoon salt and pepper. In a large skillet, brown veal in 2 tablespoons butter on both sides. Transfer to a greased 13-in. x 9-in. x 2-in. baking dish.

In the same skillet, saute onions and mushrooms in remaining butter until tender. Stir in cracker crumbs, cream, wine or broth and remaining salt; cook and stir until mixture comes to a boil. Stir in parsley; pour over veal.

Cover and bake at 350° for 20 minutes. Uncover; sprinkle with cheese. Bake 5 minutes longer or until cheese is melted. **Yield:** 6 servings.

HOLIDAY MENU SUGGESTIONS

TO MAKE holiday meal planning a little easier, our home economists offer five mouthwatering menus that are perfect for fancy sit-down dinners or more casual get-togethers.

Each meal features an entree from this chapter and side dishes and desserts from other areas of this book.

- **Casual Grill-Side Supper.** For a fun twist, fire up the grill for Flavorful Grilled Flank Steak (page 66). Broccoli with Tangy Horseradish Sauce (page 159) and baked potatoes are easy accompaniments. Then cool things down with Tangerine Cranberry Sorbet (page 153).
- **Dinner for Four.** When you're expecting a smaller number of people at your table, Barbecued Cornish Hens (opposite page) are just the right size. Chive Red Potatoes (page 162) and Pumpkin Gingerbread with Caramel Sauce (page 106) round out this perfectly portioned dinner.
- **Fine Dining.** For an easy way to impress guests, prepare Beef Tenderloin with Roasted Vegetables (page 62) and Herbed Cheddar Crescents (page 120). Then, indulge in richly delicious Cappuccino Torte (page 89).
- **Luscious Lasagna.** Bring a taste of Italy to the table with an appetizer of Antipasto Kabobs (page 37). Then present a tossed salad and luscious Seafood Lasagna Alfredo (page 65). For a fitting finale, set out Almond Venetian Dessert (page 93).
- **Regal Roast.** When paired with Warm Musroom Salad (page 28) and Hazelnut Pear Tart (page 117), Wild Rice-Stuffed Pork Loin (page 67) makes for a festive winter meal.

Holiday Glazed Ham

(Pictured at right)

This easy glaze is sure to complement any holiday ham. I serve the remaining glaze on the side.
— *Tammy Harris, Deltona, Florida*

1 boneless fully cooked ham
  (5 pounds)
1/2 cup butter
2 tablespoons all-purpose flour
1 cup apple jelly
2/3 cup packed brown sugar
1/2 cup orange juice
1/4 cup sugar
1/2 teaspoon ground cinnamon
1/2 teaspoon ground nutmeg
1/4 teaspoon ground cloves

Place ham on a rack in a large roasting pan. Bake, uncovered, at 325° for 1-1/4 hours. For glaze, melt the butter in a saucepan; stir in flour until smooth. Stir in the jelly, brown sugar, orange juice, sugar, cinnamon, nutmeg and cloves. Cook and stir over medium heat until smooth.

Brush some of the glaze over ham. Bake 30-35 minutes longer or until a meat thermometer reads 140°. Let stand for 5-10 minutes before slicing. Simmer the remaining glaze and serve with ham. **Yield:** 15 servings.

Barbecued Cornish Hens

I came up with this recipe when I was just a teenager and have made it quite often since then.
— *Diane Widmer, Blue Island, Illinois*

4 Cornish game hens (20 ounces
  each)
2 tablespoons butter, softened
Salt and pepper
1 cup ketchup
1 can (6 ounces) tomato paste
1/2 cup packed brown sugar
1/3 cup cider vinegar
1/4 cup water
2 tablespoons steak sauce
1 tablespoon prepared mustard
1 teaspoon Worcestershire
  sauce
1/4 teaspoon garlic salt

Rub Cornish hens with butter; sprinkle salt and pepper inside cavity and over skin. Place on a rack in a shallow roasting pan. Bake, uncovered, at 350° for 30 minutes.

Meanwhile, combine the remaining ingredients in a saucepan. Bring to a boil. Reduce heat; simmer, uncovered, for 10 minutes. Baste hens with sauce. Bake 45 minutes longer or until juices run clear and a meat thermometer reads 180°, basting frequently. **Yield:** 4 servings.

Quick & Easy Sweets For Santa

IF VISIONS of sugarplums dance inside your head at Christmas but time seems to be eluding you, turn to these speedy sweets!

The rapid recipes look like you fussed for hours in the kitchen...but they really rely on convenience items and easy cooking methods. So even time-pressed cooks can prepare delicious Yuletide treats.

Reach for refrigerated cookie dough and create eye-catching Fruit-Filled Dainties.

Or dress up cake and pudding mixes for lovely layered Yum-Yum Cake.

Think you need a candy thermometer to make fantastic confections? Terrific Truffles are easily prepared in the microwave. (All recipes shown at right.)

TIMELESS TREATS
(Clockwise from top)

Yum-Yum Cake (p. 72)

Fruit-Filled Dainties (p. 73)

Terrific Truffles (p. 72)

Yum-Yum Cake

(Pictured on page 71)

This cake has been a family favorite ever since my mom received the recipe from a neighbor.
My husband's co-workers ask him to bring this cake for his birthday treat every year!
— Teresa Marchese, New Berlin, Wisconsin

1-1/2 cups cold milk
1 package (3.4 ounces) instant vanilla pudding mix
1 package (18-1/4 ounces) white *or* yellow cake mix
1-1/2 cups whipped topping
1 can (8 ounces) crushed pineapple, well drained
1/4 cup flaked coconut, toasted

In a small bowl, whisk the milk and pudding mix for 2 minutes. Let stand for 2 minutes or until soft-set; cover and refrigerate.

Grease the bottom of two 8-in. square baking pans. Prepare cake batter according to package directions; pour into prepared pans. Bake at 350° for 20-25 minutes or until a toothpick inserted near the center comes out clean. Cool for 5 minutes before removing from pans to wire racks to cool completely.

Fold whipped topping into pudding until blended. Level cake tops if necessary. Place one cake on a serving plate; spread with half of the pudding mixture. Top with pineapple, and the remaining cake and pudding mixture. Sprinkle with coconut. Store in the refrigerator. **Yield:** 12-16 servings.

Terrific Truffles

(Pictured on page 70)

I spend the week before Christmas baking a selection of cakes, cookies and other goodies
for friends and family. These candies couldn't be easier.
—Amy Short, Lesage, West Virginia

1 package (8 ounces) cream cheese, softened
3 cups confectioners' sugar
12 squares (1 ounce *each*) semisweet chocolate
1-1/2 teaspoons vanilla extract
3/4 cup crushed peppermint candy, flaked coconut *or* ground nuts

In a large mixing bowl, beat cream cheese. Gradually add confectioners' sugar; mix well. In a microwave-safe bowl, melt chocolate; stir until smooth. Add chocolate and vanilla to cream cheese mixture; beat until blended. Refrigerate for 1 hour.

Shape into 1-in. balls. Roll in crushed peppermint, coconut or nuts. Store in an airtight container in the refrigerator. **Yield:** about 5 dozen.

Fruit-Filled Dainties

(Pictured at right and on page 70)

Refrigerated cookie dough can be shaped into cookies or tarts in this recipe from our Test Kitchen. Use one filling or make them both.

CRAN-ORANGE FILLING:
   2 cups orange-flavored dried
      cranberries
   9 tablespoons orange
      marmalade
APRICOT-ORANGE FILLING:
   9 tablespoons orange
      marmalade
4-1/2 teaspoons water
2-1/4 cups chopped dried apricots
DOUGH:
   1 tube (18 ounces) refrigerated
      sugar cookie dough, softened
   1/4 cup all-purpose flour
Confectioners' sugar

Prepare either the cran-orange or apricot-orange filling. For cran-orange filling, combine cranberries and marmalade in a food processor; cover and process until finely chopped. For apricot-orange filling, combine the marmalade, water and apricots in a food processor; cover and process until finely chopped.

In a large mixing bowl, beat cookie dough and flour until smooth. Divide into thirds. Work with one portion at a time, keeping remaining dough covered.

To prepare cookies: On a floured surface, roll out one portion of dough to 1/8-in. thickness. Cut into 2-1/2-in. squares or cut with a 2-1/2-in. round cookie cutter. Place 1 in. apart on ungreased baking sheets. Repeat with remaining dough.

Place a slightly rounded teaspoon of filling in the center of each square or circle. Shape by folding two opposite points of squares over one another or by folding edges of circles together; press to seal. Bake at 350° for 9-12 minutes or until lightly browned. Cool for 2 minutes before removing to wire racks. Dust with confectioners' sugar.

To prepare tarts: Shape one portion of dough into twelve 1-in. balls. Press onto the bottom and up the sides of ungreased miniature muffin cups. Repeat with remaining dough. Bake at 350° for 10-12 minutes or until lightly browned.

Using the end of a wooden spoon handle, gently make a 3/8- to 1/2-in.-deep indentation in the center of each tart. Cool for 10 minutes before removing from pans to wire racks. Dust with confectioners' sugar. Spoon about a tablespoon of filling into each tart. **Yield:** 3 dozen.

Editor's Note: Each type of filling makes enough to fill the entire batch of cookies. If you would like to use both fillings, make two batches of the dough.

Almond Date Confections

For our first Christmas together, I made these fast candies for my then-boyfriend.
He has begged me for them every holiday since...and we've been married for more than 10 years!
—Katherine Job, Carmel, Indiana

1 tube (7 ounces) almond paste
3/4 cup confectioners' sugar
1 teaspoon almond extract
1/4 to 1 teaspoon water, optional
18 pitted dates, halved
1-1/2 cups semisweet chocolate chips
Flaked coconut *or* finely chopped almonds, toasted

In a bowl, combine the almond paste, confectioners' sugar and extract. Knead until mixture forms a ball, adding water if mixture is too crumbly. Cut dates in half widthwise. Wrap about 1-1/2 teaspoons of almond mixture around each date half and roll into a ball.

In a microwave-safe bowl, melt chocolate chips; stir until smooth. Dip balls in chocolate, then roll in coconut or almonds. Place on a waxed paper-lined baking sheet. Refrigerate until chocolate is set, about 30 minutes. Store in a covered container at room temperature. **Yield:** 3 dozen.

MAKE A DATE WITH DATES

DATES are high in fiber and contain iron and potassium. They are also one of the sweetest of fruits—70% of their weight can be made up of sugar.

To prevent sticking when slicing or chopping dates, spray your scissors or knife with nonstick cooking spray...or frequently dip in cold water.

Dried dates stay fresh for 1 year in the refrigerator and for up to 5 years in the freezer.

Chip-Topped Butter Cookies

The chocolate center in these crisp butter cookies makes them a winner.
Embellish them with a quick dusting of confectioners' sugar if you like.
—Ruth Hodgdon, East Quogue, New York

1/2 cup butter, softened
1/4 cup sugar
1 cup all-purpose flour
2/3 cup semisweet chocolate chips
Confectioners' sugar, optional

In a large mixing bowl, cream butter and sugar. Add flour and beat until well mixed. Shape into 1-in. balls. Place 1 in. apart on ungreased baking sheets. Using the end of a wooden spoon handle, make a wide indentation in the center of each ball; fill with five chocolate chips.

Bake at 350° for 12-15 minutes or until edges are lightly browned. Cool for 2 minutes before removing from pans to wire racks. Just before serving, dust with confectioners' sugar if desired. **Yield:** 3 dozen.

Mint Sandwich Cookies

(Pictured at right)

Chocolate-covered mint candies are the "filling" in these doctored-up sugar cookies from our Test Kitchen. You can use colored sugar to suit the season.

1 tube (18 ounces) refrigerated sugar cookie dough, softened
1/4 cup all-purpose flour
1/8 teaspoon peppermint extract
Coarse sugar
40 chocolate-covered thin mints

In a large mixing bowl, beat the cookie dough, flour and extract until blended. Roll into 1/2-in. balls. Place 2 in. apart on greased baking sheets. Coat the bottom of a glass with nonstick cooking spray, then dip in coarse sugar. Flatten balls with prepared glass to 1/4-in. thickness, dipping in additional sugar as needed.

Bake at 350° for 7-9 minutes or until set. Carefully remove one cookie from baking sheet and immediately place a mint on the bottom of the cookie; top with another cookie, pressing lightly. Repeat with remaining cookies and mints. Cool on wire racks. **Yield:** 40 cookies.

Editor's Note: This recipe was tested with Necco chocolate-covered thin mints.

Nutty Fingers

This classic Christmas cookie has stood the test of time.
The recipe makes a nice-sized batch, which gets you in and out of the kitchen.
—Elsie Hendrickson, Hays, Kansas

1/2 cup butter, softened
1/3 cup confectioners' sugar
1 teaspoon vanilla extract
1 cup all-purpose flour
1/4 teaspoon salt
1 cup finely chopped pecans
Additional confectioners' sugar

In a small mixing bowl, cream butter and sugar. Beat in vanilla. Combine flour and salt; gradually add to creamed mixture. Stir in pecans. Shape tablespoonfuls of dough into 2-in. logs. Place 2 in. apart on ungreased baking sheets.

Bake at 375° for 9-11 minutes or until edges are lightly browned. Roll warm cookies in confectioners' sugar. Cool on wire racks. **Yield:** about 2 dozen.

Cherry Cream Tarts

This recipe is one of my favorites. It can be made for holidays, wedding receptions...
or anytime a special dessert is needed.
—*Michelle Mirich, Youngstown, Ohio*

1-1/2 cups butter, softened
    3 cups all-purpose flour
  3/4 cup confectioners' sugar
FILLING:
    1 package (8 ounces) cream
      cheese, softened
1-1/2 cups confectioners' sugar
  1/2 teaspoon vanilla extract
    1 carton (8 ounces) frozen
      whipped topping, thawed
Maraschino cherries, quartered

In a large mixing bowl, cream butter until light and fluffy. Combine the flour and confectioners' sugar; add to creamed mixture and beat until a soft dough forms. Shape into 1-in. balls. Press onto the bottom and up the sides of ungreased 2-in. tart pans or miniature muffin cups.

If using tart pans, place on baking sheets. Bake at 350° for 12-14 minutes or until lightly browned. Cool for 5 minutes before removing from pans to wire racks to cool completely.

In a small mixing bowl, beat the cream cheese, confectioners' sugar and vanilla until fluffy. Add whipped topping; beat until smooth. Pipe into tart shells. Top each with a cherry piece. **Yield:** about 4-1/2 dozen.

Pecan-Caramel Cheesecake Pie

This cheesecake pie takes very little time to prepare, so I make it often.
My husband tries to beat our son-in-law to the last piece!
—*Darlene Smith, Rockford, Illinois*

    2 packages (8 ounces *each*)
      cream cheese, softened
  1/2 cup sugar
    2 eggs
    1 teaspoon vanilla extract
  20 caramels
    2 tablespoons milk
    1 chocolate crumb crust (8 *or* 9
      inches)
  1/2 cup chopped pecans
  1/2 cup milk chocolate chips
Pecan halves, optional

In a large mixing bowl, beat the cream cheese, sugar and eggs until smooth. Beat in vanilla; set aside. In a small saucepan, heat caramels and milk over low heat until caramels are melted; stir until smooth. Pour into crust. Sprinkle with chopped pecans. Pour cream cheese mixture over the top.

Bake at 350° for 40-45 minutes or until center is nearly set. Cool for 10 minutes. Sprinkle with chocolate chips and pecan halves if desired. Cool completely on a wire rack. Refrigerate leftovers. **Yield:** 8 servings.

FREEZING AND CHOPPING NUTS

NUTS can turn rancid over time, so it's best to store them in the freezer. To thaw them before chopping and using in baked goods, spread in a pie plate. Put in the oven for a few minutes as the oven preheats.

Frosted Peanut Butter Cookies

(Pictured at right)

Are you looking for a quick way to dress up an ordinary cookie mix? Try this trick from our Test Kitchen. The frosting can be used on a variety of cookies, including sugar and chocolate chip.

1 package (17-1/2 ounces)
   peanut butter cookie mix
2 cups confectioners' sugar
1/4 cup baking cocoa
1/4 cup hot water
1 teaspoon vanilla extract
Sliced almonds *or* pecan halves

In a large mixing bowl, prepare cookie dough according to package directions. Shape into 1-in. balls. Place 2 in. apart on ungreased baking sheets. Bake at 375° for 8-10 minutes or until edges are golden brown. Cool for 1 minute before removing to wire racks.

For frosting, in a bowl, combine the confectioners' sugar, cocoa, water and vanilla. Spread over cookies; top with nuts. **Yield:** about 2 dozen.

Almond Chocolate Cake

*When our son and daughter were teenagers, our house was the hang-out for them
and their friends. This rich cake was a regular on the menu.*
—Char Safley, Raleigh, North Carolina

1 package (18-1/4 ounces)
  German chocolate cake mix
1 package (3.9 ounces) instant
  chocolate fudge pudding mix
1-1/4 cups water
1/2 cup vegetable oil
4 eggs
3 teaspoons almond extract
2-3/4 cups semisweet chocolate
  chips, *divided*
6 tablespoons refrigerated
  regular *or* amaretto-flavored
  nondairy creamer
1 tablespoon sliced almonds

In a large mixing bowl, combine the cake and pudding mixes, water, oil, eggs and extract; beat until combined. Stir in 2 cups chocolate chips. Pour into a greased and floured 10-in. fluted tube pan. Bake at 350° for 65-70 minutes or until a toothpick inserted near the center comes out clean. Cool for 10 minutes before removing from pan to a wire rack to cool completely.

In a small saucepan, combine the creamer and remaining chocolate chips. Cook over low heat until chips are melted; stir until smooth. Cool for 45 minutes. Drizzle over cake. Garnish with almonds. **Yield:** 12-16 servings.

Angel Food with Caramel Fluff

*My mother received this recipe from her neighbor, who made the most glorious
angel food cake. It's a dessert that always impresses guests.*
—Dixie Terry, Marion, Illinois

2 cups heavy whipping cream
3/4 cup packed brown sugar
1 teaspoon vanilla extract
1 prepared angel food cake
  (8 inches)

In a large mixing bowl, beat the cream, brown sugar and vanilla just until blended. Cover and refrigerate for 30 minutes. Beat until stiff peaks form.

Split cake horizontally into three layers. Place bottom layer on a serving plate; spread with some of the whipped cream mixture. Repeat. Top with remaining layer. Frost top and sides of cake with remaining whipped cream mixture. Refrigerate for at least 2 hours before serving. Refrigerate leftovers. **Yield:** 12-16 servings.

Puttin'-on-The-Ritz Candy

(Pictured at right)

Enlist the kids to help assemble these fun and tasty turtle-like candies. They make great holiday gifts from the kitchen.
—Brenda Amyx, Robert Lee, Texas

1 jar (12-1/4 ounces) caramel
    ice cream topping
1 cup chopped pecans
36 butter-flavored crackers
1 cup (6 ounces) semisweet
    chocolate chips
1 tablespoon shortening

In a microwave-safe bowl, heat the caramel topping and pecans on high for 5-7 minutes, stirring frequently until mixture is thickened. Cool for 5 minutes. Place the crackers on waxed paper-lined baking sheets. Spoon 1 teaspoon caramel mixture over each cracker. Refrigerate for 1 hour.

In a microwave-safe bowl, melt chocolate chips and shortening; stir until smooth. Dip the bottom of each cracker in chocolate; shake off excess. Place caramel side down on waxed paper-lined pans. Refrigerate for 1 hour or until set. Store in an airtight container. **Yield:** 3 dozen.

Editor's Note: This recipe was tested in a 1,100-watt microwave.

Frozen Peppermint Cream

*My mother made this when I was young and it's still a favorite dessert of mine
on Christmas Eve. It's the perfect dessert for a big holiday dinner.*
—Maureen Collop, Bothell, Washington

1-1/2 **cups graham cracker crumbs,
    divided**
    2 **tablespoons butter, melted**
    1 **pint heavy whipping cream**
    2 **teaspoons vanilla extract**
    1 **cup crushed peppermint
    candy**
    1 **cup miniature marshmallows**
1/2 **cup chopped walnuts**

In a small bowl, combine 1 cup graham
cracker crumbs and butter. Press into
a greased 11-in. x 7-in. x 2-in. dish. Refrigerate for 15 minutes.

In a large mixing bowl, beat cream

until it begins to thicken. Add vanilla; beat until stiff peaks
form. Fold in the peppermint candy, marshmallows and walnuts. Spread over crust. Sprinkle with remaining graham
cracker crumbs. Cover and freeze overnight. Remove from
the freezer 30 minutes before serving. **Yield:** 8-12 servings.

Caramel Marshmallow Treats

*I created this candy by combining my husband's favorite cookie recipe and my mom's caramel dip.
These sweets really appeal to kids...plus, they can help make them!*
— Tamara Holschen, Kaktovik, Alaska

    5 **cups crisp rice cereal,
    coarsely crushed**
    1 **can (14 ounces) sweetened
    condensed milk**
    1 **package (14 ounces) caramels**
    1 **cup butter, cubed**
    1 **teaspoon ground cinnamon**
1/2 **teaspoon vanilla extract**
    1 **package (16 ounces) large
    marshmallows**

Line two baking sheets with waxed paper; set aside. Place
cereal in a shallow bowl. In a large saucepan, cook and stir
the milk, caramels and butter over low heat until melted and
smooth. Remove from the heat; stir in the cinnamon and
vanilla.

With a toothpick, dip each marshmallow into warm
caramel mixture; turn to coat. Press marshmallow bottoms
in cereal; place on prepared pans. Let stand until set.
Yield: 5 dozen.

Raspberry Cheesecake Pie

(Pictured at right)

This creamy cheesecake pie with a raspberry layer is a light dessert after a heavy meal.
—Steve Josserand, Decatur, Illinois

   2 packages (8 ounces *each*)
     cream cheese, softened
1/2 cup sugar
1/2 teaspoon vanilla extract
   2 eggs
   1 chocolate crumb crust (8 *or* 9
     inches)
1-1/2 teaspoons unflavored gelatin
   2 tablespoons cold water
1/2 cup seedless raspberry jam
   1 cup heavy whipping cream
   2 tablespoons confectioners'
     sugar

In a large mixing bowl, beat the cream cheese, sugar and vanilla until smooth. Add eggs; beat on low speed just until combined. Pour into crust. Bake at 325° for 25-30 minutes or until the center is almost set. Cool on a wire rack for 1 hour. Refrigerate overnight.

In a small saucepan, sprinkle gelatin over cold water; let stand for 1 minute. Cook over low heat, stirring until gelatin is completely dissolved. Stir in jam. Refrigerate for 10 minutes.

In small mixing bowl, beat cream until it begins to thicken. Add confectioners' sugar; beat until stiff peaks form. Remove 1/2 cup for garnish; cover and refrigerate. Gently stir 3/4 cup whipped cream into raspberry mixture just until blended. Fold in the remaining whipped cream; spread over cheesecake. Refrigerate for at least 1 hour. Garnish with reserved whipped cream. **Yield:** 6-8 servings.

SOFT AND STIFF PEAK SECRETS

RECIPES often call for beating whipping cream or egg whites until soft or stiff peaks form. To ensure the cream or egg whites reach full volume, make sure the bowl and beaters are free from oil and the egg whites contain no specks of yolk. Whipping cream should be cold and egg whites should be room temperature before beating them.

Begin by beating with an electric mixer on medium speed until the peaks curl down when the beaters are lifted up. This is the soft peak stage.

For stiff peaks, continue beating on high speed until the volume increases and the mixture thickens even more. Lift up the beaters— the peaks should stand straight up, and if you tilt the bowl, the mixture should not slide around.

Whipped Cream Pound Cake

This cake never lasts long at family gatherings. Slices taste terrific
whether served alone or when topped with fresh fruit.
—*Shirley Tincher, Zanesville, Ohio*

1 **cup butter, softened**
3 **cups sugar**
6 **eggs**
1 **teaspoon lemon extract**
1 **teaspoon vanilla extract**
3 **cups all-purpose flour**
1 **cup heavy whipping cream**
Sliced fresh fruit, optional

In a large mixing bowl, cream butter and sugar. Add eggs, one at a time, beating well after each addition. Stir in the extracts. Add flour alternately with cream, beating just until combined.

Pour into two greased and floured 9-in. x 5-in. x 3-in. loaf pans. Bake at 325° for 80-85 minutes or until a toothpick inserted near the center comes out clean. Cool for 10 minutes before removing from pans to wire racks to cool completely. Serve with fruit if desired. **Yield:** 2 cakes (10-12 servings each).

KEEP A CAKE HANDY!

THE RECIPE for Whipped Cream Pound Cake makes two loaves. You can enjoy one now and freeze one for up to 6 months. Thaw at room temperature.

Chocolate-Topped Macaroon Crisps

What a combination! Delicate macaroons drizzled with sweet chocolate can't be beat.
The recipe comes from a co-worker's daughter, who makes us a huge batch every Christmas.
—*Rosemary Areias, Turlock, California*

1 **package (14 ounces) flaked coconut**
4 **egg whites**
1 **cup sugar**
1 **teaspoon vanilla extract**
2 **cups (12 ounces) semisweet chocolate chips**
2 **teaspoons vegetable oil**

In a food processor, finely chop coconut; set aside. In a large mixing bowl, beat egg whites until soft peaks form. Gradually add sugar, beating until stiff and glossy. Fold in vanilla and coconut. Drop by rounded tablespoonfuls 2 in. apart onto lightly greased baking sheets.

Bake at 325° for 18-19 minutes or until golden brown. Immediately remove to wire racks to cool. In a microwave-safe bowl, melt chocolate chips and oil; stir until smooth. Drizzle over cookies. **Yield:** 3-1/2 dozen.

Cobblestone Brownies

(Pictured at right)

My family enjoys the combination of chocolate and coconut. So I stirred coconut extract into brownie batter and added flaked coconut to the cream cheese filling. These fudgy bars are the tasty result!
—*Phyllis Perry, Vassar, Kansas*

1 package fudge brownie mix
   (13-inch x 9-inch pan size)
1/2 cup vegetable oil
2 eggs
1/2 teaspoon coconut extract
FILLING:
1 package (8 ounces) cream
   cheese, softened
2 eggs
1 teaspoon coconut extract
1 teaspoon vanilla extract
3-3/4 cups confectioners' sugar
1 cup flaked coconut

In a large mixing bowl, beat the brownie mix, oil, eggs and extract on medium speed until blended (batter will be stiff). Set aside 1 cup for topping. Spread the remaining batter into a greased 13-in. x 9-in. x 2-in. baking pan. Bake at 350° for 10-15 minutes or until edges crack.

For filling, in a small mixing bowl, beat the cream cheese, eggs, extracts and confectioners' sugar until smooth and creamy. Fold in the coconut. Carefully spread over brownies. Drop reserved batter by teaspoonfuls over filling. Bake for 45-50 minutes or until a knife inserted near the center comes out clean. Cool on a wire rack. Store in the refrigerator. **Yield:** 3 dozen.

Cherry Pinwheels

*When you need an elegant yet easy dessert to serve company, try these pretty pinwheels from our
Test Kitchen. Garnish with whipped cream and fresh mint for an attractive presentation.*

1 can (16 ounces) pitted dark
  sweet cherries
1 tablespoon sugar
2 tablespoons cornstarch
4 sheets phyllo dough (14
  inches x 9 inches)
2 tablespoons butter, melted

Drain cherries, reserving juice. If necessary, add enough water to juice to measure 3/4 cup. In a small saucepan, combine sugar and cornstarch; whisk in juice until smooth. Bring to a boil; cook and stir for 2 minutes or until thickened. Remove from the heat. Set aside 16 cherries. Cut remaining cherries in half and add to sauce; set aside.

Place one sheet of phyllo dough on a work surface; cut into six 4-in. squares. Discard trimmings. (Keep remaining phyllo covered with plastic wrap and a damp towel to prevent drying out.) On a baking sheet, layer phyllo squares, brushing with butter between each. Cut diagonally through dough from each corner 1-1/2 in. toward the center. Place a whole cherry between each cut; fold alternating points over cherries and toward the center. Brush with butter. Repeat with remaining phyllo sheets, cherries and butter.

Bake at 375° for 8-9 minutes or until golden brown. Serve over cherry sauce. **Yield:** 4 servings.

Crispy Peanut Butter Truffles

*This is just one of the many candies I make at Christmastime. White candy coating
makes them a nice change from the more common chocolate candies.*
—Florence Robinson, Lenox, Iowa

1 cup sugar
1/2 cup light corn syrup
1 cup peanut butter
2 cups crisp rice cereal
1 pound white candy coating,
  coarsely chopped

In a large saucepan, combine sugar and corn syrup. Cook and stir over medium heat until sugar is dissolved. Bring just to a boil. Remove from the heat; stir in peanut butter until smooth. Stir in the cereal until combined. Roll into 1-in. balls. Place on waxed paper-lined baking sheets to cool.

In a microwave-safe bowl, melt candy coating, stirring often until melted and smooth. With a fork, dip peanut butter balls in coating; return to waxed paper until set. Store in an airtight container. **Yield:** 3 dozen.

Chocolate-Caramel Mousse Parfaits

(Pictured at right)

Our home economists came up with this tempting dessert that only requires three ingredients. The contrasting layers look lovely in tall, clear glasses.

4 cups heavy whipping cream, *divided*
5 squares (1 ounce *each*) semisweet chocolate, chopped
1/3 cup caramel ice cream topping

For chocolate mousse, heat 2 cups cream in a small heavy saucepan over medium heat until it begins to simmer, about 180°. Remove from the heat; whisk in chocolate until smooth. Transfer to a mixing bowl; refrigerate until chilled. Beat until soft peaks form.

For caramel mousse, beat remaining cream in a large mixing bowl until it begins to thicken. Add caramel topping; beat until soft peaks form.

Spoon 3 tablespoons chocolate mousse into six parfait glasses; top with 3 tablespoons caramel mousse. Repeat layers. Refrigerate until serving. **Yield:** 6 servings.

DECORATING PURCHASED COOKIES

EVEN if you don't have time to bake, you and your family can still enjoy special Christmas cookies. It just takes a trip to the grocery store and a little creativity! Here are tricks for making purchased cookies your own works of art:

- Melt some vanilla or white baking chips. Dip gingersnaps halfway into melted chips...or drizzle the melted chips over the cookies.

- Tint your favorite vanilla frosting with food coloring. Use to pipe holiday designs on sugar cookies.
- Purchase chocolate-covered mint cookies; drizzle with contrasting melted white chocolate.
- Frost chocolate chip cookies with purchased or homemade chocolate frosting. Decorate with colored sugar or sprinkles.

Decked Out in Desserts

DIEHARD dessert lovers would say that festive finales are the real stars of seasonal dinners.

After all, there's no better time of year to save room for dessert and indulge in a decadent treat!

Chocoholics will fall for Cappuccino Torte's fudgy, coffee-flavored layers.

If you prefer something fresh and fruity, individual Strawberry Meringue Desserts fit the bill.

And Shortbread Lemon Tart is a tried-and-true treat no matter what the season. (All recipes shown at right.)

With tasty tortes, luscious cheesecakes, pleasing pies and more, the festive finales on the pages that follow will make every holiday meal *mmm*erry!

Shortbread Lemon Tart

(Pictured on page 86)

For a change from ordinary lemon bars, our home economists added orange peel to both the crust and filling and turned the recipe into a tart.

3 eggs
1/4 cup lemon juice
1-1/4 cups sugar
1 tablespoon grated orange peel
1/4 cup butter, melted
CRUST:
1 cup all-purpose flour
1/3 cup confectioners' sugar
1/2 cup ground almonds
1 teaspoon grated lemon peel
1 teaspoon grated orange peel
1/2 cup cold butter
Additional confectioners' sugar

For filling, in a blender, combine the eggs, lemon juice, sugar and orange peel. Cover and blend on high until smooth. Add butter; cover and process on high just until smooth. Set aside.

In a food processor, combine the flour, confectioners' sugar, almonds, lemon peel, orange peel and butter; cover and process until mixture forms a ball. Press pastry onto the bottom and up the sides of an ungreased 9-in. tart pan with removable bottom.

Pour filling into crust. Bake at 350° for 25-30 minutes or until center is almost set. Cool on a wire rack. Just before serving, sprinkle with confectioners' sugar. **Yield:** 10-12 servings.

Glazed Bananas in Phyllo Cups

I enjoy making this fast yet fancy dessert for my wife. The phyllo cups can be baked, cooled and stored in an airtight container up to one day in advance.
—Scott Maynard, Lafayette, Louisiana

3/4 cup shelled pistachios
1/2 cup sugar
1 teaspoon ground cinnamon
2 sheets phyllo dough (18 inches x 14 inches)
1/4 cup butter, melted
SAUCE:
3/4 cup butter, cubed
3/4 cup packed brown sugar
3 medium firm bananas, sliced
1/4 teaspoon ground cinnamon
3 to 4 cups vanilla ice cream

In a food processor, process pistachios and sugar until very finely chopped. Transfer to a bowl; stir in cinnamon. Cut each sheet of phyllo dough into nine 5-in. squares (discard trimmings). Stack squares and cover with plastic wrap.

One at a time, brush each square with melted butter and sprinkle with a heaping tablespoonful of pistachio mixture. Stack three squares, turning each one at an angle so the corners are not aligned. Press each stack onto the bottom and up the sides of a greased 8-oz. custard cup. Bake at 350° for 15-20 minutes or until golden brown. Cool for 5 minutes before removing to a wire rack to cool completely.

For sauce, melt butter and brown sugar in a saucepan. Bring to a boil; reduce heat. Gently stir in bananas and cinnamon; heat through. Fill phyllo cups with ice cream; top with banana sauce. Serve immediately. **Yield:** 6 servings.

Cappuccino Torte

(Pictured at right and on page 86)

Holidays are a time to spend with family and friends...it's also a chance to enjoy every bite of rich desserts like this!
—Marcia Orlando
Boyertown, Pennsylvania

1-1/4 cups graham cracker crumbs
  1/4 cup sugar
  1/3 cup butter, melted
GANACHE:
  2 cups heavy whipping cream
2-1/2 cups semisweet chocolate
    chips
  1/2 cup butter, cubed
  2 tablespoons corn syrup
CAPPUCCINO BUTTERCREAM:
  6 egg yolks
2-1/2 cups packed brown sugar
  1/2 cup water
1-1/2 cups cold butter
  1 tablespoon instant coffee
    granules
  1 tablespoon hot water
  4 squares (1 ounce *each*)
    unsweetened chocolate,
    melted and cooled
COFFEE WHIPPED CREAM:
1-1/4 cups heavy whipping cream
  2 teaspoons instant coffee
    granules
  2 tablespoons confectioners'
    sugar
  1/2 teaspoon vanilla extract
Chocolate curls, optional

In a bowl, combine the crumbs, sugar and butter; press onto the bottom of an ungreased 9-in. springform pan. Chill.

For ganache, in a large saucepan, bring cream to a boil. Reduce heat to low. Add chocolate chips; cook and stir until chocolate is melted. Remove from the heat. Add butter and corn syrup; stir until smooth. Cool to room temperature, stirring occasionally. Pour over crust. Chill until firm, about 2 hours.

For buttercream, place egg yolks in a large mixing bowl; let stand for 30 minutes. In a large saucepan, combine brown sugar and water; cook and stir over medium-high heat until sugar is dissolved. Bring to a boil; cook and stir for 2 minutes.

Beat egg yolks on high speed until thick and lemon-colored. Reduce speed to low; with mixer running, carefully and gradually add boiling brown sugar syrup. Gradually increase mixer speed to medium; beat until thickened, about 15 minutes. Add butter, 1 tablespoon at a time, beating until well mixed. Dissolve coffee in water; add to yolk mixture. Beat in melted chocolate. Spread over ganache layer. Cover and refrigerate for 4 hours or overnight.

Several hours before serving, prepare coffee whipped cream. In a small mixing bowl, combine 1 tablespoon cream and coffee; stir until coffee is dissolved. Beat in remaining cream until it begins to thicken. Add confectioners' sugar and vanilla; beat until stiff peaks form.

Carefully run a knife around edge of springform pan to loosen; remove sides. Frost top and sides of torte with whipped cream; garnish with chocolate curls if desired. Refrigerate until serving. **Yield:** 14 servings.

Editor's Note: A stand mixer is recommended for beating the frosting after it reaches 160°.

Double-Layer Pumpkin Pie

This no-bake pumpkin pie includes a delicious cream cheese layer.
It's a terrific make-ahead dessert because it needs to refrigerate a few hours.
— Donna Freund, Dubuque, Iowa

4 ounces cream cheese, softened
1 tablespoon sugar
1 tablespoon milk
1 carton (8 ounces) frozen whipped topping, thawed *divided*
1 graham cracker crust (9 inches)
1 cup cold milk
2 packages (3.4 ounces *each*) instant vanilla pudding mix
1 can (15 ounces) solid-pack pumpkin
1 teaspoon ground cinnamon
1/2 teaspoon ground ginger
1/4 teaspoon ground cloves

In a small mixing bowl, combine the cream cheese, sugar and milk. Fold in 1-1/2 cups whipped topping. Spoon into the crust.

In a bowl, whisk cold milk and pudding mixes for 2 minutes. Let stand for 2 minutes or until soft-set. Stir in the pumpkin, cinnamon, ginger and cloves. Spread over cream cheese layer. Spread with remaining whipped topping. Refrigerate for at least 3 hours before cutting. **Yield:** 6-8 servings.

HOMEMADE GRAHAM CRACKER CRUST

WHEN a recipe like Double-Layer Pumpkin Pie calls for a 9-in. graham cracker crust, you can make one from scratch in a pretty pie plate.

Begin by crushing 24 graham cracker squares to yield 1-1/2 cups crumbs. In a mixing bowl, combine the crumbs with 1/4 cup sugar. Melt 1/3 cup butter; add to crumb mixture and blend well. Press mixture onto the bottom and up the sides of an ungreased 9-in. pie plate. Refrigerate for 30 minutes before filling.

Strawberry Meringue Desserts

(Pictured at right and on page 87)

When time is short, use thawed whipped topping instead of making sweetened whipped cream.
—Susan Maraffa, Canfield, Ohio

4 egg whites
1-1/2 teaspoons vanilla extract, *divided*
1/4 teaspoon cream of tartar
Dash salt
1 cup sugar
1 cup (6 ounces) semisweet chocolate chips
4 teaspoons shortening
2 cups heavy whipping cream
2 tablespoons confectioners' sugar
5 cups fresh strawberries
Chocolate syrup

Place egg whites in a large mixing bowl; let stand at room temperature for 30 minutes. Line baking sheets with parchment paper. Draw twenty-four 4-in. x 2-1/2-in. rectangles on the paper; set aside.

Add 1 teaspoon vanilla, cream of tartar and salt to egg whites; beat on medium speed until soft peaks form. Gradually add sugar, 2 tablespoons at a time, beating on high for 5 minutes or until stiff peaks form and sugar is dissolved.

Insert a #12 round pastry tip in a pastry bag or heavy-duty plastic bag. Fill bag with meringue. Pipe meringue in long rows on rectangles until each is completely filled. Bake at 250° for 1 hour. Turn oven off and let meringue dry in oven for 1 hour (do not open oven door). Carefully remove meringues from baking sheet. Cool completely. Store in an airtight container.

In a microwave-safe bowl, melt chocolate chips and shortening; stir until smooth. Spread 1 tablespoon over each meringue. Let stand until chocolate is set. In a large mixing bowl, beat cream until soft peaks form. Gradually add confectioners' sugar and remaining vanilla, beating on high until stiff peaks form.

Set aside 12 strawberries; cut remaining strawberries into 1/4-in. slices. Place 12 meringues on a flat serving platter. Spread each with 2 tablespoons whipped cream; top with sliced strawberries. Spread each with 2 tablespoons whipped cream. Top with remaining meringues and whipped cream. Loosely cover; refrigerate for up to 2 hours.

Just before serving, drizzle with chocolate syrup. Cut reserved strawberries in half. Arrange cut side down over whipped cream. Refrigerate leftovers. **Yield:** 12 servings.

Chocolate Pecan Tassies

These dessert muffins capture the wonderful flavor of pecan pie.
The addition of chocolate chips makes them extra special.
—Ramona Porter, Olive Hill, Kentucky

1/2 cup butter, softened
1 package (3 ounces) cream
  cheese, softened
6 tablespoons sugar
1-1/2 cups all-purpose flour
3 tablespoons baking cocoa
PECAN FILLING:
1 cup packed brown sugar
2 tablespoons butter, softened
2 eggs
2 teaspoons vanilla extract
2/3 cup chopped pecans
2/3 cup miniature semisweet
  chocolate chips

In a large mixing bowl, cream the butter, cream cheese and sugar. Combine the flour and cocoa; gradually add to creamed mixture. Cover and refrigerate for 15 minutes. Meanwhile, for filling, combine the brown sugar and butter in a small mixing bowl. Beat in eggs and vanilla. Stir in the pecans and chocolate chips.

Roll cream cheese mixture into 1-in. balls. Press onto the bottom and up the sides of ungreased miniature muffin cups. Spoon filling into cups. Bake at 325° for 20-25 minutes or until lightly browned. Cool for 10 minutes before carefully removing from pans to wire racks. **Yield:** 3 dozen.

Red Raspberry Dessert

This refrigerator dessert can be made up to 24 hours ahead of time.
Feel free to substitute frozen strawberries for the raspberries if you prefer.
—Nancy Foust, Stoneboro, Pennsylvania

1-1/4 cups graham cracker crumbs
1/4 cup finely chopped walnuts
1/4 cup butter, melted
50 large marshmallows
1 cup milk
1 carton (8 ounces) frozen
  whipped topping, thawed
2 packages (10 ounces *each*)
  frozen sweetened raspberries,
  thawed
1-1/4 cups water, *divided*
1/2 cup sugar
2 teaspoons lemon juice
6 tablespoons cornstarch

In a bowl, combine the crumbs, walnuts and butter. Press into a greased 13-in. x 9-in. x 2-in. baking pan. Bake at 350° for 10 minutes. Cool.

In a large saucepan over medium heat, melt marshmallows with milk, stirring often. Cool to room temperature. Fold in whipped topping; spread over crust.

In a saucepan, bring raspberries, 1 cup water, sugar and lemon juice to a boil. Combine cornstarch and remaining water; stir into raspberry mixture. Bring to a boil; cook and stir for 2 minutes. Cool to room temperature. Spread over marshmallow layer. Chill until firm, about 4 hours. **Yield:** 12-16 servings.

Almond Venetian Dessert

(Pictured at right)

These beautiful bars feature three colorful cake-like layers, an apricot filling and a chocolate topping.
—Reva Becker
Farmington Hills, Michigan

1/2 cup almond paste
3/4 cup butter, softened
1/2 cup sugar
2 eggs, *separated*
1/4 teaspoon almond extract
1 cup all-purpose flour
1/8 teaspoon salt
5 drops green food coloring
4 drops red food coloring
2/3 cup apricot preserves
3 squares (1 ounce *each*) semisweet chocolate

Grease the bottoms of three 8-in. square baking dishes. Line with waxed paper and grease the paper; set aside.

Place almond paste in a large mixing bowl; break up with a fork. Add the butter, sugar, egg yolks and extract; beat until smooth and fluffy. Stir in flour and salt.

In another mixing bowl, beat egg whites until soft peaks form. Stir a fourth of the whites into the dough, then fold in the remaining whites (dough will be stiff).

Divide dough evenly into three portions, about 2/3 cup each. Tint one portion green and one portion red; leave the remaining portion white. Spread each portion into a prepared pan. Bake at 350° for 13-15 minutes or until edges are golden brown. Immediately invert onto wire racks; remove waxed paper. Place another wire rack on top and turn over. Cool completely.

Place green layer on a large piece of plastic wrap. Spread evenly with 1/3 cup apricot preserves. Top with white layer and spread with remaining preserves. Top with red layer. Bring plastic over layers. Slide onto a cookie sheet and set a cutting board on top to compress layers. Refrigerate overnight.

In a microwave-safe bowl, melt chocolate. Remove cutting board and unwrap dessert. Spread melted chocolate over top; let stand until set. With a sharp knife, trim edges. Cut into 2-in. x 5/8-in. bars. Store in an airtight container. **Yield:** about 2 dozen.

Pecan White Chocolate Cake

*This recipe comes from a small-town cookbook, which I received
as a wedding gift from my dear Aunt Virginia. Coconut and
creamy frosting give each slice the flavor of white German chocolate cake.*
—Jewell Tweedt, Council Bluffs, Iowa

1 cup butter, softened
1-3/4 cups sugar
4 eggs, *separated*
6 squares (1 ounce *each*) white baking chocolate, melted and cooled
1 teaspoon vanilla extract
2-1/2 cups cake flour
1 teaspoon baking powder
1/2 teaspoon salt
1 cup milk
1 cup flaked coconut
1 cup chopped pecans
FROSTING:
1/2 cup butter, softened
2 packages (3 ounces *each*) cream cheese, softened
3-3/4 cups confectioners' sugar
2 squares (1 ounce *each*) white baking chocolate, melted and cooled
1 teaspoon vanilla extract
1 cup chopped pecans, toasted

In a large mixing bowl, cream the butter and sugar. Add egg yolks, one at a time, beating well after each addition. Beat in the white chocolate and vanilla. Combine the flour, baking powder and salt; add to creamed mixture alternately with milk. Fold in the coconut and pecans. In a small mixing bowl, beat the egg whites until stiff peaks form. Fold into batter.

Pour the batter into a greased 13-in. x 9-in. x 2-in. baking pan. Bake at 350° for 40-45 minutes or until a toothpick inserted near the center comes out clean. Cool completely on a wire rack.

For frosting, in a mixing bowl, cream the butter and cream cheese. Gradually beat in confectioners' sugar, white chocolate and vanilla until light and fluffy. Fold in pecans. Frost cake. Store in the refrigerator. **Yield:** 15 servings.

SEPARATING EGGS

PLACE an egg separator over a custard cup; crack egg into the separator. As each egg is separated, place yolk in another bowl and empty egg whites into a mixing bowl. It is easier to separate eggs when they are cold.

Peppermint Cake Log

(Pictured at right)

Each Christmas, my husband only asks for one thing...this chocolate mint cake roll! The fluffy filling pairs well with the tender cake.
—Robyn Anderson, Sugar Grove, Illinois

1/2 cup all-purpose flour
1/3 cup baking cocoa
1/4 teaspoon baking powder
1/4 teaspoon baking soda
4 eggs, *separated*
1/3 cup plus 1/2 cup sugar, *divided*
1 teaspoon vanilla extract
1/3 cup water
1 tablespoon confectioners' sugar

FILLING:
1 cup heavy whipping cream
1/4 cup confectioners' sugar
1/3 cup crushed peppermint candies

GLAZE:
2 tablespoons butter
2 tablespoons baking cocoa
2 tablespoons water
1 cup confectioners' sugar
1/2 teaspoon vanilla extract

Line a greased 15-in. x 10-in. x 1-in. baking pan with waxed paper; grease the paper and set aside. Combine the flour, cocoa, baking powder and baking soda; set aside.

In large mixing bowl, beat egg yolks, 1/3 cup sugar and vanilla until thick and lemon-colored. Add dry ingredients alternately with water just until blended. In a small mixing bowl, beat egg whites on medium speed until soft peaks form. Gradually beat in remaining sugar, 1 tablespoon at a time, until stiff glossy peaks form. Fold into yolk mixture.

Spread batter evenly in prepared pan. Bake at 375° for 12-15 minutes or until cake springs back when lightly touched. Cool for 5 minutes. Invert cake onto a kitchen towel dusted with 1 tablespoon confectioners' sugar. Gently peel off waxed paper. Roll up cake in the towel jelly-roll style, starting with a short side. Cool completely on a wire rack.

For filling, in a small mixing bowl, beat cream until soft peaks form. Gradually beat in confectioners' sugar until stiff peaks form. Fold in crushed candies. Unroll cake; spread filling to within 1/2 in. of edges. Roll up again. Cover and refrigerate for at least 1 hour.

For glaze, combine the butter, cocoa and water in a small saucepan. Cook and stir over low heat until smooth. Remove from the heat. Whisk in confectioners' sugar and vanilla until smooth. Drizzle over cake. Refrigerate leftovers. **Yield:** 10 servings.

Praline Brownie Pie

I have a passion for creating my own recipes. I developed this pie from a favorite brownie.
I've lost track of how many recipe requests this dessert has generated.
—Michele Mazey, Centerville, Ohio

PASTRY:
  1/2 cup butter, softened
  1 cup confectioners' sugar
  1 egg
1-1/4 cups all-purpose flour
  1/4 cup baking cocoa
  1/8 teaspoon salt
PRALINE TOPPING:
  3/4 cup chopped pecans
  2 tablespoons butter, softened
  2 tablespoons sugar
  1 tablespoon brown sugar
  1/8 teaspoon salt
CARAMEL LAYER:
  2 tablespoons butter
  1/4 cup sugar
  2 tablespoons brown sugar
  2 tablespoons heavy whipping
    cream
FILLING:
  1 cup (6 ounces) semisweet
    chocolate chips, *divided*
  2 squares (1 ounce *each*)
    unsweetened chocolate
  1/2 cup butter, cubed
  1 cup sugar
  2 eggs
  1 teaspoon vanilla extract
  1/2 cup all-purpose flour
Dash salt

In a small mixing bowl, cream butter and confectioners' sugar; beat in egg. Combine the flour, cocoa and salt; gradually add to creamed mixture and mix well. Cover and refrigerate for 1 hour.

Meanwhile, for topping, combine the pecans, butter, sugars and salt. Spread in a single layer in a lightly greased 15-in. x 10-in. x 1-in. baking pan. Bake at 350° for 20 minutes, stirring every 5 minutes. Cool.

For caramel layer, combine the butter and sugars in a saucepan. Bring to a boil, stirring constantly. Boil and stir for 2 minutes. Stir in the cream; return to a boil. Remove from the heat and set aside.

For filling, in a microwave-safe bowl, melt 1/2 cup chocolate chips, unsweetened chocolate and butter; stir until smooth. Transfer to a large mixing bowl; cool slightly. Beat in the sugar. Add eggs, one at a time, beating well after each addition. Beat in vanilla. Stir in the flour and salt just until blended; set aside.

On a lightly floured surface, roll out pastry to fit an 11-in. fluted tart pan with removable bottom. Transfer pastry to pan; trim even with top edge. Spread filling into crust. Top with caramel mixture; cut through with a knife to swirl. Sprinkle with topping and remaining chocolate chips. Bake at 350° for 35-45 minutes or until a toothpick inserted near the center comes out clean. Cool on a wire rack. **Yield:** 16-20 servings.

Taffy Apple Cheesecake Pie

(Pictured at right)

I prepare this dessert many times during apple season. But it's actually great for any occasion. The pie combines the fabulous flavors of caramel apples and cheesecake.
—Leona Rothbauer, Bloomer, Wisconsin

3/4 cup packed brown sugar, *divided*
2 tablespoons butter
5 cups thinly sliced peeled tart apples
21 caramels
1/2 cup half-and-half cream
1 package (8 ounces) cream cheese, softened
1 egg
1-1/2 teaspoons vanilla extract
1 teaspoon pumpkin pie spice, *divided*
1 unbaked deep-dish pastry shell (9 inches)
3/4 cup chopped pecans
1/2 cup milk chocolate chips, chopped
2 cups whipped topping

In a large skillet, combine 1/4 cup brown sugar and butter. Cook over medium-high heat until sugar is dissolved, stirring occasionally. Add apples. Cook, uncovered, for 12-15 minutes or until apples are tender, stirring occasionally; drain and set aside.

In a large heavy saucepan, combine caramels and cream; cook over low heat, stirring frequently. Remove from the heat; keep warm. In a large mixing bowl, beat cream cheese and remaining brown sugar until fluffy. Beat in the egg, vanilla and 1/2 teaspoon pumpkin pie spice until smooth.

Stir half of caramel mixture into apples. Pour into pastry shell. Combine pecans and chocolate chips; set aside 2 tablespoons for topping. Sprinkle remaining pecan mixture over apples. Fold remaining caramel mixture into cream cheese mixture. Spread over pecan mixture.

Cover edges loosely with foil. Bake at 375° for 20 minutes. Remove foil; bake 15-20 minutes longer or until filling is set. Cool on a wire rack. Chill for 30 minutes. Combine whipped topping and remaining pumpkin pie spice; spread over pie just before serving. Sprinkle with reserved pecan mixture. Refrigerate leftovers. **Yield:** 8-10 servings.

Raspberry Sauce

(Pictured at right)

Use this Raspberry Sauce from our Test Kitchen to garnish any number of store-bought or homemade desserts. It's nice to have in the refrigerator for last-minute entertaining.

2/3 cup sugar
4 teaspoons cornstarch
1/4 cup water
2-1/2 cups fresh *or* frozen
    raspberries
2 teaspoons lemon juice

In a small saucepan, combine sugar and cornstarch; stir in water until smooth. Add raspberries. Bring to a boil; cook and stir for 2 minutes or until thickened. Remove from the heat; strain to remove seeds. Stir in lemon juice. Transfer to a small bowl. Store in the refrigerator. **Yield:** about 1 cup.

DESSERT PLATE PRESENTATION

WHEN entertaining, it's fun to focus on the presentation of food. The contrasting colors and flavors of Raspberry Sauce and Sour Cream Topping (recipes above and on opposite page) make them perfect partners for garnishing individual dessert plates.

Prepare the recipes as directed. Then use the following techniques with a variety of desserts, including Traditional Cheesecake (opposite page), Cappuccino Torte (page 89), Glazed Bananas in Phyllo Cups (page 88) and Red Raspberry Dessert (page 92).

1. Spread Raspberry Sauce on a dessert plate. Pipe dots of Sour Cream Topping near the edge of the sauce.

2. Spread the Sour Cream Topping on a dessert plate. Pipe Raspberry Sauce around the outside edge of the topping.

3. Spread Raspberry Sauce on a dessert plate. Pipe several vertical lines of Sour Cream Topping over the top. Starting at the top of the plate, drag a skewer through all of the parallel lines from one side of the plate to the other. Work your way down to the bottom of the plate, changing the direction of each "pull."

Traditional Cheesecake

(Pictured at right)

Our Test Kitchen shares this recipe for a basic cheesecake that tastes great alone or with any number of garnishes.

    1 cup graham cracker crumbs
    1 tablespoon sugar
    3 tablespoons cold butter
FILLING:
    4 packages (8 ounces *each*)
      cream cheese, softened
1-1/4 cups sugar
    1 tablespoon lemon juice
    2 teaspoons vanilla extract
    3 eggs, lightly beaten
Raspberry Sauce (opposite page)
  and Sour Cream Topping
  (below), optional

In a small bowl, combine the cracker crumbs and sugar; cut in butter until crumbly. Grease the sides only of a 9-in. springform pan; press crumb mixture onto bottom of pan. Place on a baking sheet. Bake at 350° for 10 minutes. Cool on a wire rack.

In a large mixing bowl, beat the cream cheese, sugar, lemon juice and vanilla until smooth. Add eggs; beat on low speed just until combined. Pour over crust. Return pan to baking sheet.

Bake at 350° for 45-55 minutes or until center is almost set. Cool on a wire rack for 10 minutes. Carefully run a knife around edge of pan to loosen; cool 1 hour longer. Refrigerate overnight. Just before serving, remove sides of pan. Garnish individual slices with Raspberry Sauce and Sour Cream Topping if desired. Refrigerate leftovers. **Yield:** 12 servings.

Sour Cream Topping

(Pictured above)

Our home economists use this sweet and tangy Sour Cream Topping to complement the Raspberry Sauce on the opposite page.

1/2 cup sour cream
    2 tablespoons confectioners'
      sugar

In a small bowl, combine sour cream and confectioners' sugar until smooth. Transfer to a pastry or plastic bag; cut a small hole in the corner of bag. Pipe desired design. **Yield:** 1/2 cup.

Jolly Gingerbread

IT JUST wouldn't be the Christmas season without the spicy aroma of gingerbread coming from the kitchen.

This year, add the rich russet color of gingerbread to your table in a host of unique ways.

Forego the common cookie cutter gingerbread treatment and make Butterscotch Gingerbread Cookies with snowflake cutters or Gingerbread Biscotti.

Pumpkin Gingerbread with Caramel Sauce is a dressed-up version of a classic dessert. (All recipes shown at right.)

In addition to newfound favorites (such as Gingerbread Pancakes), this chapter offers traditional treats (like a Mini Gingerbread House) that never go out of style!

SPICED JUST RIGHT
(Clockwise from top right)

Gingerbread Biscotti (p. 103)

Pumpkin Gingerbread with Caramel Sauce (p. 106)

Butterscotch Gingerbread Cookies (p. 105)

Surprise Gingerbread Muffins

Cranberry-raspberry sauce is the luscious surprise tucked inside these mouth-watering muffins.
—*Edie DeSpain, Logan, Utah*

1/2 cup butter, softened
1/2 cup sugar
1/2 cup packed brown sugar
  2 eggs
1/2 cup molasses
  3 cups all-purpose flour
1-1/2 teaspoons ground cinnamon
  1 teaspoon baking soda
1/4 teaspoon *each* ground ginger,
    cloves and allspice
  1 cup buttermilk
1/2 cup cranberry-raspberry
    sauce

In a large mixing bowl, cream butter and sugars. Add eggs, one at a time, beating well after each addition. Beat in the molasses. Combine the flour, cinnamon, baking soda, ginger, cloves and allspice; add to the creamed mixture alternately with buttermilk.

Fill 16 paper-lined muffin cups half full; spoon about 1-1/2 teaspoons cranberry-raspberry sauce over each. Top with remaining batter. Bake at 350° for 25-30 minutes or until a toothpick comes out clean. Cool for 10 minutes before removing from pans to wire racks to cool completely. **Yield:** 16 muffins.

Gingerbread Pancakes

My daughter's family enjoyed gingerbread pancakes at a restaurant and decided to serve them at home. The lemon syrup is a nice change from maple syrup.
—*Noreen Larson, Wainwright, Alberta*

1-1/3 cups all-purpose flour
  1 teaspoon baking powder
  1 teaspoon ground cinnamon
1/2 teaspoon ground ginger
1/4 teaspoon baking soda
1/4 teaspoon salt
  1 egg
1-1/4 cups milk
1/4 cup molasses
  3 tablespoons vegetable oil
LEMON SYRUP:
1/2 cup sugar
  1 tablespoon cornstarch
Pinch ground nutmeg
  1 cup cold water
  2 tablespoons butter, melted

  2 tablespoons lemon juice
1/2 teaspoon grated lemon peel

In a large mixing bowl, combine the flour, baking powder, cinnamon, ginger, baking soda and salt. In another bowl, whisk the egg, milk, molasses and oil. Add to the dry ingredients; beat just until blended.

Pour batter by 1/4 cupfuls onto a greased hot griddle. Turn when bubbles form on top of pancake; cook until the second side is golden brown.

For syrup, combine the sugar, cornstarch and nutmeg in a saucepan. Stir in water until smooth. Bring to a boil; cook and stir for 1-2 minutes or until thickened. Remove from the heat. Stir in the butter, lemon juice and peel. Serve with pancakes. **Yield:** 10 pancakes (1-1/3 cups syrup).

Gingerbread Biscotti

(Pictured at right and on page 101)

Cranberries and almonds pair well with the mild gingerbread flavor in these cookies from our Test Kitchen. The crisp cookies taste terrific with a steaming cup of coffee.

3 eggs
1 cup sugar
1/3 cup vegetable oil
1/4 cup molasses
3-3/4 cups all-purpose flour
3 teaspoons baking powder
3 teaspoons ground ginger
2-1/4 teaspoons ground cinnamon
1/4 teaspoon ground nutmeg
3/4 cup slivered almonds
1/2 cup dried cranberries

In a large mixing bowl, beat the eggs, sugar, oil and molasses. Combine the flour, baking powder, ginger, cinnamon and nutmeg; gradually add to the egg mixture. Turn onto a floured surface. Knead in almonds and cranberries.

Divide dough in half; shape each portion into a 14-in. x 3-in. rectangle. Transfer to a greased baking sheet. Bake at 375° for 24-26 minutes or until lightly browned. Cool for 5 minutes.

Transfer to a cutting board; with a serrated knife, cut each rectangle into 18 slices. Place slices cut side down on greased baking sheets. Bake for 10-15 minutes or until firm and crisp, turning once. Remove to wire racks to cool. Store in an airtight container. **Yield:** 3 dozen.

TWICE-COOKED COOKIE

BISCOTTI is derived from "bis" (twice) and "cotto" (cooked). This crunchy confection has its roots in the Tuscan region of Italy in a city called Prato. Because it could be stored for a long time, biscotti was ideal for sailors, soldiers and fishermen, and it's said Columbus carried some on his voyage.

Most European countries have adopted their own version of biscotti. For example, England has rusks and Germany has zwieback.

Blueberry Gingerbread Cake

The addition of blueberries in this gingerbread cake may be unusual, but the flavor is wonderful!
The mild ginger flavor appeals to all palates.
—*Vera Springer, Woodstock, Illinois*

1 cup plus 2 tablespoons sugar, *divided*
1/2 cup vegetable oil
3 tablespoons molasses
1/2 teaspoon salt
1 egg
2 cups plus 1 tablespoon all-purpose flour, *divided*
1 teaspoon ground cinnamon
3/4 teaspoon baking powder
1/2 teaspoon baking soda
1/2 teaspoon ground ginger
1/2 teaspoon ground nutmeg
1 cup buttermilk
1 cup fresh *or* frozen blueberries

In a large mixing bowl, combine 1 cup sugar, oil, molasses and salt. Beat in egg. Combine 2 cups flour, cinnamon, baking powder, baking soda, ginger and nutmeg; add to the sugar mixture alternately with buttermilk. Place the remaining flour in a resealable plastic bag; add blueberries and shake lightly to coat. Fold into batter.

Pour into a greased 11-in. x 7-in. x 2-in. baking dish. Sprinkle with remaining sugar. Bake at 350° for 35-40 minutes or until a toothpick inserted near the center comes out clean. Cool on a wire rack. **Yield:** 12 servings.

Editor's Note: If using frozen blueberries, do not thaw before adding to batter.

Baked Ginger Pudding

This recipe comes from a 1900 cookbook, although I've made some adjustments to suit
today's ingredients and cooking methods. Everyone loves this timeless soft baked pudding!
—*Jennifer Musgrove, Wheatland, Iowa*

4 cups cold milk, *divided*
1 cup cornmeal
3/4 cup molasses
1/4 cup butter, softened
3 tablespoons sugar
1/2 teaspoon salt
1/4 teaspoon *each* ground ginger, cinnamon and nutmeg
2 eggs, beaten
Whipped topping *or* vanilla ice cream, optional

In a saucepan, heat 3 cups milk over medium heat until bubbles form around sides of pan. In a small bowl, combine cornmeal and remaining cold milk; gradually add to heated milk. Cook over medium-low heat for 10 minutes, stirring occasionally. Remove from the heat. Stir in the molasses, butter, sugar, salt, ginger, cinnamon and nutmeg. Cool for 10 minutes. Whisk in the eggs.

Pour into a greased 11-in. x 7-in. x 2-in. baking dish. Bake at 325° for 1 hour or until center is almost set. Let stand for 30 minutes. Serve warm with whipped topping or ice cream if desired. **Yield:** 8 servings.

Butterscotch Gingerbread Cookies

(Pictured at right and on page 100)

Every time I make these wonderful cookies, the spicy aroma takes me back to my childhood. I helped Mom make them and delivered them to neighbors.
— *Kara Cook, Elk Ridge, Utah*

1 cup butter, softened
1 cup packed brown sugar
2 eggs
3 cups all-purpose flour
2 packages (3-1/2 ounces *each*) cook-and-serve butterscotch pudding mix
3 teaspoons ground ginger
1 teaspoon baking powder
1 teaspoon ground cinnamon

In a large mixing bowl, cream the butter and brown sugar. Beat in the eggs. Combine the flour, pudding mixes, ginger, baking powder and cinnamon; gradually add to creamed mixture. Cover and refrigerate for 1 hour or until easy to handle.

On a lightly floured surface, roll out dough to 1/4-in. thickness. Cut with floured 3-in. cookie cutters. Place 1 in. apart on ungreased baking sheets. Bake at 350° for 6-8 minutes or until firm. Remove to wire racks to cool.
Yield: about 3 dozen.

GET CREATIVE WITH CUTTERS

ANY SHAPE of cookie cutter can be used when making Butterscotch Gingerbread Cookies.

If you're looking for different kinds of cutters (like the snowflake shape shown here), stop by a specialty cooking store or visit the Wilton Industries, Inc. Web site at www.wilton.com.

Pumpkin Gingerbread With Caramel Sauce

(Pictured on page 101)

Instead of making ordinary gingerbread, I like to rely on this dressed-up version. The pumpkin gingerbread features a nutty crust and delicious caramel sauce.
—*Mitzi Sentiff, Alexandria, Virginia*

2-1/4 cups all-purpose flour
1/2 cup sugar
1-1/2 teaspoons ground ginger
1 teaspoon baking soda
1/2 teaspoon ground cinnamon
1/4 teaspoon salt
1/4 teaspoon ground cloves
2/3 cup cold butter
1 egg
1 cup buttermilk
1/2 cup canned pumpkin
1/2 cup molasses
3/4 cup chopped pecans
CARAMEL SAUCE:
1/2 cup butter
1-1/4 cups packed brown sugar
2 tablespoons light corn syrup
1/2 cup heavy whipping cream
9 pecan halves, optional

In a large bowl, combine the first seven ingredients. Cut in butter until mixture resembles fine crumbs. Combine the egg, buttermilk, pumpkin and molasses; stir into crumb mixture just until moistened. Stir in chopped pecans. Pour into a greased 9-in. square baking pan. Bake at 350° for 40-45 minutes or until a toothpick inserted near the center comes out clean.

For sauce, melt butter in a saucepan. Stir in the brown sugar and corn syrup; bring to a boil. Reduce heat to medium; cook until sugar is dissolved, about 1 minute. Stir in cream. Return to a boil; remove from the heat. Serve over warm gingerbread. Top with pecan halves if desired. **Yield:** 9 servings.

Family Traditions

INSTEAD of buying each other Christmas presents, my youngest sister and I give the gift of time. We set aside one day to bake cookies—gingerbread men and other family favorites. Spending the day together catching up and laughing is better than any gift we could buy!
—*Sandy Schmidt*
Madison, Wisconsin

Gingerbread Waffles

(Pictured at right)

So folks could enjoy the flavor of gingerbread at breakfast, our Test Kitchen home economists share this recipe. The waffles are so pretty with a sprinkling of confectioners' sugar.

1 cup all-purpose flour
1-1/2 teaspoons baking powder
1 teaspoon ground ginger
3/4 teaspoon ground cinnamon
1/2 teaspoon baking soda
1/4 teaspoon salt
1/8 teaspoon ground cloves
1/3 cup packed brown sugar
1 egg, *separated*
3/4 cup buttermilk
1/4 cup molasses
3 tablespoons butter, melted
1/8 teaspoon cream of tartar
Confectioners' sugar, optional

In a large bowl, combine the first seven ingredients. In a small mixing bowl, beat the brown sugar and egg yolk until fluffy; add the buttermilk, molasses and butter. Stir into dry ingredients just until combined.

In a small mixing bowl, beat the egg white and cream of tartar until stiff peaks form. Gently fold into batter. Quickly spoon onto a preheated waffle iron. Bake according to manufacturer's directions until golden brown. Sprinkle with confectioners' sugar if desired. **Yield:** 8 waffles.

Mini Gingerbread House
(Pictured at right)

*Our Test Kitchen shows just one way to decorate this cute little gingerbread house.
Prepare several batches of dough (one batch at a time) and decorate a number
of houses in different ways to create a gingerbread village!*

1/2 cup shortening
1/2 cup packed dark brown sugar
1/2 cup dark corn syrup
1/2 cup molasses
  1 tablespoon ground ginger
  1 tablespoon ground cinnamon
  4 cups all-purpose flour
ICING AND ASSEMBLY:
  2 egg whites
2-2/3 cups confectioners' sugar
1/4 teaspoon cream of tartar
Pastry tip-round #5
Covered board (12 inches x 7 inches)
  2 Pirouette cookies
42 Tootsie Roll Midgees
Edible glitter
16 snowflake-shaped sprinkles
  3 *each* vanilla and chocolate
    chewy pudding snack bites
  9 miniature semisweet
    chocolate nonpareils
  1 milk chocolate candy bar
    (1.55 ounces)
  6 ice cream sugar cones

Using parchment or waxed paper, make gingerbread house pattern pieces according to the diagrams on page 109; set aside.

In a heavy saucepan, cook and stir the shortening, brown sugar, corn syrup and molasses over medium heat until sugar is dissolved. Remove from the heat; stir in ginger and cinnamon. Stir in flour, 1 cup at a time, until dough can be formed into a ball. With a lightly floured rolling pin, roll out dough directly onto a greased baking sheet to 1/4-in. thickness.

Position patterns on dough; cut out. Remove dough scraps; cover and save to reroll if necessary. Bake at 350° for 10-15 minutes or until gingerbread springs back when lightly touched. Immediately place patterns over gingerbread; cut around edges to trim. Cool on baking sheet for 3-4 minutes or until gingerbread begins to harden. Carefully remove to a wire rack; cool.

For icing and assembly: In a large mixing bowl, beat the egg whites, confectioners' sugar and cream of tartar on low speed for 1 minute. Beat on high for 6-8 minutes or until stiff.

Cut a small hole in the corner of a pastry or plastic bag; insert pastry tip. Place some icing in bag. Pipe icing along base and sides of front wall and one side wall. Position at right angles to each other and place on covered board; prop with small bottles or jars. Repeat with second side section and back. Let dry; remove bottles. For side supports, carefully cut Pirouette cookies widthwise in half. Pipe icing along one side of each; position at the corners of the house.

For roof: Pipe icing along peak of roof. Position roof pieces; let dry. For roof tiles, cut Tootsie Rolls widthwise in half. Flatten with a rolling pin; cut each flattened piece in half. Pipe an icing line 1/2 in. from bottom of one side of roof. Curve Tootsie Roll pieces around your finger or a wooden spoon handle and press along icing; repeat until one horizontal row is finished. Repeat six times, slightly overlapping each row until one roof piece is covered.

Repeat on other side. Pipe a thick line of icing along top, front and back roof seams. Using the same technique, place a row of Tootsie Roll pieces at a right angle to direction of roof tiles along the top, front and back seams; let dry. Pipe a few thick clusters of icing onto roof tiles to resemble snow. Sprinkle with edible glitter.

For finishing touches: In a bead pattern, pipe icing around front door. Pipe 1-in. squares on both sides of door and on each side of house for windows. Pipe windowpanes. Decorate the corners with snowflake-shaped sprinkles.

For wreath over door, attach pudding bites and nonpareils to front of house using icing. On covered board, spread icing into a 1-in. curved strip from the front door to the edge of the board for path. Cut candy bar into small rectangles; press side by side into icing. Let dry.

Using scissors, cut sugar cones to varying heights. If desired, pipe a thick circle of icing around open end of each cone to help hold in place. Position cones around house. **Yield:** 1 house.

Editor's Note: Icing is for decorative purposes only because it is made with uncooked egg whites. Edible glitter can be ordered by mail from Wilton Industries, Inc. Call 1-800/794-5866 or visit their Web site, www.wilton.com.

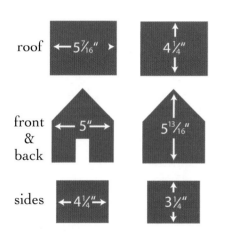

MAKING A MINI GINGERBREAD HOUSE

1. On sturdy paper, cut out patterns for your gingerbread house. Roll out one portion of dough; position one pattern on top and cut out. Repeat with remaining dough and patterns. Continue with the recipe as directed.

2. Align walls at right angles to each other. Prop with small spice bottles for stability. Let dry before removing bottles.

Frosted Gingerbread Nut Cookies

(Pictured at right)

I received the recipe for these soft ginger cookies from a dear lady, who has since passed away. A comforting classic like this always satisfies.
—Karyn Rogers, Hemet, California

1/2 cup butter, softened
2/3 cup sugar
1 egg
1/2 cup molasses
2-3/4 cups all-purpose flour
1 teaspoon baking soda
1 teaspoon ground cinnamon
1 teaspoon ground ginger
1/2 teaspoon salt
1/4 teaspoon ground cloves
1/2 cup buttermilk
1/2 cup chopped walnuts

FROSTING:
1-1/2 cups confectioners' sugar
4-1/2 teaspoons butter, softened
1/2 teaspoon vanilla extract
2 to 3 tablespoons half-and-half cream
Walnuts halves, optional

In a large mixing bowl, cream butter and sugar. Beat in the egg and molasses. Combine the flour, baking soda, cinnamon, ginger, salt and cloves; add to creamed mixture alternately with buttermilk. Stir in chopped walnuts.

Drop by tablespoonfuls 2 in. apart onto greased baking sheets. Bake at 350° for 10-12 minutes or until cookies spring back when lightly touched. Remove to wire racks to cool.

For frosting, in a small bowl, combine the confectioners' sugar, butter, vanilla and enough cream to achieve desired consistency. Frost cooled cookies. Top each with a walnut half if desired. **Yield:** 5 dozen.

Spiced Ginger Coffee

Our Test Kitchen shows how you can enjoy the flavor of gingerbread around the clock with this unique coffee recipe!

1/2 cup molasses
1/4 cup packed brown sugar
1 teaspoon ground ginger
3/4 teaspoon ground cinnamon
Hot brewed coffee
Milk, whipped cream and
  additional ground cinnamon,
  optional

In a small bowl, combine the molasses, brown sugar, ginger and cinnamon; mix well. Store in a covered container in the refrigerator for up to 2 weeks.

To prepare coffee: Place about 2 teaspoons molasses mixture in a mug. Add 1 cup of hot coffee; stir until combined. Serve with milk, whipped cream and cinnamon if desired. **Yield:** 2/3 cup molasses mixture (about 15 servings).

Gingerbread Candle Holders

(Pictured at right)

These clever candle holders from our Test Kitchen would make a lovely Christmas centerpiece when grouped together. Or use them at individual place settings as pretty party favors.

3 cups self-rising flour
2 teaspoons ground ginger
1/2 teaspoon ground cloves
1/2 cup cold butter, cubed
2/3 cup packed brown sugar
1/3 cup molasses
1 egg, lightly beaten
ICING:
2-2/3 cups confectioners' sugar
1 tablespoon meringue powder
1/4 teaspoon cream of tartar
3 tablespoons water

In a food processor, combine the flour, ginger and cloves. Add butter; cover and process until mixture resembles coarse crumbs. Add the brown sugar, molasses and egg; cover and process until mixed. Wrap dough in plastic wrap; refrigerate for at least 30 minutes or until firm.

Unwrap dough; knead until smooth, about 8 times. On a lightly floured surface, roll out dough to 1/4-in. thickness. Cut out eight trees with a floured 5-in. tree-shaped cookie cutter. Cut out eight 3-in. round circles, rerolling dough scraps if necessary.

Place 2 in. apart on a greased baking sheet. Bake at 400° for 6 minutes. Using a plastic straw, cut out circles in a random pattern on the trees (so candlelight can shine through). Bake 6-7 minutes longer or until firm. Remove to wire racks to cool.

For icing, in a large mixing bowl, combine the confectioners' sugar, meringue powder and cream of tartar. Add water; beat on low speed for 1 minute or until very stiff.

Cut a small hole in the corner of a pastry or plastic bag; insert a #5 round pastry tip. Outline trees and decorate trees with garland and ornaments as desired. Pipe icing onto the bottom edge of each tree; set tree on a round base about 1/2 in. from edge. For additional support, pipe another line of icing along the back of tree where it joins the base. Prop trees with small glasses until icing has set. Let stand overnight to dry completely. Store in an airtight container.

Place a votive candle or tea light on the base of holder behind the tree, or attach a birthday candle with a dab of icing on the base. Be aware that the heat will eventually soften the icing. **Yield:** 8 candle holders.

Editor's Note: As a substitute for *each* cup of self-rising flour, place 1-1/2 teaspoons baking powder and 1/2 teaspoon salt in a measuring cup. Add all-purpose flour to measure 1 cup. Meringue powder can be ordered by mail from Wilton Industries, Inc. Call 1-800/794-5866 or visit their Web site, www.wilton.com.

GIVING
Thanks

Looking for a way to liven up your standard Thanksgiving turkey? Try basting it with an unforgettable fruity glaze! For a twist on your traditional menu, whip up some deliciously different side dishes. Fresh cranberries are a mainstay in fall cooking. In this chapter, we offer a classic collection of recipes featuring those crimson beauties. And brimming bowls of steaming soup will warm the body and soul when cool autumn winds blow!

GIVING *Thanks*

Traditional Turkey Dinner

FOR MOST families, Thanksgiving is one of the most anticipated holidays of the year. At no other time are food and family the main focus of the day.

Such a special occasion calls for a show-stopping entree like Fruit-Glazed Turkey. An apple-raisin stuffing is tucked inside the tender bird, which is basted with a fruity spiced glaze as it bakes.

Round out the meal with a selection of sides such as Blue Cheese Romaine Salad, Squash Supreme, Herbed Cheddar Crescents and, of course, your family's favorite mashed potatoes.

Want to pass on plain old pumpkin pie this year? Serve your delighted guests slices of Hazelnut Pear Tart!

A FEAST FOR THE EYES

(Left to right)

Hazelnut Pear Tart (p. 117)

Fruit-Glazed Turkey (p. 118)

THANKSGIVING DAY TIMELINE

A Few Weeks Before:

- Prepare two grocery lists—one for non-perishable items to purchase now and one for perishable items to purchase a few days before Thanksgiving Day.
- Order a fresh turkey or buy and freeze a frozen turkey.
- Gather materials for the Sheaves of Wheat Centerpiece (page 121).
- Bake the Herbed Cheddar Crescents; cool. Freeze in a heavy-duty resealable plastic bag.

Four to Five Days Before:

- Thaw the frozen turkey in a pan in the refrigerator. (Allow 24 hours of thawing for every 5 pounds.)

Two to Three Days Before:

- Buy remaining grocery items, including the fresh turkey if you ordered one.

The Day Before:

- Set the dinner table and arrange the centerpiece.
- Make the Hazelnut Pear Tart; store in the refrigerator.
- For the Blue Cheese Romaine Salad, bake the pine nuts in butter as directed; cool and store at room temperature in an airtight container. Make the salad dressing; cover and chill. Wash, dry and tear the romaine; refrigerate in a resealable plastic bag.
- Prepare the mayonnaise mixture for the Cucumber Dill Dip; cover and chill. Cut up any vegetables for dipping; place in individual resealable plastic bags and refrigerate.
- Assemble the Squash Supreme casserole but don't sprinkle with bread crumbs and paprika or drizzle with butter. Cover and refrigerate.
- Make the glaze for Fruit-Glazed Turkey; cover and chill.

Thanksgiving Day:

- In the morning, thaw Herbed Cheddar Crescents in the refrigerator.
- Make the apple-raisin stuffing, stuff the turkey and bake, basting with the fruit glaze as directed.
- Just before guests arrive, peel, seed and chop cucumber; stir into the Cucumber Dill Dip mayonnaise mixture. Serve with vegetables and/or crackers.
- Remove Squash Supreme from the refrigerator 30 minutes before baking. Sprinkle bread crumbs and paprika on top; drizzle with the melted butter. Bake as directed. (If the casserole has been refrigerated overnight, you may need to bake it a little longer than the recipe specifies.)
- If desired, wrap Herbed Cheddar Crescents in foil. Reheat in a 325° oven for 15 to 20 minutes.
- Let the cooked turkey stand for 20 minutes. Meanwhile, make the gravy. Remove the stuffing and carve the turkey.
- Slice the apples or pears for Blue Cheese Romaine Salad. Stir the dressing and assemble the salad as directed.
- For dessert, serve Hazelnut Pear Tart.

Hazelnut Pear Tart

(Pictured at right and on page 114)

Alongside your traditional pumpkin pie, our home economists encourage you to slice wedges of this pretty, pleasing pear tart.

1 cup butter, softened
1/2 cup confectioners' sugar
1 teaspoon vanilla extract
2 cups all-purpose flour
1/2 cup finely chopped blanched hazelnuts

FILLING:
1/3 cup apricot preserves
2/3 cup chopped blanched hazelnuts, toasted
1/2 cup sugar
1 tablespoon all-purpose flour
6 tablespoons butter, softened
1 egg, lightly beaten
2-3/4 pounds pears, peeled, cored and sliced

In a large mixing bowl, cream butter and confectioners' sugar. Beat in vanilla, flour and hazelnuts. Press into a greased 11-in. tart pan with removable bottom. Bake at 400° for 10 minutes. Remove from the oven; reduce heat to 350°.

Spread apricot preserves over crust. In a bowl, combine the hazelnuts, sugar, flour, butter and egg. Spoon over preserves. Arrange pear slices over filling in a concentric circle, slightly overlapping slices. Bake for 40-45 minutes or until golden brown. Cool on a wire rack. Store in the refrigerator. **Yield:** 10-12 servings.

Fruit-Glazed Turkey

(Pictured on page 115)

*I came up with this recipe one holiday when my family asked that I make something
other than the same old turkey. They loved this fruity version.*
—Christal Helman, Lisbon, Ohio

1 **package (14 ounces)
  unseasoned stuffing cubes**
1 **small onion, chopped**
1 **medium tart apple, peeled
  and chopped**
1 **celery rib, chopped**
1 **cup raisins**
1 **cup hot water**
1 **cup butter, melted**
1 **tablespoon poultry seasoning**
1 **turkey (10 to 12 pounds)**
GLAZE:
2 **cans (8 ounces *each*)
  unsweetened crushed
  pineapple, undrained**
1 **can (11 ounces) mandarin
  oranges, undrained**
1/8 **teaspoon ground cinnamon**
1/8 **teaspoon ground cloves**
GRAVY:
3 **tablespoons all-purpose flour**
1/2 **teaspoon salt**
1/4 **teaspoon pepper**

In a large bowl, combine the first eight ingredients. Loosely stuff into turkey just before baking. Place remaining stuffing in a greased 1-qt. baking dish; cover and refrigerate until ready to bake. Skewer turkey openings; tie drumsticks together. Place breast side up on a rack in a roasting pan. Bake, uncovered, at 325° for 1 hour.

Meanwhile, in a blender, combine the glaze ingredients; cover and process until smooth. Cover and refrigerate 1 cup for gravy. Brush turkey with some of the remaining glaze. Add 1/2 in. of hot water to roasting pan. Bake 2-1/2 to 3 hours longer or until a meat thermometer reads 180° for turkey and 165° for stuffing, basting two to three times with glaze and occasionally with pan drippings (cover loosely with foil if turkey browns too quickly). Discard any unused basting glaze.

Cover and bake additional stuffing for 30-40 minutes. Uncover; bake 10 minutes longer or until lightly browned. Cover turkey and let stand for 20 minutes before removing stuffing and carving turkey.

For gravy, loosen browned bits from roasting pan. Pour pan drippings and browned bits into a bowl. Skim fat, reserving 1/4 cup. In a 2-cup measuring cup, combine pan drippings and enough water or broth to measure 2 cups.

In a large saucepan, combine the flour, salt and pepper; gradually whisk in the reserved 1/4 cup fat and dripping mixture until blended. Cook and stir over medium-high heat until thickened and bubbly. Stir in the reserved glaze. Bring to a boil; cook and stir for 2 minutes or until thickened. Serve with turkey. **Yield:** 10-12 servings (2-1/2 cups gravy).

Blue Cheese Romaine Salad

(Pictured at right)

A light lemon vinaigrette makes this salad deliciously different from all others.
—Mindy Oswalt, Winnetka, California

1/2 cup pine nuts
1 tablespoon butter, melted
6 cups torn romaine
3/4 cup crumbled blue cheese
2 medium green apples *or* pears, sliced

LEMON VINAIGRETTE:
1/3 cup lemon juice
1 tablespoon brown sugar
1 garlic clove, peeled
1/4 teaspoon salt
1/8 teaspoon pepper
1/2 cup olive oil

Combine pine nuts and butter; spread on a baking sheet. Bake at 350° for 4-6 minutes or until golden brown, stirring once. Cool on a wire rack. In a serving bowl, combine romaine and blue cheese. Add apples and pine nuts.

In a food processor or blender, combine the lemon juice, brown sugar, garlic, salt and pepper; cover and process until smooth. While processing, gradually add oil in a steady stream. Drizzle over salad and toss to coat. Serve immediately. **Yield:** 6 servings.

Cucumber Dill Dip

This cool and creamy dip keeps the oven free for other foods on Thanksgiving.
You can make the base in advance, then stir in the cucumber just before serving.
—Judith Smith, Wymore, Nebraska

1/2 cup mayonnaise
1/2 cup sour cream
1/4 cup finely chopped onion
1 teaspoon dill weed
1/2 teaspoon salt
1/2 teaspoon pepper

2 cups finely chopped seeded peeled cucumber
Assorted vegetables *and/or* crackers

In a small bowl, combine the mayonnaise, sour cream, onion, dill, salt and pepper. Cover and refrigerate for at least 2 hours. Just before serving, stir in cucumber. Serve with vegetables and/or crackers. **Yield:** about 2-1/4 cups.

Herbed Cheddar Crescents

Our son won the Champion Dinner Rolls title with this recipe. Cheddar cheese and Italian seasoning are unique additions to the dough.
—Rosalie Flanagan, Buchanan, Michigan

4-1/4 cups all-purpose flour
1 cup (4 ounces) shredded cheddar cheese
2 tablespoons plus 1-1/2 teaspoons sugar
2 packages (1/4 ounce *each*) active dry yeast
1-1/2 teaspoons Italian seasoning
1 teaspoon salt
1-1/2 cups milk
7 tablespoons butter, *divided*
1 egg yolk
1 tablespoon water

In a large mixing bowl, combine 3 cups flour, cheese, sugar, yeast, Italian seasoning and salt. In a saucepan, heat milk and 4 tablespoons butter to 120°-130°. Add to dry ingredients; beat until smooth. Stir in enough remaining flour to form a soft dough (do not knead). Cover and let rise in a warm place until doubled, about 1 hour.

Punch dough down. Turn onto a lightly floured surface; divide into thirds. Roll each portion into a 10-in. circle. Melt remaining butter; brush over dough. Cut each circle into eight wedges. Roll up wedges from the wide end and place pointed side down 2 in. apart on greased baking sheets. Curve ends down to form crescent shape. Cover and let rise until doubled, about 50 minutes.

Beat egg yolk and water; brush over crescents. Bake at 375° for 15-20 minutes or until golden. Remove from pans to wire racks. Store in the refrigerator. **Yield:** 2 dozen.

Squash Supreme

We enjoy this casserole every Thanksgiving and Christmas. Ranch dressing gives ordinary squash a boost!
—Sherri Johnson, Burns, Tennessee

2 pounds yellow summer squash, peeled and cubed
3 eggs, beaten
1 cup (4 ounces) finely shredded sharp cheddar cheese
1 cup mayonnaise
3/4 cup crushed butter-flavored crackers (about 19 crackers)
1 medium onion, finely chopped
1 envelope buttermilk ranch salad dressing mix
1/3 cup dry bread crumbs
1/8 teaspoon paprika
3 tablespoons butter, melted

Place squash in a saucepan and cover with water; bring to a boil. Reduce heat; cover and simmer for 15-20 minutes or until very tender. Drain well in a fine mesh strainer, pressing water out with the back of a large spoon.

Transfer squash to a large bowl; mash. Add the eggs, cheese, mayonnaise, cracker crumbs, onion and dressing mix; mix well. Pour into a greased 1-1/2-qt. baking dish. Sprinkle with bread crumbs and paprika. Drizzle with butter. Bake, uncovered, at 325° for 45-50 minutes or until a thermometer reads 160°. **Yield:** 8 servings.

Sheaves of Wheat Centerpiece

(Pictured above)

THANKSGIVING is a holiday when we celebrate our bounty of food, family and friends. It's also a time when cooks spend days planning menus and preparing food. So a simple yet stunning tabletop is in order!

Wheat has long been a symbol of abundance, making it a natural item to include in this easy, elegant Thanksgiving Day centerpiece.

Dried wheat bundles are inexpensive and can be found in craft and department stores. To display the striking stalks, we purchased three tall glass vases. The vases have a narrow opening, which keeps the wheat standing upright.

If the traditional browns, reds and oranges associated with Thanksgiving don't appeal to you, choose another color, like the gorgeous green candles shown here. For a little more interest, use the same shade of candle in a variety of heights and set them on an assortment of candleholders.

Either arrange the vases and candles in the middle of your table or place each item in a line down the length of the table.

GIVING Thanks

A Bounty of Side Dishes

IF TURKEY on Thanksgiving Day is a timeless tradition your family just won't let you change, have a little fun by adding deliciously different side dishes to your menu!

Guests will leave the table satisfied after sampling colorful Glazed Carrots and Peas.

You'll harvest a host of compliments when you dish out Savory Orange Dressing. With orange juice and peel, it's a tasty twist to standard stuffing.

To complement your selection of oven-fresh sides, serve hearty helpings of refreshing Marinated Asparagus Salad. (All recipes shown at right.)

FIT FOR FALL
(Clockwise from top right)

Glazed Carrots and Peas (p. 124)

Marinated Asparagus Salad (p. 126)

Savory Orange Dressing (p. 125)

Glazed Carrots and Peas

(Pictured on page 123)

Here's a low-fat way to dress up vegetables. Carrots and peas are so pretty on the table.
—Shirley Bedzis, San Diego, California

2 teaspoons cornstarch
2 teaspoons sugar
1/4 cup chicken broth
1 tablespoon soy sauce
1 teaspoon crushed garlic
1-1/2 teaspoons minced fresh
    gingerroot
4 cups thinly sliced carrots
4 cups sugar snap peas
1/2 cup sherry *or* additional
    chicken broth
2 tablespoons lemon juice

In a bowl, combine cornstarch and sugar. Stir in the broth and soy sauce until smooth; set aside. In a nonstick skillet coated with nonstick cooking spray, saute garlic and gingerroot for 30 seconds. Add the carrots, peas and sherry or additional broth. Reduce heat to low; cook for 8-10 minutes or until vegetables are tender.

Stir soy sauce mixture and add to vegetables. Bring to a boil; cook and stir for 2 minutes or until thickened. Stir in lemon juice. **Yield:** 8 servings.

READ UP ON GINGERROOT

FRESH gingerroot is available in your grocer's produce section. It should have a smooth skin. If wrinkled and cracked, the root is dry and past its prime.

When stored in a heavy-duty resealable plastic bag, unpeeled gingerroot can be frozen for up to 1 year. When needed, simply peel and grate.

Molasses New Potatoes

Molasses gives this potato dish a little sweetness while walnuts add some pleasant crunch.
—Janet Dingler, Cedartown, Georgia

2-1/2 pounds new red potatoes,
    quartered
2 tablespoons vegetable oil
2 tablespoons molasses
2 tablespoons balsamic vinegar
1 teaspoon dried thyme,
    crushed
1/2 teaspoon salt
1/2 cup coarsely chopped walnuts
1/4 cup minced chives

Place potatoes in a 13-in. x 9-in. x 2-in. baking dish coated with nonstick cooking spray. In a small bowl, combine the oil, molasses, vinegar, thyme and salt. Drizzle over potatoes and toss to coat.

Bake, uncovered, at 350° for 30 minutes. Stir in walnuts. Bake 30-35 minutes longer or until potatoes are tender, stirring once. Sprinkle with chives. **Yield:** 6 servings.

Savory Orange Dressing

(Pictured at right and on page 122)

*This recipe was in my files for years
before I finally tried it one Thanksgiving.
My family loves the combination
of orange and carrots.*
—Dixie Terry, Marion, Illinois

    1 cup sliced celery
  1/2 cup chopped onion
  1/3 cup butter
    2 teaspoons chicken bouillon
      granules
2-1/2 cups boiling water
    1 package (14 ounces) seasoned
      stuffing cubes
  1/2 cup shredded carrot
  1/4 cup orange juice
    2 teaspoons grated orange peel

In a small skillet, saute the celery and onion in butter until
tender. In a large bowl, dissolve bouillon in boiling water.
Stir in the stuffing cubes, carrot, orange juice, peel and
celery mixture.

Spoon into a greased 13-in. x 9-in. x 2-in. baking dish.
Cover and bake at 350° for 20 minutes. Uncover; bake 15
minutes longer or until heated through. **Yield:** 10 servings.

Lemon-Pecan Wild Rice

*Rice is a unique accompaniment to turkey or any number of meaty entrees.
This dish has just the right amount of lemon and nutty flavors.*
—Diane Kensinger, Manheim, Pennsylvania

3 cups chicken broth
1 cup uncooked wild rice
1 tablespoon butter
3 tablespoons thinly sliced
  green onions
2 tablespoons minced fresh
  parsley
1 tablespoon grated lemon peel

1 tablespoon lemon juice
1/2 cup chopped pecans, toasted

In a large saucepan, bring the broth, rice and butter to a boil.
Reduce heat; cover and simmer for 50-60 minutes or until
rice is tender. Stir in the onions, parsley, lemon peel and
juice. Stir in pecans. **Yield:** 4-6 servings.

Marinated Asparagus Salad

(Pictured on page 122)

*A no-fuss side dish is great when entertaining. The asparagus is cooked and chilled
in advance, then stands at room temperature in the marinade while I visit and prepare the rest of the meal.*
—Janice Connelley, Mountain City, Nevada

2 pounds fresh asparagus,
  trimmed
3/4 cup vegetable oil
1/2 cup white wine vinegar
1 tablespoon dried basil
2 teaspoons dried oregano
1 teaspoon salt
1/2 teaspoon pepper
2 garlic cloves, minced
4 green onions, chopped

Place asparagus in a large skillet; add 1/2 in. of water. Bring to a boil. Reduce heat; cover and simmer for 3-5 minutes or until crisp-tender. Rinse in cold water; drain. Refrigerate for 2-3 hours.

Arrange asparagus in a shallow dish. Combine remaining ingredients; pour over asparagus. Let stand at room temperature for 1-2 hours before serving. **Yield:** 8-10 servings.

Baked Mushrooms with Spinach

*I love special side dishes like this that are so easy to prepare.
It's great served alongside any roasted meat.*
—Sherry Hammond, New Albany, Indiana

2 packages (10 ounces *each*)
  frozen chopped spinach,
  thawed and squeezed dry
1 pound large fresh mushrooms
2 tablespoons finely chopped
  onion
4 tablespoons butter, *divided*
4 bacon strips, cooked and
  crumbled
1 cup milk
1 cup (8 ounces) shredded
  cheddar cheese
1/2 teaspoon ground mustard
1/2 teaspoon salt
Dash pepper

Place spinach in a greased 8-in. baking dish; set aside. Remove stems from mushrooms. Set caps aside; chop stems. Saute chopped mushrooms and onion in 2 tablespoons butter; spoon over spinach. Sprinkle with bacon. Top with mushroom caps. Melt remaining butter; brush over caps.

In a large saucepan, combine the milk, cheese, mustard, salt and pepper. Cook and stir over medium-low heat until cheese is melted; pour over the top. Bake, uncovered, at 350° for 35-40 minutes or until mushrooms are tender. **Yield:** 6-8 servings.

Apple Walnut Slaw

(Pictured at right)

A co-worker shared this recipe with me. Now it's a family favorite. Apples, walnuts and raisins are a fun way to dress up coleslaw.
—Joan Hallford
North Richland Hills, Texas

6 cups shredded cabbage
1-1/2 cups shredded carrots
1 cup coarsely chopped walnuts, toasted
3/4 cup raisins
1/3 cup finely chopped red onion
3/4 cup mayonnaise
3/4 cup buttermilk
4 to 5 tablespoons sugar
4-1/2 teaspoons lemon juice
3/4 teaspoon salt
1/4 to 1/2 teaspoon pepper
2 medium apples, chopped

In a large salad bowl, toss the cabbage, carrots, walnuts, raisins and onion. In a small bowl, combine the mayonnaise, buttermilk, sugar, lemon juice, salt and pepper. Pour over cabbage mixture and toss to coat. Gently fold in apples. Cover and refrigerate until serving. **Yield:** 12 servings.

SPEEDY SLAW

TO DECREASE the preparation time of Apple Walnut Slaw, use a 16-ounce bag of coleslaw mix for the shredded cabbage and carrots.

Cheesy Corn Casserole

With just five ingredients, this zesty casserole can be assembled in no time.
—Linda Jensen, Lone Rock, Iowa

3 eggs, beaten
2 packages (16 ounces *each*) frozen white *or* shoepeg corn, thawed
1 cup (4 ounces) shredded pepper Jack cheese
1 cup (4 ounces) shredded Monterey Jack cheese
1 jar (2 ounces) diced pimientos, drained

In a large bowl, combine the eggs, corn, cheeses and pimientos. Transfer to a greased 2-qt. baking dish. Bake, uncovered, at 350° for 35-40 minutes or until bubbly. **Yield:** 10-12 servings.

Bacon Herb Zucchini

The herbs in this dish really complement a Thanksgiving turkey.
The recipe can easily be doubled to serve a larger group.
— Betty Korte, Collinsville, Illinois

    4 bacon strips, diced
1/2 cup chopped celery
1/2 cup chopped onion
3/4 cup canned diced tomatoes
    with juice
    1 tablespoon minced fresh
    parsley
1/4 teaspoon *each* dried oregano,
    savory and rubbed sage
1/4 teaspoon salt
1/8 teaspoon pepper
    4 cups sliced zucchini
    3 tablespoons grated Parmesan
    cheese

In a large skillet, cook bacon over medium heat until crisp. Using a slotted spoon, remove bacon to paper towels; drain, reserving 1 tablespoon drippings.

In the drippings, saute celery and onion until tender. Add the tomatoes, parsley, oregano, savory, sage, salt, pepper and zucchini. Bring to a boil, stirring occasionally. Reduce heat; cover and simmer for 7-10 minutes or until zucchini is tender. Sprinkle with Parmesan cheese and bacon. **Yield:** 6-8 servings.

Maple Squash 'n' Apples

I was never a fan of squash. But when I came across this recipe several years ago,
I tried making it. My family is glad I did!
— Sharon Rink, Appleton, Wisconsin

3/4 cup maple syrup
1/2 cup butter, cubed
1/4 cup apple juice
    1 teaspoon ground cinnamon
1/2 teaspoon salt
1/2 teaspoon ground allspice
    3 small butternut squash (about
    1-1/2 pounds *each*)
    4 large tart apples, peeled and
    cut into 1/4-inch slices

In a small saucepan, combine the syrup, butter and apple juice. Bring to a boil over medium heat, stirring occasionally. Cook and stir for 5 minutes or until slightly thickened. Remove from the heat; whisk in the cinnamon, salt and allspice. Set aside.

Peel squash and cut in half lengthwise. Remove seeds and cut into 1/4-in. slices. Place a third of the squash in a greased 13-in. x 9-in. x 2-in. baking dish. Layer with half of the apples and a third of the squash. Top with alternating slices of remaining squash and apples. Pour syrup mixture over the top.

Cover and bake at 400° for 30-35 minutes or until squash is almost tender. Uncover; bake 15 minutes longer, basting twice. **Yield:** 8-10 servings.

Macaroon Sweet Potato Bake

(Pictured at right)

This casserole can be made the night before and chilled. Remove from the fridge 30 minutes before baking. Top with the buttered crumbled macaroons before putting in the oven.
—William Waller, Lady Lake, Florida

6 cups mashed cooked sweet
    potatoes (about 3-1/2 pounds)
6 tablespoons plus 4-1/2
    teaspoons butter, melted,
    divided
1/2 cup packed brown sugar
1/4 cup amaretto liqueur *or* 1/4
    teaspoon almond extract
1/2 teaspoon salt
1/2 teaspoon ground ginger
1/2 cup chopped pecans
1/4 cup orange marmalade
6 macaroons, crumbled

In a large mixing bowl, combine the sweet potatoes, 6 tablespoons butter, brown sugar, amaretto or extract, salt and ginger; beat until smooth. Stir in the pecans and marmalade.

Transfer to a greased 11-in. x 7-in. x 2-in. baking dish. Toss macaroons with remaining butter; sprinkle over the top. Bake, uncovered, at 325° for 30-35 minutes or until heated through. **Yield:** 8 servings.

MAKING MASHED SWEET POTATOES

TO COOK sweet potatoes, place whole scrubbed sweet potatoes in a large kettle; cover with water. Cover and boil gently for 30 to 45 minutes or until potatoes can easily be pierced with the tip of a sharp knife. Drain. When cool enough to handle, peel and mash.

Holiday Green Bean Bake

Ham and a blend of seasonings make a plain green bean bake spectacular!
The recipe has been in my family for more than 30 years.
—Frances Whitson, Tiptonville, Tennessee

6 cups frozen cut green beans, thawed
1 cup cubed fully cooked ham
3 tablespoons butter, *divided*
1 tablespoon all-purpose flour
1/2 cup milk
1 can (10-3/4 ounces) condensed cream of mushroom soup, undiluted
4 ounces process cheese (Velveeta), cubed
1 jar (4 ounces) diced pimientos, drained
1 teaspoon Worcestershire sauce
1/2 teaspoon salt
1/4 teaspoon pepper
1/2 cup dry bread crumbs

In a large bowl, combine the beans and ham; set aside. In a saucepan, melt 1 tablespoon butter. Stir in flour until smooth; gradually add milk. Bring to a boil; cook and stir for 1 minute or until thickened. Reduce heat; add the soup, cheese, pimientos, Worcestershire sauce, salt and pepper. Cook and stir until cheese is melted. Pour over bean mixture; toss to coat.

Transfer to a greased 2-qt. baking dish. Bake, uncovered, at 350° for 40 minutes, stirring twice. Melt the remaining butter; toss with bread crumbs. Sprinkle over the top. Bake 10-15 minutes longer or until golden brown. **Yield** 8-10 servings.

Candied Parsnips

Tender strips of yellow parsnips are coated in a slightly sweet honey sauce.
Recipes like this with few ingredients are great to have on hand.
—Linda Bussing, Lake Stevens, Washington

2 pounds parsnips, trimmed
1/4 cup butter
2 tablespoons honey
1/4 teaspoon ground nutmeg
Minced fresh parsley

With a vegetable peeler, peel parsnips. In a Dutch oven, cook parsnips in a small amount of salted boiling water for 25 minutes or until tender; drain. Let stand until cool enough to handle.

Cut parsnips into slices or julienned strips. In the same pan, melt butter. Stir in honey and nutmeg. Add parsnips and stir to coat. Cook until lightly browned. Sprinkle with parsley. **Yield:** 8 servings.

Asparagus Pea Medley

(Pictured at right)

Hurried hostesses will appreciate the make-ahead convenience of this casserole. A rich and creamy sauce beautifully coats asparagus and peas.
—M. Joalyce Graham, Starke, Florida

  2 packages (10-1/2 ounces *each*)
     frozen cut asparagus
  1 package (10 ounces) frozen
     peas, thawed
  1 jar (6 ounces) sliced
     mushrooms, drained
  1 jar (2 ounces) diced pimientos,
     drained
  5 tablespoons butter, *divided*
  3 tablespoons all-purpose flour
3/4 cup milk
  1 jar (5 ounces) sharp American
     cheese spread
1/4 teaspoon salt
1/4 teaspoon pepper
1/3 cup dry bread crumbs

Cook asparagus according to package directions, omitting the salt. Drain, reserving 3/4 cup cooking liquid. Place asparagus in a greased 11-in. x 7-in. x 2-in. baking dish. Top with peas, mushrooms and pimientos; set aside.

In a small saucepan, melt 3 tablespoons butter. Stir in flour until smooth; gradually add milk and reserved cooking liquid. Bring to a boil; cook and stir for 2 minutes or until thickened. Reduce heat; add the cheese spread, salt and pepper; stir until blended. Pour over vegetables. Melt remaining butter; toss with bread crumbs. Sprinkle over cheese sauce.

Cover and refrigerate for 8 hours or overnight. Or bake, uncovered, at 350° for 35-40 minutes or until bubbly. If refrigerated before baking, remove from the refrigerator 30 minutes beforehand. **Yield:** 8-10 servings.

GIVING Thanks

Awesome Autumn Soups

WHEN cool fall winds begin to blow, nothing warms you up inside and out like a bowl brimming with steaming soup.

For a lively leftover, take your Thanksgiving turkey and turn it into a whole new creation with Creamy Turkey Vegetable Soup.

Your family will love Cajun-style Autumn Sausage Corn Soup. So get ready to ladle up second—and third—helpings!

A slice of cheesy French bread is the crowning touch on individual servings of Portobello Onion Soup. (Recipes shown at right.)

Vegetables, meat, pasta, potatoes, broth, cream...the list of ingredients to include in simmering soups is endless!

Autumn Sausage Corn Soup

(Pictured on page 132)

I cook this frequently throughout the year, but my family especially loves it on cold nights.
Cayenne pepper, sausage and ham lend to its fabulous Cajun flavor.
—Belinda Desselle, Westlake, Louisiana

3/4 pound fully cooked smoked
    sausage, sliced
1/4 cup all-purpose flour
1/4 cup vegetable oil
1/2 cup chopped onion
1/2 cup chopped green pepper
  3 green onions, chopped
3-1/2 cups water
  1 package (16 ounces) frozen
    corn
1-1/2 cups cubed fully cooked ham
  1 can (14-1/2 ounces) diced
    tomatoes, undrained
  1 cup chopped fresh tomatoes

  1 can (6 ounces) tomato paste
1/4 teaspoon salt, optional
1/8 teaspoon cayenne pepper
Hot pepper sauce to taste

In a large skillet, cook and stir sausage over medium-high heat until browned; drain well and set aside. In a Dutch oven or soup kettle, cook and stir the flour in oil over medium heat for 5 minutes or until golden brown. Add the onion, green pepper and green onions; saute until tender.

  Stir in the water, corn, ham, tomatoes, tomato paste, salt if desired, cayenne, hot pepper sauce and sausage. Bring to a boil. Reduce heat; cover and simmer for 1 hour, stirring occasionally. **Yield:** 11 servings (about 2-1/2 quarts).

Potato Clam Chowder

This recipe comes from an old college friend. Pair steaming bowlfuls with sourdough bread and a green salad.
—Kristy Doty, Riverside, California

1/2 pound sliced bacon, diced
  2 large onions, chopped
  3 cans (6-1/2 ounces *each*)
    minced clams
  3 cups diced unpeeled potatoes
1/2 cup chicken broth
  1 can (10-3/4 ounces)
    condensed cream of celery
    soup, undiluted
1-1/4 cups milk
  1 cup heavy whipping cream
  1 teaspoon salt
1/2 teaspoon pepper

In a Dutch oven or soup kettle, cook bacon over medium heat until crisp. Using a slotted spoon, remove to paper towels; drain, reserving 2 tablespoons drippings. In the drippings, saute onions until tender.

  Drain clams, reserving juice. Set clams aside. Add the potatoes, clam juice and broth to the onions. Cook over medium heat for 15 minutes or until potatoes are tender. Stir in the clams, soup, milk, cream, salt, pepper and bacon; heat through. **Yield:** 8 servings (2 quarts).

Creamy Turkey Vegetable Soup

(Pictured at right and on page 133)

*My sisters and I made this soup with our
mom when we were young. Now it's the
traditional "day-after-Thanksgiving"
soup for our own families.*
—*Lois Hofmeyer, Sugar Grove, Illinois*

1 large onion, finely chopped
2 tablespoons butter
3 cups diced unpeeled red
   potatoes
2 cans (14-1/2 ounces *each*)
   chicken broth
2 cups cubed cooked turkey
   breast

2 cups frozen mixed vegetables, thawed
1/2 teaspoon salt
1/2 teaspoon white pepper
1/2 teaspoon poultry seasoning
2 cups heavy whipping cream

In a large saucepan, saute onion in butter until tender. Add
potatoes and broth. Bring to a boil. Reduce heat; cover and
simmer for 20 minutes. Stir in the turkey, vegetables, salt,
pepper and poultry seasoning. Cook 10-12 minutes longer
or until vegetables are tender. Stir in cream; heat through
(do not boil). **Yield:** 8 servings (2 quarts).

Hearty Vegetable Soup

*I've received many recipe requests for this beefy soup loaded with winter veggies.
If you're feeding a larger group, simply double the ingredients.*
—*Arlene Adams, Grafton, Massachusetts*

1 cup chopped onion
1 cup chopped celery
2 tablespoons butter
6 cups beef broth
1 cup cubed peeled potatoes
1 cup chopped peeled turnip
2/3 cup chopped carrots
2 tablespoons minced fresh
   parsley

1/4 teaspoon dried thyme
1 cup shredded cabbage

In a large saucepan, saute onion and celery in butter until
tender. Stir in the broth, potatoes, turnip, carrots, parsley and
thyme. Bring to a boil; cover and simmer for 30 minutes. Add
cabbage; simmer, uncovered, for 5 minutes. **Yield:** 6 servings.

Portobello Onion Soup

(Pictured on page 132)

With a side salad, this makes a wonderful meal.
Portobello mushrooms are a great addition to French onion soup.
—*Melissa Fitzgerald, Jeannette, Pennsylvania*

    5 cups thinly sliced halved
        onions
    4 fresh thyme sprigs
    3 tablespoons butter, *divided*
1-1/2 pounds sliced baby portobello
        mushrooms
    3 tablespoons brandy, optional
    3 garlic cloves, minced
    8 cups vegetable broth
    1 cup white wine *or* additional
        vegetable broth
  1/4 teaspoon pepper
   12 slices French bread
   12 slices provolone cheese

In a Dutch oven or soup kettle, saute onions and thyme in 1 tablespoon butter until onions are tender, about 8 minutes. Reduce heat; cook, uncovered, over low heat for 20 minutes or until onions are golden brown, stirring occasionally. Remove onions to a bowl.

In the same pan, melt remaining butter. Add mushrooms, brandy if desired and garlic; saute for 1 minute. Return onions to pan. Add the broth, wine or additional broth and pepper; bring to a boil. Reduce heat; cover and simmer for 40-45 minutes or until onions are very tender.

Meanwhile, place French bread on a baking sheet; top each slice with provolone cheese. Broil 4-6 in. from the heat for 1-2 minutes or until cheese is melted. Discard thyme sprigs from soup. Top each serving with cheese-topped bread. **Yield:** 12 servings (about 3 quarts).

FACTS FOR FREEZING SOUP

SOUPS are great to make when you have time, then freeze for fast future meals. Here are some hints for freezing.

- To cool soup quickly before freezing, place the kettle in a sink filled with ice water. When cool, transfer to airtight freezer-safe containers, leaving 1/4-in. headspace for expansion.
- Most soups freeze nicely. The exceptions are soups made with cream and potatoes. Those are better when eaten fresh.
- Pasta in soup can get mushy in the freezer. It's best to add the pasta when ready to eat, not before freezing.
- To help retain their fantastic flavor, don't freeze soups for longer than 3 months.
- Thaw soup completely in the refrigerator and reheat in a saucepan.

Potato Soup With Beans

(Pictured at right)

Winter winds can blow strong here on the Jersey shore. But this rich soup featuring potatoes, beans and sour cream is sure to warm your body and soul!
—Christine Ecker, Linwood, New Jersey

2 medium carrots, shredded
1 tablespoon butter
4 cups chicken broth
3 medium potatoes, peeled and cubed
1 garlic clove, minced
1-1/2 teaspoons dill weed
1 can (15-1/2 ounces) great northern beans, rinsed and drained
4-1/2 teaspoons all-purpose flour
3/4 cup sour cream
Pepper to taste

In a large saucepan, cook carrots in butter for 4 minutes or until tender. Stir in the broth, potatoes, garlic and dill. Bring to a boil. Reduce heat; cover and simmer for 25 minutes or until potatoes are tender.

With a slotted spoon, remove half of the potatoes to a bowl; mash with a fork. Return to pan. Stir in the beans. In a small bowl, combine the flour, sour cream and pepper; add to soup. Cook over low heat for 5 minutes or until heated through (do not boil). **Yield:** 6 servings.

Cream of Wild Rice Soup

I used to make this soup on the evening when we would pick out our Christmas tree. But my husband enjoys it so much, I now make it throughout the year.
— Tammy Bailey, Hastings, Minnesota

1 package (6.2 ounces) long grain and wild rice mix
1 cup chopped onion
4-1/2 teaspoons butter
4-1/2 teaspoons all-purpose flour
1/2 teaspoon ground mace
Pinch white pepper
3 cans (14-1/2 ounces *each*) chicken broth

2 cups half-and-half cream
1/2 cup white wine *or* additional chicken broth

Prepare rice mix according to package directions. In a large saucepan, saute onion in butter until tender. Stir in the flour, mace and pepper until blended. Gradually stir in the broth, cream, wine or additional broth and cooked rice. Bring to a boil, stirring constantly. **Yield:** 10 servings (2-1/2 quarts).

Tomato Florentine Soup

When I get a craving for this soup in summer, I head outside and pick garden-fresh tomatoes and basil. Use whatever kind of pasta you have on hand.
—Engracia Salley, Bristol, Rhode Island

4 garlic cloves, minced
3 tablespoons olive oil
8 medium tomatoes, chopped
4 cups spicy hot V8 juice
3/4 cup uncooked small pasta shells
1/2 teaspoon salt
1/8 teaspoon pepper
1 package (6 ounces) fresh baby spinach

3 tablespoons minced fresh basil *or* 1 tablespoon dried basil

In a large saucepan, saute garlic in oil until tender. Add tomatoes; cook and stir for 5-10 minutes or until tender. Add the V8, pasta, salt and pepper; bring to a boil. Reduce heat; cover and simmer for 20-25 minutes or until pasta is tender. Stir in spinach and basil. Cook 5 minutes longer or until spinach is wilted. **Yield:** 9 servings (about 2 quarts).

Curried Pumpkin Apple Soup

Sweet apples and spicy curry combine in this rich soup, which is perfect for fall. A small serving is all you need to satisfy.
—Jane Shapton, Tustin, California

2 medium Golden Delicious apples, peeled and coarsely chopped
1 medium onion, chopped
1 medium leek (white portion only), sliced
3 garlic cloves, minced
2 tablespoons butter
2 to 3 teaspoons curry powder
1 can (15 ounces) solid-pack pumpkin
4 cups chicken broth
1 cup heavy whipping cream
Salt to taste

In a large saucepan, saute the apples, onion, leek and garlic in butter until tender. Add curry; cook and stir for 1 minute. Add pumpkin and broth; bring to a boil. Reduce heat; cover and simmer for 20 minutes.

Remove from the heat; cool slightly. In a blender, process soup in batches; return all to the pan. Stir in cream; heat through. Season with salt. **Yield:** 8 servings (2 quarts).

HOMEMADE PUMPKIN BOWLS

AS A CLEVER WAY to serve individual servings of Curried Pumpkin Apple Soup, make "bowls" with fresh pumpkins.

Purchase pie pumpkins; wash and dry. Cut a wide circle around the stem of each pumpkin, making a lid. Scrape out each pumpkin. Place pumpkins and lids in a large shallow roasting pan. Cover with foil and bake at 350° for 30 to 50 minutes or just until tender (do not overbake). Cool slightly; fill with soup.

Sausage Mushroom Soup

(Pictured at right)

After trying this soup in a restaurant,
I went home to make it myself!
— Twila Maxwell
Hermitage, Pennsylvania

1 pound bulk Italian sausage
2 cans (14-1/2 ounces *each*) beef
  broth
2 jars (4-1/2 ounces *each*) sliced
  mushrooms
1 cup finely chopped celery
1/2 cup quick-cooking barley
1/3 cup shredded carrot

In a large saucepan, cook sausage over medium heat until no longer pink; drain. Add the remaining ingredients. Bring to a boil. Reduce heat; cover and simmer for 10 minutes or until vegetables and barley are tender. **Yield:** 6 servings.

Dilled Cabbage Soup

When cold weather comes, my family always asks when I'm going to make this hearty soup.
Cabbage is a perfect partner for potatoes.
—Gwen Fritsch, Eastlake, Ohio

2 cups shredded cabbage
1 large onion, chopped
1 celery rib, chopped
2 tablespoons butter
1 can (49-1/2 ounces) chicken
  broth
3 medium potatoes, peeled,
  halved and sliced
2 tablespoons all-purpose flour
1/2 cup sour cream
2 to 3 teaspoons snipped fresh
  dill
1/4 teaspoon pepper

In a Dutch oven or large saucepan, saute the cabbage, onion and celery in butter for 1 minute. Cover and cook on low for 10 minutes. Set aside 1/2 cup broth. Add potatoes and remaining broth to cabbage mixture. Whisk flour and reserved broth until smooth; stir into cabbage mixture. Bring to a boil over medium heat. Reduce heat; simmer, uncovered, for 20 minutes, stirring occasionally.

Stir a small amount of hot broth into sour cream; return all to the pan, stirring constantly. Add dill and pepper; heat through (do not boil). **Yield:** 8 servings (2 quarts).

Vegetable Lover's Minestrone

This soup is delicious, nourishing and just the thing for warming up on a cool evening.
— Debbi Wolf, Dover, Pennsylvania

1 cup chopped onion
3 tablespoons olive oil
1 cup thinly sliced carrots
1 cup chopped celery
5 garlic cloves, minced
1-1/2 teaspoons salt
1 teaspoon dried oregano
1 teaspoon dried basil
1/4 teaspoon pepper
3-1/2 cups water
2 cups tomato puree
1 can (15-1/2 ounces) great northern beans, rinsed and drained
1 cup chopped green pepper
3 tablespoons dry red wine, optional
1 cup chopped fresh tomatoes
1/2 cup minced fresh parsley
2 to 3 teaspoons sugar
Grated Parmesan cheese

In a Dutch oven or large saucepan, saute onion in oil until tender. Stir in the carrots, celery, garlic, salt, oregano, basil and pepper. Cover and cook for 8 minutes. Add the water, tomato puree, beans, green pepper and wine if desired. Bring to a boil. Reduce heat; cover and simmer for 15 minutes.

Add the tomatoes, parsley and sugar; cover and simmer 15 minutes longer or until vegetables are tender. Serve with Parmesan cheese. **Yield:** 8 servings (2 quarts).

Italian Sausage Bean Soup

My family loves this soup, so I make it often in the winter. For a little more heat, use spicy Italian sausage.
— Lora Gross, Carson City, Nevada

1-1/2 pounds bulk Italian sausage
4 medium carrots, thinly sliced
2 celery ribs, chopped
1 small onion, chopped
1 garlic clove, minced
1/8 teaspoon crushed red pepper flakes
1 can (28 ounces) diced tomatoes, undrained
1 tablespoon Italian seasoning
3 cans (14-1/2 ounces *each*) beef broth
1 can (16 ounces) kidney beans, rinsed and drained
1 can (15-1/2 ounces) great northern beans, rinsed and drained
1/2 cup water
1/2 cup dry red wine *or* additional beef broth
1/3 cup uncooked elbow macaroni
1 can (8 ounces) tomato sauce
1/2 teaspoon salt
Grated Parmesan cheese, optional

Crumble sausage into a Dutch oven or soup kettle. Cook over medium heat until no longer pink; drain. Add the carrots, celery, onion, garlic and red pepper flakes. Cook and stir for 10 minutes. Add tomatoes and Italian seasoning; cook 10 minutes longer.

Add the broth, beans, water, wine or additional broth, macaroni, tomato sauce and salt. Bring to a boil. Reduce heat; cook, uncovered, until macaroni is tender, about 10 minutes. Serve with Parmesan cheese if desired. **Yield:** 16 servings (4 quarts).

Shrimp Soup With Sherry

(Pictured at right)

This rich soup makes a great first course when small servings are just right. It's an elegant addition to any holiday menu.
—Marilyn Graner, Metairie, Louisiana

1/4 cup sliced green onions
3 tablespoons butter
1/4 cup all-purpose flour
1 teaspoon ground mustard
Pinch cayenne pepper
2 cups half-and-half cream
1 cup chicken broth
2 tablespoons minced fresh parsley
1/8 teaspoon dried thyme
1/8 teaspoon hot pepper sauce
1/8 teaspoon Worcestershire sauce
1-1/4 cups cooked small shrimp, peeled and deveined
1/4 cup dry sherry *or* additional chicken broth
Salt and pepper to taste

In a large saucepan, saute onions in butter until tender. Stir in the flour, mustard and cayenne until blended; gradually add cream and broth. Bring to a boil; cook and stir for 2 minutes or until thickened.

Stir in the parsley, thyme, hot pepper sauce and Worcestershire sauce. Cover and cook over low heat for 10 minutes, stirring occasionally. Add shrimp and sherry or additional broth; heat through. Season with salt and pepper. **Yield:** 4 servings.

Family Traditions

I USE a king-size quilt as my Thanksgiving tablecloth. During dinner, each person shares something for which they're thankful, then lights the votive candle at their place setting. Before long, the table is beautifully lit.

At the end of the meal, we write our names on the quilt with permanent markers. Then I wash the quilt and tuck it away.

The next year, young and old alike head straight to the table to find their names from previous years. That cozy Thanksgiving tablecloth has become a wonderful memento.
—Joanie Huggins
Colorado Springs, Colorado

GIVING Thanks

Crazy for Cranberries!

CRANBERRIES have been a traditional part of Thanksgiving dinners ever since the Pilgrims found them growing wild in Massachusetts.

These days, folks are showcasing cranberries in a variety of dishes all year long.

On turkey day, pop fresh crimson cuties into Baked Cranberry Relish. One taste and you'll never again serve slices of roasted turkey with canned cranberry sauce!

Berry Nice Brisket stays moist while baking thanks to both cranberry juice and sauce.

Topped with sugared cranberries, Mallow Cranberry Cheesecake will become a fluffy favorite of your family. (All recipes shown at right.)

BERRIES MAKE IT BETTER
(Clockwise from top)

Baked Cranberry Relish (p. 147)

Mallow Cranberry Cheesecake (p. 144)

Berry Nice Brisket (p. 145)

Mallow Cranberry Cheesecake

(Pictured on page 143)

Specks of cranberry sauce dot this cool and creamy cheesecake.
The sugared cranberries on top are optional.
—*Gloria Colton, Russell, New York*

3/4 cup graham cracker crumbs
1/2 cup finely chopped
    macadamia nuts
  2 tablespoons sugar
1/4 cup butter, melted
  1 envelope unflavored gelatin
1/4 cup cold water
  2 packages (8 ounces *each*)
    cream cheese, softened
  1 jar (7 ounces) marshmallow
    creme
  1 can (16 ounces) whole-berry
    cranberry sauce
  1 cup heavy whipping cream
SUGARED CRANBERRIES:
  1 package (12 ounces) fresh
    cranberries
  1 envelope unflavored gelatin
1/4 cup cold water
2/3 cup superfine sugar

In a small bowl, combine the cracker crumbs, nuts and sugar. Stir in butter. Press onto the bottom of a greased 9-in. springform pan. Place on a baking sheet. Bake at 350° for 10 minutes or until lightly browned. Cool on a wire rack.

In a small saucepan, sprinkle gelatin over cold water; let stand for 1 minute. Heat over low heat, stirring until gelatin is completely dissolved; cool slightly. In a large mixing bowl, beat cream cheese and marshmallow creme until blended. Beat in cranberry sauce. Add cooled gelatin; mix well. In a small mixing bowl, beat cream until stiff peaks form. Fold into cream cheese mixture. Pour over crust. Refrigerate for 8 hours or overnight.

Scrub cranberries in soapy water; rinse and dry completely. In a microwave-safe bowl, sprinkle gelatin over cold water; let stand for 1 minute. Microwave on high for 1-2 minutes, stirring every 20 seconds, until gelatin is completely dissolved. Whisk until slightly frothy.

Lightly brush mixture over all sides of berries. Place on a wire rack over waxed paper; sprinkle with superfine sugar. Let stand at room temperature for up to 24 hours (do not refrigerate or the sugar will dissolve).

Just before serving, carefully run a knife around edge of pan to loosen. Remove sides of pan. Spoon sugared cranberries over cheesecake. Refrigerate leftovers. **Yield:** 12 servings.

Berry Nice Brisket

(Pictured at right and on page 142)

Cranberry juice and cranberry sauce make this brisket tender and tasty.
—*Carol Hunihan, Alamosa, Colorado*

1/4 cup all-purpose flour
1 can (14-1/2 ounces) beef broth
1 can (16 ounces) whole-berry cranberry sauce
1 cup cranberry juice
3 garlic cloves, minced
1 tablespoon minced fresh rosemary *or* 1 teaspoon dried rosemary, crushed
1 large onion, thinly sliced
1 fresh beef brisket (3 to 4 pounds)
1/2 teaspoon salt
1/4 teaspoon pepper

In a bowl, combine the flour and broth until smooth. Stir in the cranberry sauce, cranberry juice, garlic and rosemary. Pour into a large roasting pan. Top with onion slices. Season the brisket with salt and pepper; place fat side up in the pan. Cover and bake at 350° for 3 to 3-1/2 hours or until meat is tender, basting occasionally.

Remove brisket to a serving platter and let stand for 15 minutes. Thinly slice meat across the grain; serve with onion and pan juices. **Yield:** 10-12 servings.

Editor's Note: This is a fresh beef brisket, not corned beef. The meat comes from the first cut of the brisket.

Apple Cranberry Bake

Even folks who claim not to like cranberries rave about this dish.
I cherish the recipe from my mother, who inspired my love of cooking.
—*Debbie Daly, Florence, Kentucky*

1 cup sugar
1 tablespoon cornstarch
3 cups chopped unpeeled tart apples
2 cups fresh *or* frozen cranberries
1 cup old-fashioned oats
1/2 cup packed brown sugar
1/2 cup chopped pecans
1/3 cup all-purpose flour
1/3 cup cold butter

In a large bowl, combine sugar and cornstarch; stir in the apples and cranberries. Transfer to a greased 2-qt. baking dish. In another bowl, combine the oats, brown sugar, pecans and flour; cut in butter until mixture is crumbly. Sprinkle over apple mixture. Bake, uncovered, at 350° for 45-50 minutes or until golden brown. Serve warm. **Yield:** 12 servings.

Nutty Cranberry Cheddar Bread

The combination of cranberries, orange and cheese makes this bread a real taste treat.
I often give these lovely quick breads as gifts.
—Joan Hallford, North Richland Hills, Texas

        3 cups all-purpose flour
1-1/4 cups sugar
        2 teaspoons baking powder
    1/2 teaspoon baking soda
    1/4 teaspoon salt
        2 tablespoons shortening
        2 teaspoons grated orange peel
        2 teaspoons grated lemon peel
    1/2 cup orange juice
        1 tablespoon lemon juice
        3 eggs, lightly beaten
1-1/2 cups (6 ounces) shredded
        sharp cheddar cheese
1-1/2 cups fresh *or* frozen
        cranberries
        1 cup chopped walnuts

In a large bowl, combine the flour, sugar, baking powder, baking soda and salt. Cut in shortening until well blended. Stir in the orange peel and lemon peel. In a measuring cup, combine orange juice and lemon juice; add enough water to measure 1 cup. Add eggs and juice mixture to dry ingredients; stir just until moistened. Fold in the cheese, cranberries and walnuts.

Pour into three greased and floured 5-3/4-in. x 3-in. x 2-in. loaf pans. Bake at 350° for 40-45 minutes or until a toothpick inserted near the center comes out clean. Cool for 10 minutes before removing from pans to wire racks to cool completely. **Yield:** 3 mini loaves.

CRANBERRY CUES

FRESH cranberries are in season from early fall through December. When buying, look for packages with shiny, bright red (light or dark) berries. Avoid berries that are bruised, shriveled or have brown spots.

Ripe cranberries should bounce when dropped, which is why cranberries are sometimes called bounceberries.

Refrigerate fresh unwashed cranberries for about 1 month. If you don't plan on using the berries within a few days, sort out any soft or bruised ones.

For longer storage, place cranberries in a single layer in a shallow pan and freeze. When frozen, transfer to a resealable plastic freezer bag for up to 1 year.

Quickly rinse cranberries before using. Cranberries are almost 90% water, so don't thaw frozen cranberries before using or they will become soft.

When cooking cranberries to make a sauce, cook them until they crack and pop. This allows the sugar to penetrate the tart fruit.

Cranberry Spinach Salad

(Pictured at right)

I came across this recipe one year when I was looking for a special salad for the holidays.
—Deb Murata, Carmichael, California

4 cups packed torn fresh
  spinach
1/2 cup dried cranberries
1/2 medium red onion, sliced and
  separated into rings
1/2 cup pecan pieces, toasted
1/4 cup crumbled blue cheese
1/4 cup olive oil
  2 to 3 tablespoons red wine
  vinegar
  1 garlic clove, minced
Salt and pepper to taste

In a large bowl, combine spinach, cranberries, onion, pecans and blue cheese. In a small bowl, whisk oil, vinegar, garlic, salt and pepper until blended. Drizzle over salad; toss to coat. Serve immediately. **Yield:** 6-8 servings.

Baked Cranberry Relish

(Pictured on page 142)

This baked cranberry compote couldn't be easier to prepare and tastes terrific on top of sliced Thanksgiving turkey. The recipe comes courtesy of my sister-in-law.
—Betty Johnson, Eleva, Wisconsin

4 cups fresh *or* frozen
  cranberries
2 cups sugar
1 cup orange marmalade
1 cup chopped walnuts, toasted
3 tablespoons lemon juice

Combine the cranberries and sugar in an ungreased 13-in. x 9-in. x 2-in. baking dish. Cover and bake at 350° for 1 hour. In a large bowl, combine the orange marmalade, walnuts and lemon juice. Stir in cranberry mixture. Cover and refrigerate until chilled. **Yield:** 4 cups.

Walnut Cranberry Pound Cake

When a friend gifted me with this pound cake one Christmas, I just had to have the recipe.
A slice and a cup of coffee make for an enjoyable mid-day snack.
—Dorothy Matthews, Scotia, New York

1 cup butter, softened
2 cups sugar
5 eggs
1/4 cup sour cream
1/4 cup maple syrup
1 teaspoon grated orange peel
1 teaspoon vanilla extract
2-1/4 cups all-purpose flour
1/2 teaspoon salt
1-1/2 cups fresh *or* frozen
    cranberries
1 cup chopped walnuts
GLAZE:
1 cup confectioners' sugar
2 tablespoons maple syrup

1 tablespoon butter, melted
2 to 3 tablespoons milk

In a large mixing bowl, cream butter and sugar until light and fluffy. Add eggs, one at a time, beating well after each addition. Combine the sour cream, syrup, orange peel and vanilla; add to creamed mixture and mix well. Combine flour and salt; gradually add to creamed mixture until blended. Fold in cranberries and walnuts.

Transfer to a greased and floured 10-in. tube pan. Bake at 350° for 65-70 minutes or until a toothpick inserted near the center comes out clean. Cool for 10 minutes before removing from pan to a wire rack to cool completely. Combine the glaze ingredients; drizzle over cake. **Yield:** 12 servings.

Cranberry Mince Pie

Tart cranberries and apple balance the sweetness of mincemeat in this recipe.
The pie makes a regular appearance on my holiday table.
—Sharon Forney, Hinckley, Ohio

2/3 cup sugar
2 tablespoons cornstarch
2/3 cup water
1-1/2 cups fresh *or* frozen
    cranberries
2 cups diced peeled tart apples
1-1/2 cups prepared mincemeat
1 unbaked pastry shell (9 inches)
TOPPING:
1/3 cup all-purpose flour
1/3 cup packed brown sugar
1 teaspoon ground cinnamon

1/4 teaspoon ground cloves
2 tablespoons cold butter

In a saucepan, combine sugar and cornstarch; stir in water. Bring to a boil over medium heat, stirring constantly. Add cranberries; cook over medium heat until berries pop, about 15 minutes. Combine apples and mincemeat; spread over the bottom of pastry shell. Top with cranberry mixture.

For topping, combine the flour, brown sugar, cinnamon and cloves in a small bowl; cut in butter until crumbly. Sprinkle over filling. Bake at 400° for 25-30 minutes or until crust is golden brown and filling is bubbly. Cool on a wire rack. Store in the refrigerator. **Yield:** 6-8 servings.

Cranberry Swirl Loaf

(Pictured at right)

My mother made this bread with dates, but I use cranberries instead.
—Darlene Brenden, Salem, Oregon

3 to 3-1/2 cups all-purpose flour
1/3 cup sugar
1 package (1/4 ounce) quick-rise yeast
1/2 teaspoon salt
1/2 cup water
1/2 cup milk
1/3 cup butter

FILLING:
1 cup chopped fresh *or* frozen cranberries
1/4 cup packed brown sugar
1/4 cup water
1 tablespoon butter
1/2 cup chopped walnuts
1 tablespoon lemon juice

TOPPING:
2 tablespoons all-purpose flour
2 tablespoons sugar
2 tablespoons cold butter, *divided*

In a large mixing bowl, combine 1 cup flour, sugar, yeast and salt. In a saucepan, heat the water, milk and butter to 120°-130°. Add to dry ingredients; beat until combined. Stir in enough remaining flour to form a soft dough.

Turn onto a floured surface; knead until smooth and elastic, about 5-7 minutes. Place in a greased bowl, turning once to grease top. Cover and let rise in a warm place until doubled, about 1 hour.

For filling, combine the cranberries, brown sugar and water in a small saucepan. Cook over medium heat until berries pop, about 15 minutes. Remove from the heat; stir in the butter, walnuts and lemon juice. Cool.

Punch dough down. Turn onto a lightly floured surface; roll into a 20-in. x 10-in. rectangle. Spread cooled filling to within 1/2 in. of edges. Roll up jelly-roll style, starting with a long side; pinch seam to seal. Place in a zigzag pattern in a greased 9-in. x 5-in. x 3-in. loaf pan.

For topping, combine flour and sugar in a small bowl; cut in 1 tablespoon butter until crumbly. Melt remaining butter; brush over dough. Sprinkle with topping. Cover and let rise until doubled, about 40 minutes. Bake at 350° for 40-45 minutes or until bread sounds hollow when tapped. Carefully remove from pan to a wire rack to cool. **Yield:** 1 loaf.

SHAPING CRANBERRY SWIRL LOAF

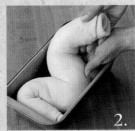

1. Spread cranberry filling over dough to within 1/2 in. of edge. Starting with a long side, roll up jelly-roll style; pinch seam to seal.

2. Place dough in a zigzag pattern in a greased 9-in. x 5-in. x 3-in. loaf pan.

Pork Tenderloin with Cranberry Sauce

Our Test Kitchen came up with this easy, elegant entree. The pork medallions are so pretty on the table.

2 pork tenderloins (1 pound *each*)
Salt and pepper to taste
2 teaspoons butter
1 can (16 ounces) whole-berry cranberry sauce
1/2 cup cranberry juice
1/3 cup heavy whipping cream
1/4 cup burgundy wine *or* additional cranberry juice
1-1/2 teaspoons cornstarch
1/4 cup unsweetened apple juice

Cut tenderloins into 1/2-in. slices; flatten to 1/4-in. thickness. Sprinkle with salt and pepper. In a skillet over medium-high heat, brown pork on both sides in butter in batches. Remove and keep warm.

In a bowl, combine the cranberry sauce, cranberry juice, cream and wine or additional juice. Pour into the skillet; simmer, uncovered, for 7-10 minutes or until reduced by half. Combine cornstarch and apple juice until smooth; gradually stir into cranberry mixture. Bring to a boil. Reduce heat; cook and stir for 2 minutes or until thickened. Pour over pork. **Yield:** 6 servings.

Banana Cranberry Dessert

This cool, creamy dessert prompts recipe requests whenever I take it to covered-dish dinners. The mellow flavor of bananas complements the tart cranberries.
—Zelda Patterson, Grand Prairie, Texas

2 cups crushed vanilla wafers (about 44 wafers), *divided*
1 can (14 ounces) sweetened condensed milk
6 tablespoons lemon juice
3 teaspoons vanilla extract
1 cup chopped pecans
1 to 2 medium firm bananas, sliced and quartered
2 cups chopped fresh *or* frozen cranberries
2/3 cup sugar
1 cup heavy whipping cream
2 tablespoons confectioners' sugar

Sprinkle 1 cup wafer crumbs in an 8-in. square dish coated with nonstick cooking spray. In a bowl, combine the milk, lemon juice and vanilla. Pour over crumbs and spread to cover. Sprinkle with pecans.

In another bowl, combine the bananas, cranberries and sugar. Spread over pecans. In a large mixing bowl, beat the cream until it begins to thicken. Add confectioners' sugar; beat until stiff peaks form. Spread over fruit layer. Sprinkle with remaining wafer crumbs. Refrigerate until chilled. **Yield:** 9 servings.

Cranberry Cream Pie

(Pictured at right)

This recipe cleverly combines cheesecake and cranberry pie in one fantastic dessert. Make it a day ahead for added convenience.
—Pamela Brown, Ingersoll, Ontario

2-1/2 cups whole-berry cranberry
     sauce
    1 pastry shell (9 inches), baked
    1 package (8 ounces) cream
     cheese, softened
  2/3 cup sugar
    2 eggs, lightly beaten
    3 tablespoons all-purpose flour
    1 teaspoon vanilla extract

Spread cranberry sauce over the bottom of pastry shell. In a small mixing bowl, beat cream cheese and sugar until smooth. Beat in eggs, flour and vanilla on low speed just until combined. Pour over cranberry layer.

Bake at 350° for 35-40 minutes or until center is set. Cool on a wire rack. Cover and refrigerate for at least 4 hours before cutting. **Yield:** 8 servings.

Cherry Cranberry Punch

My husband is a pastor, and our church has many functions, which allows me to try out a selection of recipes. This lovely red punch is one of my favorites to serve.
—Christine Fletcher, Bronx, New York

    1 package (3 ounces) cherry
     gelatin
    1 cup boiling water
    4 cups cranberry juice
    3 cups cold water
  3/4 cup lemonade concentrate
3-1/2 cups club soda, chilled
Lemon sherbet, optional

In a large bowl, dissolve gelatin in boiling water. Stir in the cranberry juice, cold water and lemonade concentrate. Refrigerate until chilled. Just before serving, stir in the soda. Top with scoops of sherbet if desired. **Yield:** 16 servings (3 quarts).

Thanksgiving Cranberry Gelatin

This salad has graced my mother's Thanksgiving table for as long as I can remember.
— Tiffany Anderson-Taylor, Gulfport, Florida

1 package (6 ounces) cherry
  gelatin
1/3 to 1/2 cup sugar
2 cups boiling cranberry juice
1-1/2 cups ice cubes
2 celery ribs, finely chopped
1 medium pear, peeled, cored
  and finely chopped
1 cup chopped fresh *or* frozen
  cranberries
3/4 cup ground walnuts, *divided*
1 package (3 ounces) lemon
  gelatin
1 cup boiling water
1 cup mayonnaise
1 carton (8 ounces) frozen
  whipped topping, thawed,
  divided

In a large bowl, dissolve cherry gelatin and sugar in boiling cranberry juice. Add the ice cubes; stir until dissolved. Refrigerate until thickened, about 45 minutes. Fold in the celery, pear, cranberries and 1/2 cup walnuts. Transfer to a 13-in. x 9-in. x 2-in. dish coated with nonstick cooking spray. Refrigerate until firm, about 50 minutes.

Meanwhile, in another bowl, dissolve lemon gelatin in water. Refrigerate until slightly thickened, about 35 minutes. Whisk in 1/4 cup mayonnaise; fold in the remaining mayonnaise. Fold in half of the whipped topping. Carefully spoon over cherry layer. Refrigerate until firm, about 45 minutes.

Spread with remaining whipped topping. Sprinkle with remaining walnuts. Refrigerate for at least 3 hours. Cut into squares. **Yield:** 16-20 servings.

White Chocolate Cranberry Fudge

This no-bake recipe is at the top of my list when I head to the kitchen to make holiday treats.
Chewy, tart cranberries pair well with salty, crunchy almonds.
—Lois Aitken, Dauphin, Manitoba

1 teaspoon butter
12 squares (1 ounce *each*) white
  baking chocolate, chopped
2/3 cup sweetened condensed
  milk
1 cup roasted salted almonds,
  coarsely chopped
1/2 cup dried cranberries
2 teaspoons grated orange peel

Line an 8-in. square pan with foil and grease the foil with 1 teaspoon butter; set aside. In a large microwave-safe bowl, combine the chocolate and milk. Microwave, uncovered, at 30% power for 2-3 minutes or until chocolate is almost melted; stir until smooth. Stir in the almonds, cranberries and orange peel. Spread into prepared pan.

Cover and refrigerate for 2 hours or until firm. Using foil, lift fudge out of pan. Discard foil; cut fudge into 1-in. squares. **Yield:** 1-1/2 pounds.

Editor's Note: This recipe was tested in a 1,100-watt microwave.

Tangerine Cranberry Sorbet

(Pictured at right)

This is a very easy recipe to prepare and keep in the freezer before a party. It's a light and refreshing finish to a heavy holiday meal.
—*Pamela Brown, Ingersoll, Ontario*

1-1/2 cups fresh *or* frozen cranberries
2 cups water
3 to 4 medium tangerines
2 tablespoons plus 1/2 cup sugar, *divided*
1 cup light corn syrup

In a saucepan, bring cranberries and water to a boil. Reduce heat; simmer for 5 minutes. Meanwhile, using a sharp knife or zester, peel outer layer of one tangerine into strips for garnish. Toss the strips of peel with 2 table- spoons sugar; set aside. Squeeze tangerines to yield 1 cup of juice.

Place cranberries with liquid in a sieve over a large bowl. Press berries to remove juices. Discard pulp. Add the tangerine juice, corn syrup and remaining sugar to cran- berry juice; stir until sugar is dissolved. Pour into a 9-in. square dish. Cover and freeze until firm, about 3 hours.

Remove from the freezer 30 minutes before serving. Spoon into dessert bowls. Garnish with reserved tangerine peel. **Yield:** 8 servings.

TANGERINE TIP

UNLIKE sweet oranges, tangerines are considered a loose-skinned orange because the skin easily comes off the fruit and the segments are easy to divide.

Tangerines should feel heavy for their size and be free of moldy or soft spots. They'll stay fresh for a few days at room temperature and for up to 2 weeks in the refrigerator.

EASTER
Gatherings

If you find yourself hosting a smaller group this Easter,
we have an elegant dinner perfect for a party of six.
This springtime celebration features the down-home
goodness of pork chops and potatoes, while Easter Nest
Torte—a tempting chocolate dessert—serves as the
crowning touch. Continue the confectionary feast
by indulging in an assortment of sweets that can
be tucked into colorful Easter baskets.

Elegant Easter Feast

IF YOU find yourself hosting a gathering for six on Easter Sunday, turn to this eye-catching menu that will surely please your guests' palates.

Cilantro-Lime Pork Chops sizzling in a skillet are the centerpiece in this special celebration supper.

For two colorful sides that highlight the beauty of spring, lovely Chive Red Potatoes and Broccoli with Tangy Horseradish Sauce can't be beat.

Then watch friends and family flock to the table to sample Easter Nest Torte, an indulgent chocolate-laden dessert topped with cute candy eggs. (All recipes shown at right.)

PRETTY IN PINK
(Clockwise from top)

Easter Nest Torte (p. 158)

Chive Red Potatoes (p. 162)

Cilantro-Lime Pork Chops (p. 160)

Broccoli with Tangy
Horseradish Sauce (p. 159)

Easter Nest Torte

(Pictured at right and on page 156)

In this delectable dessert from our home economists, a luscious cake layer nestles rich mousse and chocolate "twigs."

1/2 cup butter, softened
1/2 cup sugar
2 eggs
1/2 cup all-purpose flour
1/3 cup baking cocoa
1 teaspoon baking powder
1/4 teaspoon salt
8 squares (1 ounce *each*)
  semisweet chocolate, melted
FILLING:
1/4 cup sugar
1 teaspoon cornstarch
1-1/4 cups milk
3 egg yolks, beaten
1 envelope unflavored gelatin
3 tablespoons cold water
7 squares (1 ounce *each*)
  semisweet chocolate, chopped
1-1/4 cups heavy whipping cream
20 to 30 small candy Easter eggs

In a large mixing bowl, cream butter and sugar. Add eggs, one at a time, beating well after each addition. Combine the flour, cocoa, baking powder and salt; beat into creamed mixture.

Spread into a greased 9-in. springform pan. Bake at 350° for 15-20 minutes or until a toothpick inserted near the center comes out clean. Cool for 10 minutes. Carefully run a knife around edge of pan to loosen. Remove sides and bottom of pan. Cool completely on a wire rack.

From a large sheet of waxed paper, cut a 29-in. x 5-in. strip. Fold strip lengthwise in half. Place strip on a large sheet of waxed paper on a work surface. Spread melted chocolate evenly along one long edge of waxed paper strip; spread upward, making a wavy line to within 1/2 in. of other long edge. Let stand for 10-30 minutes until chocolate begins to set but is still pliable.

Carefully lift waxed paper strip and wrap chocolate strip around cake with straight edge on the bottom. Do not remove waxed paper. Refrigerate until chilled. Meanwhile, cover three baking sheets with waxed paper. Drizzle remaining melted chocolate from a spatula over waxed paper in both directions. Chill for 10 minutes. Peel off waxed paper; break chocolate into 2-in. to 3-in. "twigs"; set aside.

For filling, in a small saucepan, combine the sugar and cornstarch. Stir in milk until smooth. Cook and stir over medium-high heat until slightly thickened and bubbly. Reduce heat; cook and stir 2 minutes longer. Remove from the heat. Stir a small amount of hot filling into egg yolks; return all to the pan, stirring constantly. Bring to a gentle boil; cook and stir 2 minutes longer. Remove from the heat.

In a small bowl, sprinkle gelatin over water; let stand for 1 minute. Stir into custard until gelatin is dissolved. Add chopped chocolate; stir until smooth. Cover surface with plastic wrap; cool to room temperature.

In a large mixing bowl, beat cream until soft peaks form; fold into chocolate mixture. Carefully spoon over top of cake. Cover and refrigerate for 1-2 hours or until set. Remove waxed paper strip from side of cake. Position chocolate "twigs" around top of cake to create a nest. Arrange candy eggs in center. **Yield:** 12-14 servings.

1. Cut a 29-in. x 5-in. strip of waxed paper. Fold strip lengthwise in half. Place on a large sheet of waxed paper on a work surface. Melt chocolate; spread evenly along one long edge of waxed paper strip. Make a wavy line to within 1/2 in. of other long edge. Let stand for 10-30 minutes.

Meanwhile, drizzle remaining melted chocolate over waxed paper-lined baking sheets. Chill for 10 minutes. Peel off paper and break chocolate into twigs.

2. When chocolate on the strip begins to set but is still pliable, wrap the strip around the cake with the straight edge on the bottom and the wavy edge on top.

Broccoli with Tangy Horseradish Sauce

(Pictured on page 156)

A mild horseradish sauce is all you need to dress up tender broccoli spears.
Try the topping on a variety of cooked veggies.
—Janet Allen, Sarasota, Florida

2 pounds fresh broccoli, cut
    into spears
1/4 cup butter
1 tablespoon all-purpose flour
1 cup (8 ounces) sour cream
1 tablespoon minced fresh
    parsley
1 teaspoon prepared horseradish
2 tablespoons lemon juice

Place broccoli in a steamer basket; place in a large saucepan over 1 in. of water. Bring to a boil; cover and steam for 5-8 minutes or until crisp-tender.

In a small saucepan, melt butter. Whisk in flour until smooth; cook and stir for 1-2 minutes or until bubbly. Remove from the heat; whisk in the sour cream, parsley and horseradish. Gradually whisk in lemon juice. Serve with broccoli. **Yield:** 6 servings (1-1/4 cups sauce).

Cilantro-Lime Pork Chops

(Pictured on page 156)

These moist and tender chops will appeal to the entire family.
Cilantro, lime and cumin blend wonderfully for a little southwestern flavor.
—Mildred Sherrer, Fort Worth, Texas

6 tablespoons lime juice
1 tablespoon grated lime peel
1-1/2 teaspoons ground cumin
1-1/2 teaspoons chili powder
1 teaspoon salt
1/2 teaspoon garlic powder
6 bone-in pork chops (1 inch thick)
2 tablespoons olive oil
1-1/2 teaspoons cornstarch
1 cup chicken broth
1/2 cup orange juice
2 tablespoons honey
1/4 cup minced fresh cilantro

In a small bowl, combine the first six ingredients. Pour 1/3 cup marinade into a large resealable plastic bag; add pork chops. Seal bag and turn to coat; refrigerate for 20 minutes. Cover and refrigerate remaining marinade.

Drain and discard marinade from pork. In a skillet, brown chops in oil for 4-5 minutes on each side. Remove and keep warm.

In a small bowl, combine cornstarch and reserved marinade until smooth. Stir in the broth, orange juice and honey; add to skillet. Bring to a boil; cook and stir for 1-2 minutes or just until thickened. Stir in cilantro. Add pork chops; heat through. **Yield:** 6 servings.

Herbed Cheese Spread

This tasty herb spread is terrific on top of crackers or served with fresh veggies.
Preparing it in the blender yields a creamy concoction.
—Shirley Glaab, Hattiesburg, Mississippi

1 carton (12 ounces) small-curd cottage cheese
1 package (3 ounces) cream cheese, softened
1 tablespoon minced chives
1 tablespoon minced fresh parsley
1-1/2 teaspoons minced fresh thyme or 1/2 teaspoon dried thyme
3/4 teaspoon minced fresh basil or 1/4 teaspoon dried basil

3/4 teaspoon minced fresh savory *or* 1/4 teaspoon dried savory
1/8 to 1/4 teaspoon salt
Assorted crackers

Place the cottage cheese and cream cheese in a blender; cover and process until smooth. Transfer to a bowl; stir in the chives, parsley, thyme, basil, savory and salt. Cover and refrigerate for 2 hours. Serve with crackers. **Yield:** about 1-1/2 cups.

Springtime Salad

(Pictured at right)

Tender green asparagus and juicy red strawberries star in this colorful salad, which I often make for spring luncheons and showers. It tastes as terrific as it looks!
—Molly Payne, Buffalo, Minnesota

  1 **cup water**
  1 **pound fresh asparagus, trimmed**
1/4 **cup sugar**
1/4 **cup vegetable oil**
  2 **tablespoons cider vinegar**
1-1/2 **teaspoons sesame seeds**
  1 **teaspoon poppy seeds**
  1 **teaspoon grated onion**
1/4 **teaspoon salt**
1/8 **teaspoon paprika**
1/8 **teaspoon Worcestershire sauce**
  2 **cups sliced fresh strawberries**
1/4 **cup crumbled blue cheese, optional**

In a large skillet, bring water to a boil. Add asparagus; cover and boil for 3 minutes. Drain and immediately place asparagus in ice water. Drain and pat dry; set aside.

In a jar with a tight-fitting lid, combine the sugar, oil, vinegar, sesame seeds, poppy seeds, onion, salt, paprika and Worcestershire sauce; shake well. Cover and refrigerate for 1 hour.

In a bowl, combine the asparagus and strawberries. Drizzle with dressing and toss to coat. Sprinkle with blue cheese if desired. **Yield:** 6 servings.

Easter Day Agenda

A Few Weeks Before:

- Prepare two grocery lists—one for non-perishable items to purchase now and one for perishable items to purchase a few days before Easter.
- Assemble the Rose Napkin Blossoms (opposite page).

Two Days Before:

- Set the table.
- Buy remaining grocery items.

The Day Before:

- Prepare Herbed Cheese Spread; cover and chill.
- Assemble marinade for Cilantro-Lime Pork Chops; cover and refrigerate.
- Make Tangy Horseradish Sauce; cover and chill.
- For Springtime Salad, cook the asparagus and slice the strawberries; refriger-

ate in separate covered containers. Make the salad dressing; cover and chill.

- Make Easter Nest Torte (but don't add the candy eggs); refrigerate.

Easter Day:

- In the morning, remove one narrow strip of skin around each red potato. Cover potatoes with cold water and let stand at room temperature.
- As guests arrive, set out Herbed Cheese Spread and crackers.
- Marinate the pork chops, then cook as directed.
- Prepare Chive Red Potatoes.
- Reheat Tangy Horseradish Sauce in a saucepan over low heat; cook broccoli. Serve sauce with broccoli.
- Assemble Springtime Salad and set out.
- Before serving, place candy eggs on top of Easter Nest Torte.

Chive Red Potatoes

(Pictured on page 157)

These simply dressed potatoes from our Test Kitchen pair well with any meaty entree.
The color is so pretty on an Easter dinner table.

2 pounds small red potatoes
1/3 cup butter, melted
2 tablespoons minced chives
1/2 teaspoon salt
1/4 teaspoon garlic powder

With a vegetable peeler, remove a narrow strip of peel around the middle of each potato. Place potatoes in a large saucepan and cover with water. Bring to a boil. Reduce heat; cover and cook for 15-20 minutes or until tender.

In a small bowl, combine the butter, chives, salt and garlic powder. Drain potatoes; drizzle with butter mixture and toss gently to coat. **Yield:** 6-8 servings.

Rose Napkin Blossoms

(Pictured at right)

EVEN FOLKS who don't have a green thumb can bring spring blossoms to their Easter dinner table by creating beautiful Rose Napkin Blossoms!

We made vibrant pink napkin "roses" peeking out from lovely green napkin "leaves." But feel free to use whatever color "flower" works well with your dishes and linens. You could even use a variety of colored napkins to create a glorious "garden."

MAKING ROSE NAPKIN BLOSSOMS

1. For "leaves," fold a green square napkin in half diagonally to make a triangle. Fold again to make a smaller triangle; set aside.

2. For "roses," fold a square napkin in half diagonally to make a triangle. With the folded edge nearest you, fold down the point of the triangle, extending about 1 inch beyond the fold.

3. Fold down the top straight edge to about 1/4 inch from the edge of the bottom fold.

4. Starting at one narrow edge, tightly roll up the napkin to form a rose bud.

5. Place the rose bud near the center of the folded green napkin, with the top of the rose bud near the top point of the green napkin. Fold the green napkin over the rose bud, aligning the points on the bottom. Place inside a glass.

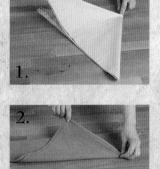

Easter Basket Treats

IN THE PAST, part of an Easter celebration included indulging in foods that were forbidden during the Lenten fast.

Even today, kids eagerly hunt for plastic eggs in anticipation of sampling the candies they've gone without for weeks.

Add to the confectionery feast by filling pretty baskets with an assortment of homemade goodies.

Chocolate-covered Easter Egg Candies rival any variety bought from a specialty store. Orange extract makes Marbled Orange Fudge a refreshing addition to the table.

We even show you how to make a White Chocolate Easter Basket to use as a centerpiece for all your sweet treats!

SPRINGTIME SWEETS
(Clockwise from top)

White Chocolate Easter Basket (p. 166)

Marbled Orange Fudge (p. 168)

Easter Egg Candies (p. 167)

White Chocolate Easter Basket

(Pictured on page 164)

This chocolate clay basket from our Test Kitchen makes a great centerpiece when filled with Easter candy.

CHOCOLATE CLAY:
   20 ounces white candy coating,
      chopped
   2/3 cup light corn syrup
BASKET:
   10 ounces white candy coating,
      chopped
   13 pretzel sticks (3 inches)
Round plastic cover (about 4-1/2
   inches in diameter)
Thin wire headband or 1 piece
   1/8-inch-thick wire (about 15
   inches long)
Thin ribbon, optional

In a microwave-safe bowl, melt 20 ounces candy coating; stir until smooth. Stir in corn syrup just until blended. Spread onto a sheet of waxed paper to 3/8-in. thickness (about a 16-in. x 8-in. rectangle). Let stand, uncovered, at room temperature for 2 hours or until dry to the touch. Wrap tightly with plastic wrap; let stand overnight. Use immediately or store for up to 2 weeks.

Melt 10 ounces candy coating; stir until smooth. Completely coat pretzel sticks; place on a wire rack. Chill for 10 minutes. Set remaining melted coating aside.

Be certain plastic cover is clean and dry. Place two dampened paper towels in the bottom of a 1-1/2-qt. bowl. Position cover on the towels (to hold it in place). Place ends of the candy-coated pretzels around outer edge of cover, resting the other ends against the side of the bowl to form the

Making a Chocolate Basket

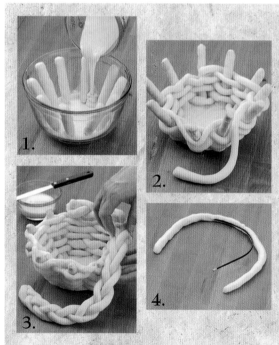

1. Set one end of the candy-coated pretzels around outer edge of bowl cover, resting the other ends against the side of the bowl. Pour or spoon melted candy coating into the plastic cover until it surrounds all of the pretzels. Chill until firm.

2. Loosely weave chocolate clay ropes around pretzels until the top of the pretzels is reached. (End one rope and begin the next on the inside of a pretzel, overlapping ropes slightly and pressing ends together.)

3. Place a drop of melted candy coating on top of each pretzel. Lay the three braided ropes on top, blending the ends to create a finished edge.

4. For basket handle, make one 15-in.-long chocolate rope. Push headband into rope, allowing 1 in. on each end to remain uncovered. Insert uncovered ends into the top braid of the basket.

upports for basket sides.

Spoon some of the reserved candy coating into plastic cover until it is 1/8 in. from the top and surrounds all of the pretzels. Chill until firm, about 30 minutes. Remove from the bowl and discard paper towels. Carefully loosen edges of plastic cover and remove. Set base on waxed paper.

Knead a 1-in. ball of chocolate clay until pliable but not sticky. Roll into a 1/4-in. rope. Beginning on the inside of a pretzel, loosely weave rope around pretzels. Repeat, adding the next rope by overlapping slightly and pressing ends together. (Always end one rope and begin the next on the inside of a pretzel.) Continue to weave between pretzels until the top of the pretzels is reached, ending the last rope on the inside of a pretzel.

Make three ropes about 20 in. long; braid and set aside. Remelt reserved coating; place a drop on the top of each pretzel. Lay braided ropes on top, blending the ends to create a finished edge. If pretzels break, "reglue" with melted coating.

For basket handle, make one rope about 15 in. long. Push headband into rope to within 1 in. of each end; mold rope around headband to cover. Insert uncovered ends of headband into top braid of basket. Decorate with ribbon if desired. **Yield:** 1 basket.

Easter Egg Candies

(Pictured at right and on page 164)

Kids will jump at the chance to help in the kitchen when you're making these Easter egg candies.
—Gloria Jarrett, Loveland, Ohio

1/2 cup butter, cubed
2 packages (3 ounces *each*) cook-and-serve vanilla pudding mix
1/2 cup milk
3-3/4 cups confectioners' sugar
1 teaspoon vanilla extract
1/2 cup chopped walnuts
1 teaspoon maple flavoring
1/2 cup flaked coconut
1/2 teaspoon coconut extract
2 cups milk chocolate chips
2 teaspoons shortening

In a large saucepan, melt butter. Stir in pudding mixes until blended. Whisk in milk. Bring to a boil; cook and stir for 2 minutes or until thickened. Remove from the heat. Stir in confectioners' sugar and vanilla until smooth.

Divide pudding mixture between two bowls. To the first bowl, add walnuts and maple flavoring; mix well. To the second bowl, add coconut and coconut extract; mix well. Cover and refrigerate for 30 minutes or until firm. Form tablespoonfuls of pudding mixture into egg shapes. Place on a waxed paper-lined pan. Chill for 30 minutes or until firm.

In a microwave-safe bowl, melt milk chocolate chips and shortening; stir until smooth. Dip eggs in chocolate. Place on waxed paper until set. Decorate as desired. Store in the refrigerator. **Yield:** 4 dozen.

Marbled Orange Fudge

(Pictured on page 165)

This soft fudge is guaranteed to get smiles because it has the familiar taste of frozen Creamsicles.
—Diane Wampler, Morristown, Tennessee

1-1/2 teaspoons plus 3/4 cup butter, *divided*
  3 cups sugar
3/4 cup heavy whipping cream
  1 package (10 to 12 ounces) vanilla *or* white chips
  1 jar (7 ounces) marshmallow creme
  3 teaspoons orange extract
12 drops yellow food coloring
  5 drops red food coloring

Grease a 13-in. x 9-in. x 2-in. pan with 1-1/2 teaspoon butter; set aside. In a heavy saucepan, combine the sugar cream and remaining butter. Cook and stir over low heat until sugar is dissolved. Bring to a boil; cook and stir for 4 minutes. Remove from the heat; stir in chips and marshmallow creme until smooth.

Remove 1 cup and set aside. Add orange extract and food coloring to the remaining mixture; stir until blended. Pour into prepared pan. Drop reserved marshmallow mixture by tablespoonfuls over the top; cut through with a knife to swirl. Cover and refrigerate until set. Cut into squares. **Yield:** about 2-1/2 pounds.

Easter Sugar Sandwich Cookies

Make these fruit-filled sugar cookies from our Test Kitchen throughout the year by using different cookie cutter shapes.

1/2 cup shortening
  1 cup sugar
  2 eggs
  1 teaspoon lemon extract
2-1/2 cups all-purpose flour
1/2 teaspoon salt
1/4 teaspoon baking soda
1/3 cup raspberry filling
1/3 cup apricot filling

In a large mixing bowl, cream shortening and sugar until light and fluffy. Beat in eggs and extract. Combine the flour salt and baking soda; gradually add to creamed mixture. Cover and refrigerate for 1 hour or until easy to handle.

Divide dough in half. On a lightly floured surface, roll out one portion to 1/8-in. thickness. Cut with a floured 2-1/2-in. round cookie cutter. Repeat with remaining dough. Using a small floured bunny- or chick-shaped cookie cutter, cut out the center of half of the cookies.

Place cookies and cutouts 1 in. apart on ungreased baking sheets. Bake at 350° for 8-10 minutes or until edges are very lightly browned. Remove to wire racks to cool. To assemble, spread bottom of solid cookies with filling; top with cookies that have cutout centers. Serve with cutouts. **Yield:** 1-1/2 dozen sandwich cookies and 1-1/2 dozen small cutouts.

Orange Jelly Candies

(Pictured at right)

Making candy is my favorite thing to do. I've been collecting candy recipes for more than 40 years and have taken several candy-making classes. These soft confections are fantastic.
—Leah Jackson, Washington, Utah

1 package (1-3/4 ounces)
    powdered fruit pectin
1/2 teaspoon baking soda
3/4 cup water
1 cup sugar
1 cup light corn syrup
1/8 teaspoon orange oil
5 drops *each* red and yellow
    food coloring

Butter a 9-in. square pan; set aside. In a large saucepan, combine the pectin, baking soda and water (mixture will be foamy). In another saucepan, combine sugar and corn syrup. Bring both mixtures to a boil. Cook until foam on pectin mixture thins slightly and sugar mixture comes to a full rolling boil, about 4 minutes. Gradually add pectin mixture to boiling sugar mixture, stirring constantly. Boil for 1 minute, stirring constantly.

Remove from the heat. Stir in orange oil and food coloring. Immediately pour into prepared pan. Let stand at room temperature for 3 hours or until set.

Sprinkle waxed paper with sugar; invert pan onto sugar. With a knife dipped in warm water, cut candy into 1-in. squares; roll in additional sugar. Place on a wire rack. Let stand, uncovered, at room temperature overnight. Store in an airtight container. **Yield:** 81 pieces.

Family Traditions

WHEN our kids were younger, we took them to our city's annual egg hunt the weekend before Easter. The Chamber of Commerce would disperse decorated eggs and assorted candy throughout the city park. Kids divided by age group were turned loose to find treasures. Our kids always looked forward to this event...and to eating the candy, of course!
—Deb Poitz, Fort Morgan, Colorado

Caramel Cashew Clusters

Several years ago, a co-worker came across candies like these in a store and asked if I could make them. After some trial and error, I came up with a winning recipe.
—*Karen Daniels, Jefferson City, Missouri*

2 pounds milk chocolate candy coating, chopped, *divided*
1 cup salted cashew halves
28 caramels
2 tablespoons heavy whipping cream

Line baking sheets with waxed paper and butter the paper; set aside. In a heavy saucepan, melt 1 pound of candy coating. Drop by scant tablespoonfuls onto prepared pans. Let stand until partially set, about 3 minutes. Top each with six or seven cashews. Let stand until completely set.

In a small heavy saucepan, combine caramels and cream. Cook and stir over low heat until melted; stir until smooth. Spoon over cashews. Reheat caramel over low heat if it thickens. Melt remaining candy coating; spoon over caramel. Let stand until set. **Yield:** 2-1/2 dozen.

Peanut Butter Coconut Balls

This recipe has been a family "secret" for generations. But I think it's too good to keep to ourselves! A glossy chocolate coating hides a crunchy coconut filling.
—*Jennifer Dignin, Westerville, Ohio*

1 cup butter, softened
1 cup crunchy peanut butter
2 tablespoons vanilla extract
3-1/2 cups confectioners' sugar
2 cups graham cracker crumbs
2 cups chopped walnuts
1-1/3 cups flaked coconut
2-1/2 cups semisweet chocolate chips
4 teaspoons shortening
Chopped nuts *or* sprinkles

In a large mixing bowl, cream the butter, peanut butter and vanilla. Add confectioners' sugar. Stir in the cracker crumbs, walnuts and coconut. Shape into 1-in. balls. Place on baking sheets; cover and refrigerate for at least 1 hour.

In a deep glass measuring cup or bowl, combine the chocolate chips and shortening. Microwave until melted, stirring every 15 seconds; stir until smooth. Dip balls into melted chocolate; shake off excess. Roll in nuts or sprinkles. Place on waxed paper until set. Store in an airtight container in the refrigerator. **Yield:** about 7 dozen.

Chocolate Popcorn Balls

(Pictured at right)

I've had this recipe for more than 20 years. They were good then...and just as great today! They're a fun change from traditional Easter candy.
—*Carolyn Hayes, Johnston City, Illinois*

4 quarts popped popcorn
2 squares (1 ounce *each*)
 unsweetened chocolate
2 cups sugar
1/2 cup light corn syrup
1 cup water

Place the popcorn in a large heatproof bowl; keep warm in a 200° oven. In a heavy saucepan, melt chocolate. Stir in sugar and corn syrup. Add water. Cook and stir over medium heat until mixture comes to a boil. Continue to cook until a candy thermometer reads 250° (hard-ball stage).

Pour over warm popcorn and stir until evenly coated. When mixture is cool enough to handle, quickly shape into 3-in. balls, dipping hands in cold water to prevent sticking. Cool; wrap in plastic wrap. **Yield:** 1 dozen.

Editor's Note: We recommend that you test your candy thermometer before each use by bringing water to a boil; the thermometer should read 212°. Adjust your recipe temperature up or down based on your test.

COOKING CANDY TO HARD-BALL STAGE

CANDY is cooked to a hard-ball stage when a candy thermometer reads 250°. Drop a small amount of the hot candy mixture into cold water. When cooled and removed from the water, the candy will form a hard yet pliable ball.

Full-of-Chips Cookies

My mom, Dolores Hartford, created this recipe with my daughter.
Mom would have these cookies ready for Karissa whenever she came home from college.
—Deana Williams, Canton, Pennsylvania

1 cup butter-flavored shortening
3/4 cup sugar
3/4 cup packed brown sugar
2 eggs
1 teaspoon vanilla extract
2-1/4 cups all-purpose flour
1 teaspoon baking soda
3/4 teaspoon salt
1/3 cup *each* semisweet chocolate chips, peanut butter chips, butterscotch chips and vanilla *or* white chips
1/3 cup milk chocolate M&M's
1/3 cup Reese's pieces candy

In a large mixing bowl, cream shortening and sugars. Add eggs, one at a time, beating well after each addition. Beat in vanilla. Combine the flour, baking soda and salt; gradually add to creamed mixture. Stir in chips and candy.

Drop by rounded tablespoonfuls 2 in. apart onto ungreased baking sheets. Bake at 375° for 7-9 minutes or until lightly browned around edges. Remove to wire racks to cool. **Yield:** about 4 dozen.

Crispy Cone Treats

Kids get a kick out of ice cream cake cones filled with a chocolate-topped rice cereal mixture.
Make them for a birthday party instead of cake.
—Vera Matheson, Portage la Prairie, Manitoba

1 cup packed brown sugar
1 cup light corn syrup
1 cup peanut butter
1 tablespoon butter
4 cups crisp rice cereal
1 cup chopped peanuts
18 ice cream cake cones
1-1/2 cups semisweet chocolate chips
1 tablespoon shortening
Colored sprinkles

In a large microwave-safe bowl, combine the brown sugar, corn syrup, peanut butter and butter. Microwave on high for 1-2 minutes or until melted, stirring twice. Stir in cereal and peanuts. Spoon into ice cream cones.

Melt chocolate chips and shortening; stir until smooth. Dip tops of cones in melted chocolate. Dip in sprinkles. Let stand until set. These treats are best served the day they are made. **Yield:** 1-1/2 dozen.

Editor's Note: This recipe was tested in a 1,100-watt microwave.

Cookies on a Stick

(Pictured at right)

As folks munch on these peanut butter cookies, they're delighted to uncover the candy bar surprise tucked inside.
— Delores Wallace, Jacobsburg, Ohio

1/2 cup butter, softened
1/2 cup peanut butter
1/2 cup sugar
1/2 cup packed brown sugar
   1 egg
   1 teaspoon vanilla extract
1-1/2 cups all-purpose flour
1/2 teaspoon baking powder
1/2 teaspoon baking soda
  20 lollipop sticks
  20 miniature Snickers candy
       bars

In a large mixing bowl, cream the butter, peanut butter and sugars. Add egg; beat well. Beat in vanilla. Combine the flour, baking powder and baking soda; gradually add to creamed mixture.

Insert a lollipop stick into one side of each candy bar until stick is nearly at the opposite side. Press 1 heaping tablespoon of dough around each candy bar until completely covered. Press dough tightly around the end of the candy bar and the stick.

Place 3 in. apart on lightly greased baking sheets. Bake at 350° for 14-16 minutes or until cookies are set. Cool for 1-2 minutes before removing from pans to wire racks to cool completely. **Yield:** 20 cookies.

SPECIAL Celebrations

Don't limit your entertaining to Christmas, Thanksgiving and Easter! Get the year going by hosting an elegant New Year's Eve party for a few close friends. As spring approaches, host a Seder meal for Passover. Celebrate two special people—Mom and the graduate— with gatherings in their honor. In the heat of summer, enjoy a refreshing July Fourth ice cream social or host a Hawaiian luau. Then bewitch family and friends with a "spook-tacular" Halloween bash!

New Year's Eve Gala

WHILE you wait for Father Time to welcome in a new year, celebrate the momentous evening with a strictly adult gathering.

Now's not the time to watch waistlines! Enjoy a sparkling sit-down dinner showcasing two elegant entrees.

Guests will count down the minutes to mealtime when Baked Lobster Tails and Gala Beef Tenderloin Fillets are on the menu. This surf-and-turf combination is so rich and satisfying you won't need to serve seconds.

Simple side dishes like Make-Ahead Artichoke Salad and New Year's Eve Potatoes round out the dazzling dinner.

After the stroke of midnight, wind down the festivities with assorted appetizers and desserts!

SURF 'N' TURF MENU

Baked Lobster Tails (p. 180)

Gala Beef Tenderloin Fillets (p. 178)

New Year's Eve Potatoes (p. 179)

Gala Beef Tenderloin Fillets

(Pictured on page 176)

A subtle garlic butter sauce tastefully tops tenderloin fillets in this recipe from our Test Kitchen.

6 beef tenderloin fillets (6 ounces *each* and 1-1/2 to 2 inches thick)
1/4 teaspoon salt
1/8 teaspoon pepper
2 tablespoons butter, *divided*
1 tablespoon olive oil
2 tablespoons finely chopped onion
2 garlic cloves, minced
1/3 cup dry red wine or beef broth

2 tablespoons minced fresh parsley
1/2 teaspoon browning sauce, optional

Season fillets with salt and pepper. In a large skillet, heat 1 tablespoon butter and oil over medium-high heat. Cook fillets for 5-8 minutes on each side or until meat reaches desired doneness (for medium-rare, a meat thermometer should read 145°; medium, 160°; well-done, 170°). Remove and keep warm.

In the same skillet, saute onion and garlic in remaining butter for 1 minute. Add wine or broth; cook and stir for 1 minute. Stir in parsley and browning sauce if desired. Drizzle over beef. **Yield:** 6 servings.

Make-Ahead Artichoke Salad

If I want leftovers when I take this salad to an event, I have to leave some at home because the bowl is always scraped clean!
—*Mary Lou Chernik, Taos, New Mexico*

1/4 cup olive oil
2 tablespoons lemon juice
1 tablespoon minced fresh parsley
1-1/2 teaspoons balsamic vinegar
1 garlic clove, minced
1/4 teaspoon salt
1/8 teaspoon pepper
1 can (14 ounces) water-packed artichoke hearts, rinsed, drained and quartered
1 can (2-1/4 ounces) sliced ripe olives, drained

1/4 pound fresh mushrooms, quartered
2/3 cup chopped red onion
1/2 cup chopped sweet yellow pepper
1/2 cup chopped sweet red pepper

In a jar with a tight-fitting lid, combine the first seven ingredients; shake well. In a large bowl, combine the artichokes, olives, mushrooms, onion and peppers. Add dressing and toss to coat. Cover and refrigerate for at least 24 hours. Remove from the refrigerator 2-3 hours before serving. Serve with a slotted spoon. **Yield:** 6 servings.

New Year's Eve Potatoes

(Pictured at right and on page 176)

I make this creamy mashed potato casserole in a 1-1/2-qt. baking dish. It's a terrific side dish for many entrees.
—Antonia Witmayer, Las Vegas, Nevada

1 pound potatoes, peeled and
    quartered
2 tablespoons milk
1 tablespoon butter
1/4 teaspoon salt
1/3 cup sour cream
1/3 cup ricotta cheese
2 tablespoons beaten egg
3 green onions, finely chopped

Place the potatoes in a large saucepan and cover with water; bring to a boil. Reduce heat; cover and cook for 20-25 minutes or until tender. Drain and place potatoes in a large mixing bowl. Add the milk, butter and salt; mash un-til light and fluffy. Fold in the sour cream, ricotta cheese, egg and onions.

Generously coat six muffin cups with nonstick cooking spray. Fill with potato mixture; smooth tops. Bake at 375° for 20-25 minutes or until edges are lightly browned. Cool for 5 minutes. Carefully run a knife around the edge of each muffin cup; invert onto a baking sheet or serving platter. **Yield:** 6 servings.

PREPARE POTATOES AHEAD

TO SAVE TIME when entertaining on New Year's Eve, assemble New Year's Eve Potatoes in the morning and put into greased muffin cups; cover and chill. Remove from the refrigerator 30 minutes before baking as directed.

Baked Lobster Tails

(Pictured on page 176)

Lobster tails are a rich and filling entree, especially when served alongside steak.
In this recipe, our home economists cut three lobster tails in half to feed six people.

3 fresh *or* frozen lobster tails
    (8 to 10 ounces *each*), thawed
1 cup water
1 tablespoon minced fresh
    parsley
1/8 teaspoon salt
Dash pepper
1 tablespoon butter, melted
2 tablespoons lemon juice
Lemon wedges and additional
    melted butter, optional

Split lobster tails in half lengthwise. With cut side up and using scissors, cut along the edge of shell to loosen the cartilage covering the tail meat from the shell; remove and discard cartilage.

    Pour water into a 13-in. x 9-in. x 2-in. baking dish; place lobster tails in dish. Combine the parsley, salt and pepper; sprinkle over lobster. Drizzle with butter and lemon juice. Bake, uncovered, at 375° for 20-25 minutes or until meat is firm and opaque. Serve with lemon wedges and melted butter if desired. **Yield:** 6 servings.

PREPARING LOBSTER TAIL HALVES

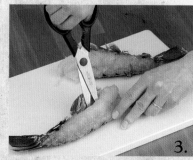

1. With a scissors, cut lengthwise through the shell on the underside of the lobster to expose the meat.

2. Cut the tail in half lengthwise with a sharp knife.

3. Place lobster tail halves cut side up on a cutting board. Using scissors, cut along the edge of shell to loosen the cartilage from the shell; remove and discard cartilage.

Jelled Champagne Dessert

(Pictured at right)

Our home economists fashioned this refreshing dessert to look like a glass of bubbling champagne, making it perfect for New Year's Eve.

1 tablespoon unflavored gelatin
2 cups cold white grape juice, *divided*
2 tablespoons sugar
2 cups champagne *or* club soda
8 fresh strawberries, hulled

In a small saucepan, sprinkle gelatin over 1 cup cold grape juice; let stand for 1 minute. Heat over low heat, stirring until gelatin is completely dissolved. Stir in sugar. Remove from the heat; stir in remaining grape juice. Cool to room temperature.

Transfer gelatin mixture to a large bowl. Slowly stir in champagne or soda. Pour half of the mixture into eight champagne or parfait glasses. Add one strawberry to each glass. Chill glasses and remaining gelatin mixture until almost set, about 1 hour.

Place the reserved gelatin mixture in a blender; cover and process until foamy. Pour into glasses. Chill for 3 hours or until set. **Yield:** 8 servings.

Peppermint Eggnog Punch

With peppermint ice cream, this is almost more of a dessert than a beverage!
—Marjorie Jane Watkins, Eugene, Oregon

1 quart peppermint ice cream, softened
1 quart eggnog, chilled
1 cup rum *or* 2 teaspoons rum extract, optional
2 cups carbonated water, chilled
Miniature candy canes, optional

Set aside a few scoops of ice cream to use as a garnish. Place the remaining ice cream in a large punch bowl; stir in the eggnog and rum or extract if desired. Add carbonated water. Top with reserved ice cream scoops. Serve with candy canes if desired. Serve immediately. **Yield:** 9 cups.

Editor's Note: This recipe was tested with commercially prepared eggnog.

Crab Wontons

(Pictured at right)

Gather guests into the kitchen as you fry these crisp seafood bundles.
We enjoy them with hot mustard as well as sweet-and-sour sauce.
—Karolee Plock, Burwell, Nebraska

- 1 **package (8 ounces) cream cheese, softened**
- 1 **envelope buttermilk ranch salad dressing mix**
- 3 **tablespoons diced celery**
- 3 **tablespoons diced sweet red pepper**
- 1 **tablespoon finely chopped onion**
- 1 **tablespoon minced fresh parsley**
- 1 **garlic clove, minced**
- 2 **cans (6 ounces *each*) crab meat, drained, flaked and cartilage removed**
- 60 **to 70 wonton wrappers**

Oil for frying
Sweet-and-sour sauce

In a small mixing bowl, combine the first seven ingredients. Stir in crab. Place 1 teaspoon crab mixture off-center on each wonton wrapper. Fold the point of the wrapper nearest the filling over the top of filling and gently tuck under filling. Gently roll toward center to within 1 in. from the opposite point. Moisten the right point; fold over the left point, pressing ends together to seal. Moisten the overlapping points.

In an electric skillet, heat 1 in. of oil to 375°. Fry wontons in batches for 1-2 minutes on each side or until golden brown. Drain on paper towels. Serve warm with sweet-and-sour sauce. **Yield:** about 5 dozen.

TIMELY WONTONS

CRAB WONTONS can be assembled in advance, covered with a damp towel and refrigerated until you're ready to fry them.

Garlic Brie Pizza

(Pictured at right)

Elegant occasions require fancy appetizers like this. Family and friends will be surprised to hear just how easy it is to prepare.
—*Gail Cawsey, Sequim, Washington*

3 whole garlic bulbs
2 tablespoons olive oil
12 ounces Brie cheese
1 prebaked Italian bread shell crust (14 ounces)
1/2 cup sliced almonds, toasted

Remove papery outer skin from garlic (do not peel or separate cloves). Cut the top off each garlic bulb. Brush with oil. Wrap each bulb in heavy-duty foil; place on a baking sheet. Bake at 425° for 30-35 minutes or until softened. Cool for 10-15 minutes. Squeeze softened garlic into a small bowl and mash.

Remove rind from Brie and discard. Cut Brie into 1/4-in. slices. Place crust on a 12-in. pizza pan. Spread with garlic. Arrange cheese slices over garlic; sprinkle with almonds. Bake at 450° for 8-10 minutes or until cheese is melted. **Yield:** 10 servings.

Italian Olives

A friend shared this recipe with me more than 25 years ago, and I still get raves when I serve them as part of an antipasto platter.
—*Jean Johnson, Reno, Nevada*

2 cans (6 ounces *each*) pitted ripe olives, drained
1 jar (5-3/4 ounces) stuffed olives, drained
2 tablespoons diced celery
2 tablespoons diced onion
2 tablespoons capers, rinsed and drained
1/4 cup olive oil
2 tablespoons red wine vinegar
2 garlic cloves, minced

1 teaspoon dried basil
1 teaspoon dried oregano
1 teaspoon crushed red pepper flakes
1/4 teaspoon salt

In a large bowl, combine the first five ingredients. In a small bowl, whisk the oil, vinegar, garlic, basil, oregano, pepper flakes and salt; pour over olive mixture and toss to coat. Cover and refrigerate for at least 3 hours before serving. Store in the refrigerator for up to 3 days. **Yield:** 4 cups.

Timely New Year's Eve Table

(Pictured above)

AT NO OTHER TIME do folks seem to watch the clock than on New Year's Eve. After all, the celebration is about the magic hour of midnight!

A collection of clocks and pocket watches set down the length of your table makes a spectacular showpiece on New Year's Eve. We used crystal and silver varieties to go with the glass dinner plates and silver chargers. (A quirky vase filled with silver metallic stars and streamers serves as a playful centerpiece.)

At each place setting, carry on the timely theme by using a wristwatch napkin ring around the Diagonal Napkin Fold. (See above right for folding instructions.)

Before guests arrive, synchronize the timepieces on the table so they strike midnight all at once!

DIAGONAL NAPKIN FOLD

1. Place a square cloth napkin wrong side up on a flat surface. Fold in two sides so they overlap and form a rectangle.

2. Fold the upper left corner down to the center of the rectangle's lower edge.

3. Fold the triangle you just made over so that it forms a square.

4. Turn the napkin over; roll two sides into the center to make a tube. Turn the napkin over so the rolled edges are underneath. Slip a wristwatch over the napkin.

Raspberry Chocolate Tart

When our son was young, he would gauge his birthday based on when the raspberries were ripe.
We'd use the fresh-picked berries to decorate this tart for his special day.
—Annie Dougherty, Fairbanks, Alaska

1 cup all-purpose flour
1/3 cup walnut pieces
3 tablespoons sugar
1/4 teaspoon salt
1/2 cup cold butter, cubed
2 egg yolks
1/3 cup seedless raspberry jam
3/4 cup plus 2 tablespoons heavy
　　whipping cream
1 cup (6 ounces) semisweet
　　chocolate chips
1 cup fresh raspberries

In a food processor, combine the flour, walnuts, sugar and salt; cover and process until walnuts are chopped. Add butter; pulse just until crumbly. Add egg yolks; process until small moist crumbs form. Shape into a ball, then flatten into a disk. Wrap in plastic wrap and refrigerate for 30 minutes.

Place dough between two pieces of waxed paper; roll into a 10-in. circle. Transfer to a greased 9-in. springform pan. Press onto the bottom and 1/2 in. up the sides of pan. Bake at 375° for 20-22 minutes or until golden brown. Spread with jam. Bake 5 minutes longer. Cool completely on a wire rack.

Meanwhile, in a heavy saucepan, heat cream over medium heat until bubbles form around sides of pan. Remove from the heat; stir in chocolate chips until melted. Cool to room temperature, about 1 hour, stirring occasionally. Pour over crust. Refrigerate until firm, about 2 hours. Remove sides of pan. Arrange raspberries over the top. **Yield:** 12 servings.

Passover Celebration

PASSOVER is an 8-day Jewish holiday marking the physical freedom of the Hebrews (under the leadership of Moses) from the Egyptian Pharaoh.

On the first 2 nights, friends and family share a festive meal called Seder, meaning "order."

Here we offer one idea for a mouth-watering meal to serve during Passover.

Veal Breast with Farfel Stuffing bakes for a few hours, resulting in a tender, tasty entree.

The pleasant flavor of rich Onion Kugel appeals to all... even folks who don't care for onions.

Refreshing Cucumber Salad is a cool and crisp complement to the oven-fresh dishes. (All recipes shown at right.)

SEDER SUPPER
(Top to bottom)

Onion Kugel (p. 189)

Veal Breast with Farfel Stuffing (p. 190)

Refreshing Cucumber Salad (p. 188)

PASSOVER DINNER PLAN

A Few Weeks Before:

- Prepare two grocery lists—one for non-perishable items to purchase now and one for perishable items to purchase a few days before your dinner.
- Order a veal breast from your butcher.
- Bake Passover Bagels; cool. Freeze in a heavy-duty resealable plastic bag.

Two Days Before:

- Set the table.
- Buy remaining grocery items, including the veal breast you ordered.
- Prepare the Refreshing Cucumber Salad; cover and chill.

The Day Before:

- Assemble the stuffing for Veal Breast with Farfel Stuffing. Cover and refrigerate. (Do not stuff into the veal breast until ready to bake.)
- Finely chop the onions for Onion Kugel. Refrigerate in an airtight container.

- Make Matzo Ball Soup. Let cool; cover and chill.
- Prepare Chicken Liver Pate; cover and refrigerate.
- Bake the Flourless Apricot Pecan Tart but don't add the garnish. Cover with foil; store at room temperature overnight.

The Day of Your Passover Dinner:

- In the morning, thaw Passover Bagels at room temperature.
- Garnish the tart and recover.
- Stuff the veal breast and bake as directed.
- As guests arrive, set out Chicken Liver Pate and assorted crackers.
- Assemble the Onion Kugel and bake.
- If desired, wrap the bagels in foil and reheat in a 350° oven for 15 to 20 minutes.
- Reheat Matzo Ball Soup and offer it as a first course.
- Serve Refreshing Cucumber Salad with a slotted spoon.
- For dessert, cut the Flourless Apricot Pecan Tart.

Refreshing Cucumber Salad

(Pictured on page 186)

This refreshing salad from our home economists can be prepared days in advance.

3 medium cucumbers, thinly sliced
1 medium onion, thinly sliced
1/3 cup lemon juice
3/4 teaspoon salt

In a large bowl, combine the cucumbers and onion. Stir in lemon juice and salt. Cover and refrigerate for 1-2 days, stirring occasionally. Serve with a slotted spoon. **Yield:** 6-8 servings.

Onion Kugel

(Pictured at right and on page 187)

This traditional dish from our Test Kitchen resembles a delicious souffle. Sliced eggplant, sliced green peppers or shredded cabbage can be used in place of the onions.

6 eggs, *separated*
2 cups finely chopped onions
1/3 cup matzo meal
1/3 cup vegetable oil
3/4 teaspoon salt
1/4 teaspoon pepper

In a large mixing bowl, beat the egg yolks on high speed for 2 minutes or until thick and lemon-colored. Add the onions, matzo meal, oil, salt and pepper; mix well. In another mixing bowl, beat egg whites on high until stiff peaks form; fold into onion mixture.

Pour into an ungreased round 2-qt. baking dish. Bake, uncovered, at 350° for 35-40 minutes or until a knife inserted near the center comes out clean. Serve immediately. **Yield:** 8 servings.

THE MEANING OF MATZAH

IT'S SAID that when Moses led the Jews to freedom, they left so quickly they didn't wait for their bread to rise. That's why the crunchy, flat bread called Matzah is eaten during Passover.

Matzo meal is finely ground from matzah. It's used as the main ingredient in matzo balls, in baking, as a breading for fried foods and as a thickening agent.

Veal Breast with Farfel Stuffing

(Pictured on page 187)

I prepare this entree often for Passover Seder. It bakes up golden brown and tastes terrific.
—*Sala Simonds, Lancaster, California*

1 cup chopped celery
1/4 cup chopped onion
1/4 cup rendered chicken fat *or*
    vegetable oil
4 cups matzo farfel
1/4 cup minced fresh parsley
1 egg, lightly beaten
1 cup chicken broth
1 teaspoon salt
1 teaspoon rubbed sage
1 teaspoon paprika
1/4 teaspoon pepper
1 bone-in veal breast with
    pocket (7 to 8 pounds)
Olive oil

In a large skillet, saute celery and onion in chicken fat until tender. Add farfel; cook and stir over medium heat until lightly browned. Stir in the parsley. Combine the egg, broth, salt, sage, paprika and pepper; add to farfel mixture. Cook over low heat until liquid is absorbed, stirring occasionally.

Just before baking, evenly fill the veal breast pocket with stuffing; close and tie several times with kitchen string. Place in a shallow greased roasting pan. Brush veal with olive oil. Bake, uncovered, at 350° for 1-3/4 to 2 hours or until a meat thermometer reads 160° for veal and 165° for stuffing, basting occasionally. Let stand for 10 minutes before slicing. **Yield:** 8-10 servings.

STORY OF THE SEDER PLATE

DURING the Seder, the story of the Exodus is reenacted using a special Seder Plate (like the one shown on page 186). It contains the following key elements of Passover:

- Betzah (a roasted or boiled egg), commemorating the destruction of the Temple in Jerusalem.
- Charoset (a fruit and nut mixture), symbolizing the mortar used by Jews to build Egyptian structures.
- Karpas (spring greens such as radishes, onions, parsley or celery). The Karpas is dipped in salted water, which symbolizes the tears shed by the Jewish people. The spring greens and the salted water together symbolize life.
- Marror (bitter herbs), usually horseradish or romaine lettuce, commemorating the harsh conditions of slavery in ancient Egypt.
- Zeroa (roasted or boiled meat or poultry), recalling the Pascal sacrifice of the original Exodus.

In addition, red wine is consumed during the course of the Seder to commemorate the redemption of the Jewish people.

Matzo Ball Soup

(Pictured at right)

Our Test Kitchen shares the recipe for this traditional soup. You can make the soup a day ahead and reheat it just before serving.

10 cups water
12 garlic cloves, peeled
 3 medium carrots, cut into chunks
 3 small turnips, peeled and cut into chunks
 2 medium onions, cut into wedges
 2 medium parsnips, peeled and cut into chunks
 1 medium leek (white portion only), sliced
1/4 cup minced fresh parsley
 2 tablespoons snipped fresh dill
 1 teaspoon salt
 1 teaspoon pepper
3/4 teaspoon ground turmeric
MATZO BALLS:
 3 eggs, *separated*
 3 tablespoons water *or* chicken broth
 3 tablespoons rendered chicken fat
1-1/2 teaspoons salt, *divided*
3/4 cup matzo meal
 8 cups water

For broth, combine the first 12 ingredients in a large soup kettle or stockpot. Bring to a boil. Reduce heat; cover and simmer for 2 hours.

Meanwhile, in a mixing bowl, beat the egg yolks on high speed for 2 minutes or until thick and lemon-colored. Add the water, chicken fat and 1/2 teaspoon salt. In another mixing bowl, beat egg whites on high until stiff peaks form; fold into yolk mixture. Fold in matzo meal. Cover and refrigerate for at least 1 hour or until thickened.

In another large stockpot, bring water to a boil; add remaining salt. Drop eight rounded tablespoonfuls of matzo ball dough into boiling water. Reduce heat; cover and simmer for 20-25 minutes or until a toothpick inserted into a matzo ball comes out clean (do not lift cover while simmering).

Strain broth, discarding vegetables and seasonings. Carefully remove matzo balls from water with a slotted spoon; place one matzo ball in each soup bowl. Add broth. **Yield:** 8 servings.

Passover Bagels

We use these traditional bagels to make sandwiches throughout Passover.
But they can also be served as rolls with dinner.
—Myrna Lief, Burlington, Massachusetts

1 cup water
1/2 cup vegetable oil
1 tablespoon sugar
1/4 teaspoon salt
1 cup matzo meal
4 eggs

In a large saucepan, bring the water, oil, sugar and salt to a boil. Add matzo meal all at once and stir until a smooth ball forms. Remove from the heat; let stand for 5 minutes. Add eggs, one at a time, beating well after each addition. Continue beating until mixture is smooth and shiny.

Drop dough into 12 mounds 3 in. apart on two greased baking sheets. Bake at 450° for 10 minutes. Reduce heat to 350°; bake 12-15 minutes longer or until golden brown. Remove to wire racks. Immediately cut a slit in each to allow steam to escape; cool. **Yield:** 1 dozen.

Chicken Liver Pate

My family loves this spread with crackers.
But I've also put it to use as a sandwich filling with lettuce and tomato.
—Roberta Wolff, Waltham, Massachusetts

1 pound chicken livers
1 small onion, chopped
1/3 cup rendered chicken fat *or* margarine
1/2 pound fresh mushrooms, quartered
2 hard-cooked eggs, quartered
1 to 2 tablespoons sherry *or* chicken broth
3/4 teaspoon salt
1/4 teaspoon pepper
Melba toast *or* assorted crackers

In a skillet, saute chicken livers and onion in chicken fat for 10 minutes or until livers are no longer pink. Transfer to a food processor; cover and process until chicken livers are coarsely chopped.

Add the mushrooms, eggs, 1 tablespoon sherry or broth, salt and pepper. Cover and process until smooth, adding more sherry or broth if needed for pate to reach desired consistency. Transfer to a bowl. Cover and refrigerate for at least 3 hours. Serve with melba toast or crackers. **Yield:** 12 servings.

Flourless Apricot Pecan Tart

(Pictured at right)

Apricot and chocolate are pleasing partners in this elegant dessert created in our Test Kitchen. It doesn't contain flour, so it's appropriate for people with gluten allergies.

12 ounces dried apricots, chopped
1 cup water
6 tablespoons sugar
1 tablespoon minced fresh gingerroot
1 tablespoon lemon juice
1 teaspoon grated lemon peel

CRUST:
1 tablespoon matzo meal
4 cups pecan halves, toasted
1-1/2 cups sugar
1/2 teaspoon ground ginger
1/4 teaspoon salt
2 eggs
4 squares (1 ounce *each*) semisweet chocolate

GARNISH:
2 squares (1 ounce *each*) semisweet chocolate
1/2 cup pecan halves
Dried apricots

In a heavy saucepan, combine the apricots, water, sugar, gingerroot, lemon juice and peel; bring to a boil. Reduce heat; cover and simmer for 30-35 minutes or until apricots are tender. Uncover; simmer 5-10 minutes longer or until thickened and liquid is absorbed.

Transfer to a food processor; cover and pulse five times or until mixture is smooth and thickened. Pour into a bowl; cool.

Trace the removable bottom of an 11-in. tart pan on waxed paper; set aside. Grease tart pan; dust with matzo meal and set aside.

In a food processor, combine the pecans, sugar, ginger and salt; cover and process until pecans are finely ground. Add eggs; cover and process until mixture forms a moist ball. Place half of the dough in a bowl; cover and refrigerate. Press remaining dough over the bottom and up the sides of prepared pan.

Bake at 350° for 12-15 minutes or until crust is puffed and lightly browned. Press bottom of crust lightly to flatten if necessary. Cool on a wire rack.

In a microwave, melt chocolate; stir until smooth. Spread over crust. Chill for 10 minutes or until set. Spread apricot filling over chocolate. Press remaining dough over waxed paper circle. Invert dough over filling; carefully peel off waxed paper and discard. Press edges of dough to edge of tart pan to seal.

Bake at 350° for 35-40 minutes or until lightly browned and dry to the touch. Cool completely in pan on a wire rack. Cover with foil and let stand overnight.

For garnish, melt chocolate; stir until smooth. Drizzle 2 tablespoons over tart. Dip pecans halfway in remaining chocolate. Garnish tart with dipped pecans and dried apricots. **Yield:** 12-14 servings.

Make Mother's Day Special

ONE WAY to make Mom feel like a million on Mother's Day is by having Dad rouse the kids and whisk them to the kitchen to prepare breakfast in bed for her!

Golden Oat Pancakes and Green Onion Scrambled Eggs deliciously prove that great-tasting foods don't require complicated recipes. (Dishes shown at right.)

Do you prefer not to disturb Mom on her special morning? Skip the breakfast and serve up a soup and sandwich lunch at the kitchen table. Or dish out a hearty helping of pasta salad.

We even offer timetables that make menu planning extra easy!

RISE-AND-SHINE SURPRISE

Golden Oat Pancakes (p. 197)

Green Onion Scrambled Eggs (p. 197)

MOTHER'S DAY BREAKFAST PLAN

One Week Before:

- Come up with the menu and make a grocery list.
- Have the kids make a card or draw a picture for Mom. (If desired, pick up an inexpensive photo frame for the drawing. See page 203 for one idea.)
- Look at home for a breakfast tray or pick one up from the store. You don't have to use a tray with legs...any tray (even a plastic one for outdoor entertaining) will do.

Two Days Before:

- Stop at the grocery store for any needed items.
- Put marbles in a drinking glass. Surround with a ponytail holder and crayons if desired. (See page 203 for directions.) Hide the glass from Mom!

The Day Before:

- Make Lemon-Blueberry Tea Bread and cool completely. Store in a resealable plastic bag on the counter overnight.
- Combine the flour, baking powder, brown sugar and salt for Golden Oat Pancakes. Place in an airtight container; store at room temperature.

Mother's Day Morning:

- Get up early with the kids and let Mom sleep in!
- Have older kids add water and fresh-cut flowers from your yard to the marble-filled drinking glass; set on the breakfast tray along with the kid-crafted greeting card or framed drawing.
- Slice Lemon-Blueberry Tea Bread.
- Make Fruit Smoothies or pour Mom a cup of coffee, orange juice or her favorite morning beverage.
- While the Golden Oat Pancakes are cooking on the griddle, prepare Green Onion Scrambled Eggs in a skillet.
- Top the pancakes with fresh fruit or syrup.
- Serve Mom breakfast in bed!

Golden Oat Pancakes

(Pictured at right and on page 194)

My husband's face lights up when I serve these country-style flapjacks. Serve them with fresh fruit or syrup.
—Raymonde Bourgeois, Swastika, Ontario

1-1/3 cups milk
  1 cup old-fashioned oats
  2 eggs, lightly beaten
  3 tablespoons vegetable oil
2/3 cup all-purpose flour
  4 teaspoons baking powder
  4 teaspoons brown sugar
1/4 teaspoon salt

In a bowl, combine the milk and oats; let stand for 5 minutes. Stir in eggs and oil. Combine the flour, baking powder, brown sugar and salt; stir into oat mixture just until moistened. Pour batter by 1/4 cupfuls onto a greased hot griddle; turn when bubbles form on top of pancakes. Cook until second side is lightly browned. **Yield:** 10 pancakes.

Green Onion Scrambled Eggs

(Pictured above and on page 194)

Our Test Kitchen home economists added cream cheese and green onions to create these deliciously different scrambled eggs.

  4 green onions, chopped
  2 tablespoons butter
  8 eggs
  1 package (3 ounces) cream
    cheese, cubed
1/2 teaspoon seasoned salt

In a large skillet, saute onions in butter for 2 minutes. In a bowl, beat the eggs; add cream cheese and seasoned salt. Pour into the skillet. As eggs set, gently move a spatula across bottom and sides of pan, letting uncooked portion flow underneath. Continue cooking and stirring until the eggs are completely set. **Yield:** 4 servings.

Lemon-Blueberry Tea Bread

Moist slices of this cake-like bread are bursting with blueberries and lots of lemon flavor.
— Wendy Masters, Grand Valley, Ontario

1/2 cup butter, softened
1 cup sugar
2 eggs
1 teaspoon grated lemon peel
1-1/2 cups all-purpose flour
1 teaspoon baking powder
1/4 teaspoon salt
1/2 cup milk
1 cup fresh *or* frozen blueberries
1/4 cup confectioners' sugar
1 tablespoon lemon juice

In a small mixing bowl, cream the butter and sugar. Add the eggs, one at a time, beating well after each addition. Beat in lemon peel. Combine the flour, baking powder and salt; add to creamed mixture alternately with milk. Fold in blueberries.

Pour into a greased 8-in. x 4-in. x 2-in. loaf pan. Bake at 350° for 65-70 minutes or until a toothpick inserted near the center comes out clean. Cool for 10 minutes before removing from pan to a wire rack. In a small bowl, combine confectioners' sugar and lemon juice until smooth; drizzle over warm bread. **Yield:** 1 loaf.

Editor's Note: If using frozen blueberries, do not thaw before adding to batter.

Fruit Smoothies

Instead of pouring a glass of ordinary orange juice, our Test Kitchen suggests
making Mom this refreshing smoothie that's quickly prepared in a blender.

2 cups milk
1 cup frozen unsweetened
  peach slices
1 cup frozen unsweetened
  strawberries
1/4 cup orange juice
2 tablespoons honey

In a blender, combine all ingredients. Cover and blend until smooth. Pour into chilled glasses; serve immediately. **Yield:** 4 servings.

Strawberry Swirl Mousse Tarts

(Pictured above)

Our Test Kitchen created a delicious dessert that requires only six ingredients.

1-1/2 cups cold milk
   1 package (3.3 ounces) instant
      white chocolate pudding mix
   1 cup whipped topping
   1 package (6 count) individual
      graham cracker tart shells
 1/4 cup strawberry ice cream
      topping
   6 fresh strawberries

In a small bowl, gradually whisk milk and pudding for 2 minutes. Let stand for 2 minutes or until soft-set. Gently fold in whipped topping. Spoon into tart shells. Drizzle with strawberry topping. Refrigerate for at least 30 minutes. Garnish with strawberries. **Yield:** 6 servings.

PLATE OF DISTINCTION

IN THE PHOTO above, we used the well-known "You Are Special Today" plate by Waechtersbach.

This stunning, signature red plate is a fun, family heirloom that's wonderful to have on hand to celebrate many occasions throughout the year.

Pineapple Chicken Salad Sandwiches

(Pictured on page 199)

These sandwiches are always welcome at lunchtime around our home.
Sweet pineapple and crunchy pecans are nice additions to ordinary chicken salad.
—*Carol Alexander, Midland, Michigan*

2 cups cubed cooked chicken breast
1/2 cup crushed pineapple, drained
1/4 cup chopped pecans
1/4 cup chopped celery
2 tablespoons finely chopped onion
2 tablespoons sweet pickle relish
1/2 cup mayonnaise
1/4 teaspoon onion salt
1/4 teaspoon garlic salt
1/4 teaspoon paprika
6 lettuce leaves
6 sandwich rolls, split

In a small bowl, combine the first six ingredients. Combine the mayonnaise, onion salt, garlic salt and paprika; add to chicken mixture and mix well. Serve on lettuce-lined rolls. **Yield:** 6 servings.

GETTING COOKED CHICKEN

WHEN recipes like Pineapple Chicken Salad Sandwiches call for cubed cooked chicken, stop by the deli counter and have them cut a thick slice of cooked chicken breast sandwich meat for you to cut up at home.

Speedy Spud Soup

(Pictured on page 199)

I'm a busy wife and mother with not a lot of time to spend in the kitchen.
This time-saving soup recipe relies on frozen potatoes and canned soup.
—*Stacy Barron, Bentonville, Arkansas*

1 package (24 ounces) frozen shredded hash brown potatoes, thawed
1/2 cup chopped onion
1/2 cup butter, cubed
4 cups milk
1 can (10-3/4 ounces) condensed cream of chicken soup, undiluted

1 cup (4 ounces) shredded cheddar cheese
1/2 teaspoon garlic salt
Cooked crumbled bacon

In a large saucepan, cook and stir the potatoes and onion in butter over medium-low heat for 10 minutes. Stir in the milk, soup, cheese and garlic salt. Cook, uncovered, for 20 minutes or until potatoes are tender. Garnish with bacon. **Yield:** 8 servings (2 quarts).

Crab Pasta Salad

(Pictured at right)

The medley of crab, pasta and vegetables in a creamy dressing make this a special salad for company as well as everyday.
—Estelle Hardin, Kanab, Utah

 2 cups uncooked tricolor spiral pasta
 2 cups imitation crabmeat, chopped
 1 cup (8 ounces) sour cream
 1/2 cup mayonnaise
 3/4 teaspoon celery seed
 3/4 teaspoon garlic powder
 1/4 teaspoon salt
Pepper to taste
 1 cup fresh broccoli florets
 1 cup fresh cauliflowerets

Cook pasta according to package directions; drain and rinse in cold water. In a bowl, combine the crab, sour cream, mayonnaise, celery seed, garlic powder, salt and pepper. Stir in the pasta, broccoli and cauliflower. Cover and refrigerate for at least 2 hours before serving. **Yield:** 6-8 servings.

Cinnamon Dip

This creamy dip can be prepared the night before and chilled.
Serve with apple wedges or an assortment of cookies for a sweet anytime snack.
—Jessica Flory, Queen Creek, Arizona

 1 package (8 ounces) cream cheese, softened
 3 tablespoons milk
 2 tablespoons brown sugar
 1 teaspoon vanilla extract
 1 teaspoon ground cinnamon
1/4 teaspoon ground nutmeg
Apple wedges

In a small mixing bowl, combine the cream cheese, milk, brown sugar, vanilla, cinnamon and nutmeg; beat until smooth. Transfer to a serving bowl. Refrigerate until serving. Serve with apple wedges. **Yield:** 1 cup.

MOTHER'S DAY LUNCH TIMETABLE

One Week Before:

- Decide if you want to serve Crab Pasta Salad as the only main course or the Pineapple Chicken Salad Sandwiches with Speedy Spud Soup.
- Prepare a grocery list.
- Have the kids make a card or draw a picture for Mom. (If desired, pick up an inexpensive photo frame for the drawing. See opposite page for one idea.)

Two Days Before:

- Stop at the grocery store for any needed items.
- Put marbles in a drinking glass. Surround with a ponytail holder and crayons if desired. (See opposite page for directions.) Hide the glass from Mom!

The Day Before:

- Make the Crab Pasta Salad or the filling for Pineapple Chicken Salad Sandwiches; refrigerate in an airtight container.
- Prepare Cinnamon Dip; cover and chill.

Mother's Day:

- As a mid-morning snack, serve Mom the Cinnamon Dip with apple wedges.
- Enlist the kids to set a special seat at the table for Mom.
- Have older kids add water and fresh-cut flowers from your yard to the marble-filled drinking glass; set on the table along with the kid-crafted greeting card or framed drawing.
- About 45 minutes before lunchtime, assemble Strawberry Swirl Mousse Tarts; place on a baking sheet and refrigerate until ready to serve.
- If serving Speedy Spud Soup, make it about 30 minutes before lunch. While the soup is simmering, assemble Pineapple Chicken Salad Sandwiches.
- Make Mom a plate of Crab Pasta Salad. Or serve her the soup and sandwich combination. Don't forget to pour Mom a beverage!
- For dessert, offer Mom the Strawberry Swirl Mousse Tarts.

Mementos for Mom

(Pictured above)

THE GIFTS that Mom cherishes most are the ones hand-crafted by her own kids. When you present Mom with a mouth-watering breakfast in bed or a lovely lunch at the kitchen table, have the kids make their mark with a one-of-a-kind tray or table topper.

Instead of buying a greeting card, enlist the little ones to make a card at home. Or have them draw a pretty picture and place it in a frame. (Inexpensive canvas or paper-covered photo frames are available at craft stores.)

Fresh-picked daisies bring a touch of spring inside...and a kid-crafted vase is the perfect way to display the bright bouquet!

While you start making the meal, have the kids hunt down some of their marbles and place them in a regular drinking glass. Tuck daisy stems into the marbles, then fill with water.

For an even more colorful arrangement, place a decorative ponytail holder around the marble-filled glass. Slide crayons between the glass and holder until the entire glass is covered.

Graduation Get-Together

WHEN you have a child graduating, your days leading up to the big event are packed with endless extra-curricular activities.

Address your dilemma of what to serve on commencement day by preparing the pleasing picnic meal shown at right.

With hot pork sausage and a special sauce, Sweet 'n' Spicy Meatballs make the grade for all of your hungry guests.

You'll earn top honors when you serve Crowd-Pleasin' Muffuletta as your main course.

For a stellar side that never fails to satisfy, dish out Marinated Vegetable Salad.

A purchased sheet cake from a local bakery concludes the memorable feast.

CUISINE
WITH CLASS
(Clockwise from top right)

Sweet 'n' Spicy
Meatballs (p. 209)

Marinated
Vegetable Salad (p. 206)

Crowd-Pleasin'
Muffuletta (p. 207)

Marinated Vegetable Salad

(Pictured on page 205)

I was known only as an average cook before I first made this lip-smacking salad!
—*Mrs. Earl Anderson Jr., Stockton, California*

4 cups fresh broccoli florets
4 cups fresh cauliflowerets
5 medium carrots, cut
   into 2-inch thin strips
2 cups grape tomatoes
1 can (15 ounces) whole baby
   corn, drained and cut width
   wise into quarters
1 can (6 ounces) pitted ripe
   olives, drained and halved
1 cup olive oil
2/3 cup white wine vinegar
1/3 cup sherry *or* chicken broth
4 teaspoons Dijon mustard
3 garlic cloves, minced
2 teaspoons salt
1/2 teaspoon pepper

Place the broccoli, cauliflower and carrots in a large steamer basket; place in a large saucepan over 1 in. of water. Bring to a boil; cover and steam for 4-6 minutes or until crisp-tender. Place basket in ice water for 1-2 minutes or until vegetables are cooled; drain well.

Transfer the cooled vegetables to a large resealable plastic bag. Add the tomatoes, corn and olives. In a bowl, whisk the oil, vinegar, sherry or broth, mustard, garlic, salt and pepper. Pour over vegetables. Seal bag and turn to coat; refrigerate for at least 8 hours or overnight.

Remove from the refrigerator 30 minutes before serving. Turn bag to coat; pour salad into a serving bowl. Serve with a slotted spoon. **Yield:** 15 servings.

Sweet Heat Drumettes

Sweet maple syrup plays down the heat from the cayenne pepper in these finger-lickin'-good drumettes. Use a chafing dish to keep them warm at a party.
—*Deb Zurawski, Jamesport, New York*

1 cup maple syrup
1 cup chili sauce
1/2 cup minced chives
1/4 cup soy sauce
2 teaspoons ground mustard
1/2 to 1 teaspoon cayenne pepper
4 pounds frozen chicken
   drumettes *or* wingettes,
   thawed

In a bowl, combine the syrup, chili sauce, chives, soy sauce, mustard and cayenne. Set aside 2/3 cup for basting. Divide remaining marinade between two large resealable plastic bags; add chicken. Seal bags and turn to coat. Cover and refrigerate for 1 hour.

Drain and discard marinade. Place chicken in two greased 15-in. x 10-in. x 1-in. baking pans. Bake, uncovered, at 375° for 30 minutes; drain. Turn chicken over; baste with some of the reserved marinade. Bake for 10 minutes; turn and baste again. Bake 10-15 minutes longer or until juices run clear and sauce is thickened. **Yield:** about 4 dozen.

Crowd-Pleasin' Muffuletta

(Pictured at right and on page 204)

A garlic-olive paste is the delicious difference in this hearty make-ahead sandwich.
—*Jeannie Yee, Fremont, California*

1 cup stuffed olives, finely chopped
1 cup pitted ripe olives, finely chopped
2/3 cup olive oil
1/2 cup chopped roasted sweet red peppers
3 tablespoons minced fresh parsley
2 tablespoons red wine vinegar
3 garlic cloves, minced
1 round loaf (2 pounds) unsliced Italian bread
1 pound thinly sliced deli turkey
12 ounces thinly sliced mozzarella cheese (about 16 slices)
1 pound thinly sliced hard salami
1 pound thinly sliced deli ham

In a large bowl, combine the first seven ingredients; set aside. Cut bread in half horizontally. Carefully hollow out top and bottom, leaving a 1-in. shell (save removed bread for another use).

Spread 1-1/2 cups olive mixture over bottom of bread shell. Spread remaining olive mixture over top of bread shell. In bottom of bread, layer the turkey, half of the cheese, salami, remaining cheese and ham. Replace bread top. Wrap tightly in plastic wrap. Refrigerate for 4 hours or overnight. Cut into wedges to serve. **Yield:** 12-14 servings.

MEATLESS MUFFULETTA

IF YOU PREFER, make Crowd-Pleasin' Muffuletta without meat. Replace the turkey, salami and ham with grilled portobello mushroom caps, fresh tomato slices and spinach leaves. You could also sprinkle some drained and rinsed cannellini beans on top.

Old-Fashioned Potato Salad

I've been making this comforting salad since I was old enough to help Mom in the kitchen.
—*Karen Taylor-Guthrie, Cedar Point, North Carolina*

3 tablespoons sugar
4-1/2 teaspoons all-purpose flour
3 teaspoons salt, *divided*
3/4 cup milk
1 egg, lightly beaten
1/4 cup cider vinegar
1 tablespoon prepared mustard
5 pounds red potatoes
12 hard-cooked eggs
3 cups finely chopped celery
1 medium sweet onion, finely chopped
2 cups mayonnaise
3/4 teaspoon pepper

In a small saucepan, combine the sugar, flour and 1 teaspoon salt. Stir in milk until smooth. Cook and stir over medium-high heat until thickened and bubbly. Reduce heat; cook and stir 2 minutes longer.

Remove from the heat. Stir a small amount of hot mixture into egg; return all to the pan, stirring constantly. Bring to a gentle boil; cook and stir 2 minutes longer. Remove from the heat. Gently stir in vinegar and mustard. Cool without stirring to room temperature.

Cut potatoes into 1/2-in. cubes; place in a large kettle and cover with water. Bring to a boil. Reduce heat; cover and simmer for 8-10 minutes or until tender. Drain; rinse in cold water and drain again.

Set aside one hard-cooked egg for garnish; chop the remaining eggs. In a large bowl, combine the potatoes, chopped eggs, celery and onion. Whisk the mayonnaise, pepper and remaining salt into cooled milk mixture. Pour over potato mixture; toss gently to coat. Cover and refrigerate for at least 2 hours. Garnish with reserved egg. **Yield:** 22 servings.

Southern Barbecued Pork

My dear friend Ruby gave me this authentic recipe when my family lived in North Carolina. Ruby has since passed away and we've moved North, but these zesty sandwiches bring back memories!
—*Sue Alleva, Lake Elmo, Minnesota*

1 boneless pork shoulder roast (3 to 4 pounds), trimmed
1 large onion, chopped
1 cup white vinegar
1/2 cup Worcestershire sauce
1/2 cup ketchup
3 tablespoons brown sugar
3 tablespoons ground mustard
1 teaspoon salt
1/2 teaspoon cayenne pepper
12 kaiser rolls, split
3 cups deli coleslaw, optional

Place the pork roast and onion in a Dutch oven. In a small bowl, whisk the vinegar, Worcestershire sauce, ketchup, brown sugar, mustard, salt and cayenne; pour over roast. Cover and bake at 325° for 3-4 hours or until meat is very tender.

Remove roast; shred meat with two forks. Skim fat from pan juices. Return meat to the pan. Use a slotted spoon to serve on rolls. Top with coleslaw if desired. **Yield:** 12 servings.

Cherry Cream Trifle

(Pictured at right)

Not only is this dessert cool and creamy, it's a conversation piece when presented in a punch bowl!
—Juanita Davis, Martin, Tennessee

1 package (18-1/4 ounces) yellow cake mix
2 packages (3.4 ounces *each*) instant vanilla pudding mix
2 cans (21 ounces *each*) cherry pie filling
2 cans (20 ounces *each*) crushed pineapple, drained
2 cartons (16 ounces *each*) frozen whipped topping, thawed
2 cups chopped pecans

Prepare and bake cake according to package directions for a 13-in. x 9-in. x 2-in. pan. Cool on a wire rack. Prepare pudding according to package directions.

Cut cake into 1-1/2-in. cubes; place a third of the cubes in an 8-qt. punch bowl. Top with a third of the pie filling, pineapple, pudding, whipped topping and pecans; repeat layers twice. Cover and refrigerate until serving. **Yield:** 25-30 servings.

Sweet 'n' Spicy Meatballs

(Pictured on page 205)

You'll usually find a batch of these meatballs in my freezer. The slightly sweet sauce nicely complements the spicy pork sausage.
—Genie Brown, Roanoke, Virginia

2 pounds bulk hot pork sausage
1 egg, lightly beaten
1 cup packed brown sugar
1 cup red wine vinegar
1 cup ketchup
1 tablespoon soy sauce
1 teaspoon ground ginger

In a large bowl, combine the sausage and egg. Shape into 1-in. balls. Place in a greased 15-in. x 10-in. x 1-in. baking pan. Bake at 400° for 15-20 minutes or until meat is no longer pink. Meanwhile, in a saucepan, combine the brown sugar, vinegar, ketchup, soy sauce and ginger. Bring to a boil. Reduce heat; simmer, uncovered, until sugar is dissolved.

Transfer meatballs to a 3-qt. slow cooker. Add the sauce and stir gently to coat. Cover and keep warm on low until serving. **Yield:** about 4 dozen.

Cream-Filled Cake Bars

This recipe has been circulated around our church for years.
Keep a batch in the freezer for a cool summer snack at the ready.
—*Pearl Stuenkel, Spokane Valley, Washington*

1 package (18-1/4 ounces)
  chocolate cake mix
1-1/3 cups water
1/2 cup vegetable oil
3 eggs
FILLING:
5 tablespoons all-purpose flour
1-1/2 cups milk
1 cup shortening
1/2 cup butter, softened
1 cup sugar
1 teaspoon vanilla extract
FROSTING:
1 cup sugar
1 cup packed brown sugar
1/2 cup butter, cubed
1/2 cup milk
1 cup (6 ounces) semisweet
  chocolate chips
1 teaspoon vanilla extract

In a large mixing bowl, combine the cake mix, water, oil and eggs. Pour into two greased 13-in. x 9-in. x 2-in. baking pans. Bake at 350° for 18-20 minutes or until a toothpick inserted near the center comes out clean. Cool on wire racks.

For filling, in a small saucepan, combine flour and milk until smooth. Bring to a boil; cook and stir for 2 minutes or until thickened. Cool. In another mixing bowl, cream the shortening, butter and sugar. Add the cooled milk mixture and vanilla; beat until smooth and fluffy, about 5 minutes. Spread evenly over cakes. Cover and refrigerate for 1 hour.

For frosting, in a large saucepan, combine the sugars, butter and milk. Bring to a boil; cook and stir for 2 minutes or until sugar is dissolved. Remove from the heat. Add chocolate chips and vanilla; stir until chips are melted. Transfer to a large mixing bowl; cool to room temperature. Beat on medium speed until light and fluffy. Spread over filling. Cut into bars. **Yield:** about 3 dozen.

Praline Cereal Crunch

A sweet and salty snack like this is hard to resist. The recipe makes 10 cups,
so it's great to make when hosting a party.
—*Gelene Bolin, Paradise, California*

8 cups Crispix cereal
2 cups pecan halves
1/2 cup packed brown sugar
1/2 cup light corn syrup
1/2 cup butter, cubed
1 teaspoon vanilla extract
1/2 teaspoon baking soda

In a 13-in. x 9-in. x 2-in. baking pan, combine cereal and pecans; set aside. In a microwave-safe bowl, combine the brown sugar, corn syrup and butter. Microwave, uncovered, on high for 2 to 2-1/2 minutes or until mixture comes to a boil, stirring occasionally. Stir in vanilla and baking soda.

Pour over cereal mixture; stir to coat evenly. Bake at 250° for 1 hour, stirring every 20 minutes. Turn onto waxed paper to cool. Break into bite-size pieces. **Yield:** 10 cups.

Artichoke Veggie Pizza

(Pictured at right)

Our Test Kitchen home economists used sun-dried tomato spread as the base for this vegetable-laden appetizer.

1 tube (13.8 ounces) refrigerated pizza crust
1 package (8 ounces) cream cheese, softened
1/2 cup sun-dried tomato spread
1 can (14 ounces) water-packed artichoke hearts, rinsed, drained and finely chopped
1/2 cup chopped sweet onion
1 can (4-1/4 ounces) chopped ripe olives, drained
3/4 cup sliced carrots
3/4 cup chopped green pepper
1-1/2 cups fresh broccoli florets, chopped
1 cup (4 ounces) shredded Italian-blend cheese

Press pizza dough into a greased 15-in. x 10-in. x 1-in. baking pan. Prick dough thoroughly with a fork. Bake at 400° for 13-15 minutes or until golden brown. Cool.

In a small mixing bowl, beat cream cheese and tomato spread until blended. Stir in the artichokes. Spread over crust. Sprinkle with onion, olives, carrots, green pepper, broccoli and cheese; press down lightly. Chill for 1 hour. Cut into squares. Refrigerate leftovers. **Yield:** 3 dozen.

Saucy Baked Beans

My family enjoys these baked beans with corn bread, but they also round out any cookout. Canned pork and beans make preparation easy.
—Phyllis Schmalz, Kansas City, Kansas

2 cans (31 ounces *each*) pork and beans
1-1/2 cups packed brown sugar
1/2 pound sliced bacon, cooked and crumbled
1 cup finely chopped onion
1 cup ketchup
1 cup cola
2 tablespoons ground mustard

In a large bowl, combine all ingredients. Pour into a greased 3-qt. baking dish. Bake, uncovered, at 325° for 1-1/4 hours or until bubbly. **Yield:** 12-15 servings.

Greek Tortellini Salad

A bold homemade dressing gives this pasta salad a burst of flavor. Watch it disappear from your buffet table!
—*Sue Braunschweig, Delafield, Wisconsin*

16 to 18 ounces refrigerated *or*
    frozen cheese tortellini
1 medium sweet red pepper,
    julienned
1 medium green pepper,
    julienned
3/4 cup sliced red onion
1/4 cup sliced ripe olives
1/2 cup olive oil
1/2 cup white wine vinegar
3 tablespoons minced fresh
    mint *or* 1 tablespoon dried
    mint flakes
3 tablespoons lemon juice

1-1/2 teaspoons seasoned salt
1 teaspoon garlic powder
1/2 teaspoon pepper
1/8 to 1/4 teaspoon crushed red pepper flakes
1/2 cup crumbled feta cheese

Cook tortellini according to package directions; drain and rinse in cold water. In a large bowl, combine the tortellini, peppers, onion and olives.

In a jar with a tight-fitting lid, combine the oil, vinegar, mint, lemon juice, seasoned salt, garlic powder, pepper and pepper flakes; shake well. Pour over salad and toss to coat. Cover and refrigerate for at least 4 hours. Just before serving, sprinkle with feta cheese. **Yield:** 10 servings.

GRADE-A GRADUATION PARTY!

Get the Grad's Input. Ask the graduate if he or she would like a big bash with lots of relatives and friends or a more intimate gathering with immediate family.

Pick a Date. With last-minute school events, work schedules and other graduation parties to attend, choosing a date may be your biggest challenge. Consider hosting the party later in the summer when you're less harried and when most other parties have already taken place.

Chose a Setting. Backyards and parks are great places to host a casual graduation party. Make sure to offer enough seating and some shelter from bad weather. (Consider renting tables, chairs and even a tent.) If you'll be going to a restaurant, call for reservations well in advance.

Pick a Theme. Although school colors are a natural choice when decorating for a grad-

uation party, the sky's the limit so get as creative as you desire!

Spotlight the grad with a table filled with memorabilia…awards and honors, prom photos, senior pictures, diploma, mortarboard, pompons, yearbooks, pennants, etc.

Address and Mail Invitations. Most schools offer graduation announcements and invitations, which gives you one less thing to think about. (But again, feel free to be creative!) Send out the invitations about 4 weeks before the party. Include directions or small maps if you're expecting out-of-town guests.

Plan the Menu. When hosting a party for a large group, buffets are the way to go. There's no serving involved, which allows you to mingle while keeping an eye on the table for refills. Look for recipes that can be prepared ahead. Save foods with lots of last-minute preparation for smaller, intimate gatherings.

Graduation Caps

(Pictured at right)

I made these cute treats for my daughter's graduation. They really topped off the party fun!
—Margy Stief, Essington, Pennsylvania

24 miniature peanut butter cups
 1 tube (6 ounces) decorating frosting in color of your choice
24 After Eight thin mints
24 milk chocolate M&M's in color of your choice *or* 24 semisweet chocolate chips

Remove paper liners from peanut butter cups; place upside down on waxed paper. Place a small amount of frosting on each peanut butter cup; center a mint on each. Using frosting, make a loop for the cap's tassel. Place an M&M on top of loop. **Yield:** 2 dozen.

July 4th
Ice Cream Social

IT SEEMS like the heat of summer has a habit of hitting on Independence Day.

So as you celebrate our country's birthday with family and friends, cool things off with a tried-and-true ice cream social.

Why settle for store-bought when you can serve scoops of tasty Strawberry Ice Cream in home-made Ice Cream Bowls?

Kids will create lasting memories when they sip Old-Fashioned Ice Cream Sodas. (And older "kids" will fondly recall days gone by!)

For a terrific do-ahead treat that can be kept in the freezer for a week, rely on Delicious Ice Cream Dessert. (All recipes shown at right.)

ICE CREAM,
YOU SCREAM!
(Clockwise from top right)

**Old-Fashioned
Ice Cream Sodas** (p. 218)

Strawberry Ice Cream (p. 220)
in Ice Cream Bowls (p. 218)

**Delicious Ice Cream
Dessert** (p. 216)

Delicious Ice Cream Dessert

(Pictured on page 214)

We appreciate a cool and creamy dessert like this in summer.
It stays fresh in the freezer for one week. Top with the fudgy sauce before serving.
—*Mrs. Earl Brewer, Jackson, Mississippi*

1 package (12 ounces) vanilla
    wafers, crushed
1/2 cup chopped pecans
3/4 cup butter, melted
1/2 gallon vanilla ice cream (in
    rectangular package)
FUDGE TOPPING:
1 cup sugar
5 tablespoons baking cocoa
3 tablespoons all-purpose flour
1 cup milk
2 tablespoons butter, softened

In a bowl, combine the wafer crumbs, pecans and butter. Press half of the mixture into a 13-in. x 9-in. x 2-in. dish. Freeze for 30 minutes. Remove ice cream from package; cut into slices and place over crust. Sprinkle with remaining crumb mixture. Cover and freeze for at least 4 hours.

For topping, combine the sugar, cocoa and flour in a small saucepan; stir in milk until smooth. Bring to a boil, stirring constantly; cook and stir for 2 minutes. Stir in butter. Serve over dessert. **Yield:** 12-16 servings.

Hot Fudge Topping

(Pictured at right)

I've been making this thick and tasty hot fudge sauce for years.
Use it to top ice cream, cake or any other dessert!
—*Judy Carl, Duluth, Minnesota*

1 package (11-1/2 ounces) milk
    chocolate chips
4 squares (1 ounce *each*)
    unsweetened chocolate
1 cup butter, cubed
2 cans (14 ounces *each*)
    sweetened condensed milk
1/3 cup evaporated milk

In a large saucepan over low heat, combine the chocolate chips, chocolate squares and butter; heat until melted, stirring occasionally. Gradually stir in condensed milk and evaporated milk; heat through. Store leftovers in the refrigerator. **Yield:** 5-1/2 cups.

Mint Chocolate Chip Ice Cream

(Pictured at right)

Our sons enjoy helping me make this rich and creamy ice cream. It's better than any store-bought variety.
—Marcia Peters, Baldwin City, Kansas

2 quarts half-and-half cream
2 cups sugar
1 can (14 ounces) sweetened
   condensed milk
1 pint heavy whipping cream
1 package (3.4 ounces) instant
   vanilla pudding mix
3 tablespoons vanilla extract
1 teaspoon peppermint extract
1-1/2 cups miniature semisweet
   chocolate chips
Green food coloring
Hot Fudge Topping (recipe on
   opposite page), optional

In a large saucepan, heat half-and-half to 175°. Add sugar and milk; stir until sugar is dissolved. Remove from the heat; cool completely.

In a bowl, whisk whipping cream and pudding mix until smooth (mixture will be thick). Add extracts. Stir into cooled cream mixture. Stir in chocolate chips and enough food coloring to tint mixture light green. Cover and refrigerate for at least 30 minutes.

Fill cylinder of ice cream freezer two-thirds full; freeze according to manufacturer's directions. Refrigerate remaining mixture until ready to freeze, stirring before freezing each batch. Allow to ripen in ice cream freezer or firm up in the refrigerator freezer for 2-4 hours before serving. Serve with Hot Fudge Topping if desired. **Yield:** 3 quarts.

Old-Fashioned Ice Cream Sodas

(Pictured on page 215)

I keep the ingredients for these ice cream sodas on hand so I can enjoy a treat any time I want.
You can easily make more when feeding a crowd.
—Anna Erickson, Terrebonne, Oregon

3/4 cup chocolate syrup
1 cup milk
4 cups carbonated water, chilled
8 scoops chocolate *or* vanilla ice cream
Whipped cream in a can, optional

Place 3 tablespoons chocolate syrup in each of four 16-oz. glasses. Add 1/4 cup milk and 1 cup carbonated water to each; stir until foamy. Add two scoops of ice cream to each glass. Top with whipped cream if desired. **Yield:** 4 servings.

Ice Cream Bowls

(Pictured on page 214)

Once you sample these homemade waffle ice cream bowls from our Test Kitchen,
you'll want to serve them time and again! You can either prepare them with pretty designs
in a special pizzelle cookie maker or without designs in the oven.

3 eggs
3/4 cup sugar
1/2 cup butter, melted
2 teaspoons vanilla extract
1-1/2 cups all-purpose flour
2 teaspoons baking powder

In a small mixing bowl, beat eggs on medium speed until blended. Gradually beat in sugar. Add butter and vanilla. Combine flour and baking powder; gradually add to egg mixture. Invert two 6-oz. custard cups on paper towels; coat with nonstick cooking spray.

Prepare cookies in a preheated pizzelle maker according to manufacturer's directions, using 2 tablespoons batter for each cookie. Immediately remove pizzelles and drape over inverted custard cups. To shape into bowls, place another custard cup coated with nonstick cooking spray over each pizzelle. Let stand until set. Remove from custard cups and set aside.

To make ice cream bowls in the oven, line a baking sheet with parchment paper. Draw two 7-in. circles on paper. Spread 2 tablespoons batter over each circle. Bake at 400° for 4-5 minutes or until edges are golden brown. Immediately remove cookies and drape over inverted custard cups. Shape into bowls as directed above. Store in an airtight container. **Yield:** 16 servings.

MAKING ICE CREAM BOWLS

1. Drop 2 tablespoons batter into a hot pizzelle maker; cook until both sides are golden brown. (Follow manufacturer's directions for more details.)

2. Drape hot pizzelle over inverted custard cup; top with another inverted custard cup to form the bowl.

Strawberry Banana Ice Pops

(Pictured at right)

My brothers and sisters (as well as my Dad!) are thrilled when they see me making these ice pops. They can hardly wait for them to set up in the freezer.
—*Valerie Belley, St Louis, Missouri*

1 package (3 ounces) strawberry gelatin
1/2 cup boiling water
1 package (10 ounces) frozen sweetened sliced strawberries, thawed
1 can (8 ounces) crushed pineapple, undrained
1/2 cup mashed ripe banana
1/4 to 1/2 cup chopped walnuts
1 cup (8 ounces) sour cream
1 teaspoon sugar
1/4 teaspoon vanilla extract
12 Popsicle molds *or* plastic cups (3 ounces) and Popsicle sticks

In a large bowl, dissolve gelatin in boiling water. Stir in the strawberries, pineapple, banana and nuts. Pour 2 cups into a 13-in. x 9-in. x 2-in. dish coated with nonstick cooking spray. Refrigerate until set, about 1 hour. Set remaining gelatin mixture aside.

In a small bowl, combine the sour cream, sugar and vanilla. Spread over gelatin. Top with reserved gelatin mixture. Chill for 1 hour. Spoon 1/3 cup into each mold. Freeze until firm, about 5 hours. **Yield:** 1 dozen.

Strawberry Ice Cream

(Pictured on page 214)

Nothing says "Welcome Home" to out-of-town relatives as well as homemade ice cream.
I make this for every family reunion.
—Barbara Sue Jones, Cedar City, Utah

2 cups fresh strawberries,
  crushed
3 cups sugar, *divided*
3 tablespoons all-purpose flour
3 cups half-and-half cream
2 eggs, beaten
3 cups heavy whipping cream
1-1/3 cups orange juice
1/2 cup lemon juice
1 teaspoon vanilla extract

In a small bowl, combine strawberries and 3/4 cup sugar; set aside. In a heavy saucepan, heat the half-and-half to 175°. In a large saucepan, combine the flour and remaining sugar; stir in the half-and-half until smooth.

Whisk a small amount of the hot mixture into eggs. Return all to the pan, whisking constantly. Cook and stir over low heat until mixture reaches at least 160° and coats the back of a metal spoon. Remove from the heat. Cool quickly by placing pan in a bowl of ice water; stir for 2 minutes.

Stir in whipping cream, orange juice, lemon juice, vanilla and reserved strawberry mixture. Press plastic wrap onto surface of custard. Refrigerate for several hours or overnight.

Fill cylinder of ice cream freezer two-thirds full; freeze according to manufacturer's directions. Refrigerate remaining mixture until ready to freeze. Allow to ripen in ice cream freezer or firm up in refrigerator freezer for 2-4 hours before serving. **Yield:** 4-1/2 quarts.

Tropical Sorbet

Every summer when I was young, Mother would serve her special sorbet.
The recipe has been in the family for generations.
—Charlene Jackson, Jackson, Mississippi

1 cup sugar
1 cup boiling water
1-1/2 cups orange juice
1-1/2 cups mashed ripe bananas
  (about 3 medium)
2/3 cup lemon juice
1 can (8 ounces) crushed
  pineapple, undrained

In a heat-proof bowl, dissolve sugar in boiling water; cool completely. Stir in the remaining ingredients. Chill for several hours. Fill cylinder of ice cream freezer; freeze according to manufacturer's directions. Transfer sorbet to a freezer container; cover and freeze for 4 hours or until firm. Remove from the freezer 10 minutes before serving. **Yield:** about 1-1/2 quarts.

Lemon Ice Cream

(Pictured at right)

Just five ingredients (and no ice cream maker!) are all you need to make this refreshing ice cream. We enjoy generous scoops of it in summer.
—Janet Eisner, Portland, Oregon

1 cup milk
1 cup sugar
1/3 cup lemon juice
1 cup heavy whipping cream
1/2 teaspoon vanilla extract

In a small saucepan, heat milk to 175°; stir in sugar until dissolved. Cool completely. Stir in lemon juice. In a large mixing bowl, beat cream until stiff; fold in vanilla and cooled milk mixture. Pour into a 9-in. square dish. Freeze for 4 hours or until firm, stirring at least once. Remove from the freezer 10 minutes before serving. **Yield:** 1 quart.

Very Berry Topping

Frozen berries allow me to prepare this colorful ice cream sauce all year-round. You can also stir in one 20-ounce can of drained pineapple tidbits.
—Sheri Rarick, Galloway, Ohio

1 package (16 ounces) frozen unsweetened blueberries, thawed
1 package (16 ounces) frozen unsweetened strawberries, thawed
1 package (12 ounces) frozen unsweetened raspberries, thawed
2 cups frozen unsweetened blackberries, thawed

3/4 to 1 cup sugar
3 tablespoons cornstarch

In a large bowl, combine the berries; stir in desired amount of sugar. Let stand for 1 hour. Drain and reserve the juice. Return berries to the bowl; cover and refrigerate.

In a saucepan, combine cornstarch and 1/4 cup reserved juice until smooth. Stir in the remaining juice. Bring to a boil; cook and stir for 2 minutes or until thickened. Remove from the heat. Cool to room temperature, stirring several times. Pour over berries and stir gently. **Yield:** about 6 cups.

Chocolate Fudge Bombe

Four convenience items come together in this easy yet eye-catching dessert.
It's a great way to wow guests with little effort.
—Margaret Wilson, Hemet, California

1 package fudge brownie mix
   (13-inch x 9-inch pan size)
1/2 gallon fudge ripple *or* caramel
   swirl ice cream, softened
3/4 cup chocolate frosting
1 jar (12 ounces) seedless
   raspberry jam

Prepare brownie mix for cake-like brownies and bake according to package directions in a greased 13-in. x 9-in. x 2-in. baking pan. Cool completely on a wire rack.

Cut brownies into squares; place on the bottom and up the sides of a 2-1/2-qt. bowl lined with plastic wrap. Spoon ice cream into brownie bowl; cover and freeze for 8 hours or until firm.

Place frosting in a small microwave-safe bowl; cover and microwave on high for 45 seconds or until soft. Invert brownie bombe onto a large plate; spread with frosting. Cut into wedges. Warm the jam; drizzle over dessert plates. Top with a wedge. Serve immediately. **Yield:** 12 servings.

Coffee Ice Cream

My husband doesn't drink coffee, but he can't get enough of this coffee ice cream!
—Esther Bergen, Clarendon Hills, Illinois

4 cups milk
2 cups sugar
3 cups cold strong brewed coffee
1 pint heavy whipping cream
2 teaspoons vanilla extract

In a Dutch oven, heat milk to 175°. Stir in sugar until dissolved; cool. Transfer to a 3-qt. freezer container. Stir in the coffee, cream and vanilla. Cover and freeze for 4-5 hours or until mixture is slushy. Beat with an electric mixer until smooth. Freeze until firm. Remove from the freezer 30 minutes before serving. **Yield:** 12 servings.

SANDWICH YOUR ICE CREAM

HOMEMADE ice cream sandwiches are another fun idea for an ice cream social.

Place 1/2 cup of any flavor ice cream on the flat side of a 3-in. cookie of your choice. Place another cookie, bottom side down, on top of the ice cream. Gently press cookies together until ice cream is even with the edges.

If desired, roll edges of the sandwich in toppings (like miniature chocolate chips, chopped nuts and chocolate jimmies) until covered.

Serve immediately or wrap in plastic wrap and freeze.

Creative Ice Cream Cones

(Pictured above)

EVEN an ice cream social can be made special with just a little extra effort. Your guests will be in their glory when they catch sight of assorted decorated ice cream cones at your July Fourth festivities.

Start by purchasing a variety of waffle, cake and sugar cones. Place toppings in separate small bowls. (We used flaked coconut, chopped nuts, colored sprinkles and chocolate jimmies.)

Melt white and/or milk chocolate candy coating; dip the tops of the cones into the melted chocolate. Roll the chocolate-covered top of each cone into toppings of your choice. Set decorated cones in ice cream cone holders until chocolate is set. (If making these cute cones a few days in advance, store in airtight containers at room temperature, using waxed paper to separate layers.)

Peachy Berry Shakes

I love making smoothies on summer afternoons. This fruity shake is refreshingly cool on sweltering days!
—Adrienne Hollister, Sultan, Washington

1/2 cup milk
3 cups vanilla ice cream
1-1/2 cups fresh *or* frozen sliced
    peeled peaches
1 cup fresh *or* frozen
    unsweetened strawberries
3/4 cup vanilla, peach *or*
    strawberry yogurt

Whipped cream, slivered almonds and whole fresh strawberries

In a blender, combine the milk, ice cream, peaches, strawberries and yogurt; cover and process until smooth. Pour into glasses. Garnish with whipped cream, almonds and strawberries. **Yield:** 4 servings.

Pecan Praline Sauce

As a working mother, I need fast recipes that are guaranteed to satisfy my family.
This nutty ice cream topping is a hit.
—Evelyn Logan, Fresno, California

1/2 cup sugar
1/2 cup packed brown sugar
2 tablespoons all-purpose flour
Dash salt
1 cup water
1/4 cup orange juice
1/2 cup miniature marshmallows
2 tablespoons butter
1 cup chopped pecans, toasted
1 teaspoon vanilla extract

In a large saucepan, combine the sugars, flour, salt, water and orange juice until smooth. Bring to a boil; cook and stir for 2 minutes or until thickened. Stir in the marshmallows and butter; cook and stir until blended. Remove from the heat; stir in pecans and vanilla. Serve warm. **Yield:** 2 cups.

Family Traditions

ON JULY FOURTH, my husband and I invite our four boys and their families home for a big barbecue featuring grilled chicken, fresh watermelon and a variety of picnic foods. After a day of yard games and fun, we scoop out heaping bowls of ice cream. There's nothing better than a relaxing day with good food and family.   *—Bertha Johnson*
Indianapolis, Indiana

Patriotic Sundae Bar

(Pictured above)

SUNDAE BAR fixings make a fun and festive centerpiece on the Fourth of July! For the patriotic presentation shown above, we set red, white and blue bowls on and around an attractive tiered plant stand.

Guests will forever remember this stars-and-stripes celebration when you feature color coordinated items like maraschino cherries, raspberries, blueberries, strawberries and candy-coated chocolate candies.

Don't forget to include such standbys as bananas, nuts, canned whipped cream and hot fudge. If you like, finish off the dynamic display with a daisy-filled vase.

Backyard Hawaiian Luau

IF YOU'RE not planning a trip to Hawaii any time soon, bring the flavors of the Pacific Rim to your own backyard!

It's easy to re-create the lavish luaus in Hawaii with the luscious on-the-deck dinner shown here.

Say "Aloha" to guests as they arrive out back by offering them a tall glass of Luau Refresher.

Grilled Mahi Mahi showcases a fabulous fruit salsa, which is a pleasing complement to the mild fish flavor.

Macadamia Citrus Couscous is a special side dish that can either be served warm or chilled.

A breath-taking bounty of fresh fruit rounds out the delightful dinner.

A Taste of the Tropics
(Top to bottom)

Luau Refresher (p. 229)

Macadamia Citrus Couscous (p. 230)

Grilled Mahi Mahi (p. 228)

Grilled Mahi Mahi

(Pictured on page 226)

*Instead of grilling out the usual hamburgers or chicken breasts,
prepare this mahi mahi from our Test Kitchen and reel in raves!*

3/4 cup reduced-sodium teriyaki
    sauce
2 tablespoons sherry *or*
    pineapple juice
2 garlic cloves, minced
8 mahi mahi fillets (6 ounces
    each)
TROPICAL FRUIT SALSA:
1 medium mango, peeled and
    diced
1 cup diced seeded peeled
    papaya
3/4 cup chopped green pepper
1/2 cup cubed fresh pineapple
1/2 medium red onion, chopped
1/4 cup minced fresh cilantro
1/4 cup minced fresh mint

1 tablespoon chopped seeded jalapeno pepper
1 tablespoon lime juice
1 tablespoon lemon juice
1/2 teaspoon crushed red pepper flakes

In a large resealable plastic bag, combine the teriyaki sauce, sherry or pineapple juice and garlic; add mahi mahi. Seal bag and turn to coat; refrigerate for 30 minutes. In a bowl, combine the salsa ingredients. Cover and refrigerate until serving.

Coat grill rack with nonstick cooking spray before starting the grill. Drain and discard marinade. Grill mahi mahi, covered, over medium heat for 4-5 minutes on each side or until fish flakes easily with a fork. Serve with salsa. **Yield:** 8 servings.

Editor's Note: When cutting or seeding hot peppers, use rubber or plastic gloves to protect your hands. Avoid touching your face.

Frozen Coconut Dessert

A crunchy coconut and macadamia nut garnish pairs well with this cool and creamy dessert.
—Charlotte Mallet-Prevost, Frederick, Maryland

1-1/3 cups water
2/3 cup sugar
2-1/3 cups flaked coconut, *divided*
2 teaspoons vanilla extract
1 pint heavy whipping cream
1/3 cup coarsely chopped
    macadamia nuts

In a large saucepan, bring water and sugar to a boil. Cook, uncovered, for 5 minutes. Cool. Stir in 2 cups coconut and vanilla. In a small mixing bowl, beat cream until soft peaks form; fold into coconut mixture. Pour into serving dishes. Cover and freeze overnight.

Remove from the freezer 45 minutes before serving. Toast the remaining coconut; sprinkle over dessert. Top with macadamia nuts. **Yield:** 8 servings.

Luau Refresher

(Pictured at right and on page 226)

To tie into our tropical feast, our home economists created this recipe featuring passion fruit juice. For the most fizz, stir in the soda just before serving.

4-1/2 cups sweet white wine, chilled
   3 cups passion fruit juice blend, chilled
   3 tablespoons lemon juice
   3 tablespoons lime juice
1-1/2 cups grapefruit soda *or* citrus soda, chilled
Ice cubes

In a 3-qt. pitcher or punch bowl, combine the wine and juices. Stir in soda. Serve over ice. **Yield:** 9 servings.

Cucumber Whimsies

During the heat of summer, it's nice to offer lighter fare. These cold snacks are a great addition to a picnic buffet.
—*Cheryl Stevens, Carrollton, Texas*

   2 cans (6 ounces *each*) crabmeat, drained, flaked and cartilage removed
1/4 cup mayonnaise
   1 small tomato, chopped
   2 tablespoons snipped fresh dill
   1 green onion, chopped
   1 teaspoon grated lemon peel
1/8 teaspoon cayenne pepper
Dash salt

   3 medium cucumbers, cut into 1/4-inch slices
Lemon-pepper seasoning
Dill sprigs

In a bowl, combine the first eight ingredients. Cover and refrigerate for 1 hour. Sprinkle cucumber slices with lemon-pepper. Top each with about 1-1/2 teaspoons crab mixture; garnish with a dill sprig. Refrigerate until serving. **Yield:** 5 dozen.

Macadamia Citrus Couscous

(Pictured on page 226)

Our Test Kitchen provides this tasty twist on couscous salad. It pairs well with many entrees. Or toss in some cooked shrimp for a meal on the lighter side.

1/4 cup chopped sweet onion
1 garlic clove, minced
1 teaspoon olive oil
1 cup chicken broth
1 cup passion fruit juice blend
1/2 cup orange marmalade
1 tablespoon Worcestershire sauce
1 tablespoon minced fresh gingerroot
Dash cayenne pepper
1 package (10 ounces) couscous
1 teaspoon grated orange peel

1/2 cup chopped macadamia nuts
1/2 cup orange-flavored dried cranberries
3 tablespoons minced fresh cilantro
3 green onions, sliced

In a large saucepan, saute onion and garlic in oil for 2 minutes or until tender. Add the broth, fruit juice, marmalade, Worcestershire sauce, ginger and cayenne. Bring to a boil; stir in couscous and orange peel. Cover and remove from the heat; let stand for 10 minutes. Stir in the macadamia nuts, cranberries, cilantro and green onions. Serve warm or chilled. **Yield:** 8 servings.

Papaya-Avocado Tossed Salad

Fruit is a terrific addition to green salads in summer. Here our home economists tossed in papaya and avocado.

4 cups torn red leaf lettuce
4 cups torn green leaf lettuce
1 medium papaya, peeled, seeded and sliced
1 large ripe avocado, peeled and sliced
1/2 cup sliced red onion
DRESSING:
1/4 cup olive oil
3 tablespoons lemon juice
1 tablespoon grated lemon peel
2 teaspoons white wine vinegar
1 teaspoon sugar
1/8 teaspoon salt

In a large salad bowl, gently toss the lettuce, papaya, avocado and onion. In a jar with a tight-fitting lid, combine the dressing ingredients; shake well. Drizzle over salad and toss to coat. **Yield:** 8 servings.

Shrimp on Rosemary Skewers

(Pictured at right)

Fresh sprigs of rosemary are the clever skewers for these shrimp kabobs. You can serve this as an appetizer or as a main course.
—Amber Joy Newport
Hampton, Virginia

8 fresh rosemary sprigs, about 6 inches long
1/2 cup orange marmalade
1/2 cup flaked coconut, chopped
1/4 teaspoon crushed red pepper flakes
1/4 teaspoon minced fresh rosemary
1-1/2 pounds uncooked large shrimp, peeled and deveined

Soak rosemary sprigs in water for 30 minutes. In a small bowl, combine the marmalade, coconut, pepper flakes and minced rosemary; set aside 1/4 cup for serving.

Coat grill rack with nonstick cooking spray before starting the grill. Thread shrimp onto rosemary sprigs. Grill for 4 minutes. Turn; baste with some of the remaining marmalade mixture. Grill 3-4 minutes longer or until shrimp turn pink; baste again. Serve with reserved marmalade mixture. **Yield:** 8 servings.

HISTORY OF THE LUAU

BEFORE 1819, it was a traditional Hawaiian practice for men and women to dine apart from each other. A feast where King Kamahameha II ate with women was the symbolic act ending this custom... and the luau was born.

A favorite dish at these royal feasts was called luau (a combination of leaves of the taro plant and chicken baked in coconut milk).

Mats were rolled out for people to sit on and the food was eaten with the fingers. Breath-taking centerpieces were made with ferns and native flowers.

Pineapple Apricot Bars

A buttery crust holds an apricot and pineapple filling in this dessert. The recipe comes from a cousin.
—Jane Bricker, Scottdale, Pennsylvania

1 can (20 ounces) crushed
  pineapple, undrained
1 cup diced dried apricots
1-1/2 cups sugar, *divided*
3/4 cup butter, softened
2 cups all-purpose flour
1/2 teaspoon baking soda
1/2 teaspoon salt
1-3/4 cups flaked coconut
3/4 cup finely chopped walnuts

In a large saucepan, bring the pineapple and apricots to a boil. Reduce heat; cover and simmer for 20 minutes, stirring occasionally. Stir in 1/2 cup sugar. Simmer, uncovered, for 5 minutes.

Meanwhile, in a large mixing bowl, cream butter and remaining sugar until light and fluffy. Combine the flour, baking soda and salt; gradually add to creamed mixture. Stir in coconut and nuts.

Press 4 cups of the mixture into a greased 13-in. x 9-in. x 2-in. baking pan. Bake at 375° for 10 minutes. Spread hot pineapple mixture over crust; sprinkle with the remaining coconut mixture. Bake 20-25 minutes longer or until lightly browned. Cool on a wire rack. Cut into squares. **Yield:** 2 dozen.

MAKING ORCHID LEIS

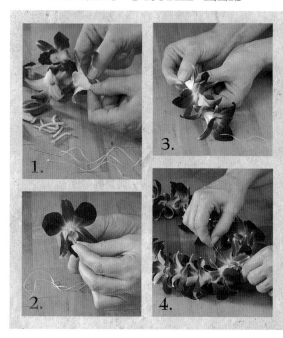

TO MAKE one lei, you'll need about 50 fresh orchids, a piece of dental floss (36 inches long), a long hand-sewing needle and scissors.

1. Thread the dental floss onto the needle; tie a knot on one end. Remove stems from the orchids.

2. Insert the threaded needle into the center of the orchid throat and out the other end.

3. Continue threading orchids onto the floss, gently sliding the orchids down to the knotted end of the floss. "Nest" the orchids so no floss is showing between them.

4. Finish the lei by nesting the first and last orchids together. Tie floss into a square knot. Trim floss close to the knot.

Tropical Turnovers

(Pictured at right)

Friends and family won't be able to stop nibbling on these tasty turnovers. Our home economists tuck a fruity filling inside tender pastry pockets.

2 cups all-purpose flour
1/4 teaspoon baking powder
1/4 teaspoon salt
5 ounces cold cream cheese, cut into small pieces
3/4 cup cold butter, cut into small pieces
3 tablespoons cold water
FILLING:
1-1/4 cups finely chopped peeled mangoes
1/2 cup guava jelly
1 tablespoon chopped fresh mint
1/2 teaspoon grated lemon peel
1 egg, lightly beaten
2 teaspoons water
2 teaspoons sugar

In a bowl, combine the flour, baking powder and salt; cut in cream cheese and butter until crumbly. Gradually add water, tossing with a fork until dough is moistened. Knead in bowl until a ball forms; flatten into a disk. Wrap in plastic wrap; refrigerate for at least 1 hour or until easy to handle.

In a bowl, combine the mangoes, jelly, mint and lemon peel; set aside. In a small bowl, whisk egg and water. On a floured surface, roll out dough to 1/8-in. thickness; cut into 4-in. circles. Spoon 2 teaspoons mango mixture into the center of each circle. Brush edges with water; fold dough over filling and seal with a fork. Brush with egg mixture; sprinkle with sugar.

Place on foil-lined baking sheets. Bake at 375° for 20-23 minutes or until golden brown. Remove to wire racks to cool. **Yield:** 2 dozen.

Dicing a Mango

MANGOES have a large flat seed that doesn't easily separate from the flesh. So the flesh needs to be cut away from the seed.

1. Slice off one of the wide sides of the mango, cutting as close as possible to the seed. Repeat on the other wide side, then slice off the other two ends.

2. Being careful not to cut through the skin, score the flesh in one direction. Then make perpendicular scores in the opposite direction.

3. With your fingers, push up on the skin so that the mango turns inside out. Slice the diced flesh off of the skin. (A small spoon can also be used to remove the flesh.)

Cutting Up a Fresh Pineapple

IF YOU FAVOR the flavor of fresh pineapple but aren't sure how to cut one up, follow these easy steps!

1. Cut off the top; trim the bottom so the pineapple stands upright. Starting at the top and working down, cut off wide strips of peel all the way around the fruit.

2. Lay the pineapple on its side. Remove the eyes by cutting narrow wedge-shaped grooves diagonally around the fruit, following the pattern of the eyes.

3. Stand the pineapple upright. Starting at the top and working down, slice off one side of the pineapple, cutting as close to the core as possible. Repeat on the remaining three sides. Cut flesh into slices or chunks.

Fruit Platter Centerpiece

(Pictured at right)

FOR A NATURAL centerpiece at your Hawaiian luau, set out a tray topped with a bounty of fresh fruits!

For the photo at right, we included family favorites such as apples, oranges, kiwi, star fruit and cantaloupe. Don't forget tropical favorites like mango, passion fruit and pineapple. (See the hints at left for cutting up mango and pineapple.) You may also want to tuck in bunches of red grapes for a burst of contrasting color.

Instead of tossing out the top of the pineapple, we placed it in the center of our platter, then tucked in fresh edible orchids. (You can also use the orchids to make a lei. See page 232 for instructions.)

Rosemary Pineapple Chicken

I brought this recipe with me from Germany. It's my family's favorite way to eat chicken.
—*Christl Haymond, Duvall, Washington*

4 bone-in chicken breast halves (8 ounces *each*)
1 tablespoon butter
1 teaspoon salt
1/2 teaspoon minced fresh rosemary
1/2 teaspoon ground ginger
1/2 teaspoon paprika
1/4 teaspoon pepper
1 medium onion, thinly sliced and separated into rings
2 cans (6 ounces *each*) unsweetened pineapple juice

In a large skillet, brown chicken in butter on both sides. Sprinkle with salt, rosemary, ginger, paprika and pepper. Transfer to a greased 13-in. x 9-in. x 2-in. baking dish. Place onion rings over chicken; pour pineapple juice over chicken. Bake, uncovered, at 350° for 45-55 minutes or until chicken juices run clear. **Yield:** 4 servings.

Eerie Halloween Evening

SCARE UP your favorite ghouls and goblins on October 31 for a haunting Halloween filled with frighteningly good food and fun!

Get the party jumping with Witch's Caviar appetizer and bubbling Magic Potion Punch.

Then bewitch hungry guests by laying Yummy Mummy Calzones upon your spine-tingling table.

You can fill these tasty Italian-inspired turnovers with any of your favorite pizza toppings.

Licorice Caramels shaped like tombstones are a spooky sweet sure to invoke the Halloween spirit in everyone.

Or put a spin on standard sugar cookies and serve Spiderweb Cookies! (Recipes shown at right.)

Yummy Mummy Calzones

(Pictured on page 236)

Family-favorite pizza toppings are the not-so-spooky surprise inside these clever calzones from our Test Kitchen. If you serve these on wood "coffins" like we did in the photo on page 236, be sure to line the surface with plastic wrap or waxed paper.

2 loaves (1 pound *each*) frozen bread dough, thawed
1-1/2 cups (6 ounces) shredded mozzarella cheese
1/2 cup pizza sauce
50 pepperoni slices
1/2 cup chopped green pepper
1 egg, beaten
2 ripe olive slices, cut in half

Roll out each piece of dough into a rounded triangle shape, about 14 in. long and 11 in. wide at the base of the triangle. Place each on a parchment-lined baking sheet with the tip of the triangle toward you. Lightly score a 4-in.-wide rectangle in the center of the triangle 2 in. from the top and bottom. On each long side, cut 1-in.-wide strips at an angle up to the score line, leaving a triangle in the top center of the wide end for the head.

Inside the scored rectangle in the center, layer cheese, pizza sauce, pepperoni and green pepper. Shape the top center triangle into a head. Starting at the head, fold alternating strips of dough at an angle across filling, stopping at the last strip on each side. Fold the bottom dough tip up over the filling, then fold the remaining two strips over the top; press down firmly.

Brush dough with egg. Cover and let rise for 15 minutes. For eyes, press olive pieces into head. Bake at 350° for 25-28 minutes or until golden brown. Let stand for 5 minutes before slicing. **Yield:** 8-10 servings.

MAKING YUMMY MUMMY CALZONES

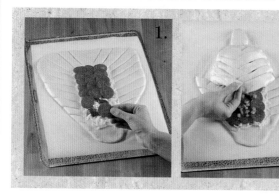

1. Form the bread dough into a rounded triangle shape and score a 4-in.-wide rectangle in the center. On each long side, cut 1-in.-wide strips at an angle up to the score line. Layer toppings in the rectangle.

2. Starting at the wide end, fold alternating strips of dough at an angle across the filling, leaving one strip on the bottom of each side. Continue with the recipe as directed.

Spiderweb Cookies

(Pictured at right and on page 236)

A clever design puts a new spin on standard sugar cookies in this recipe from our Test Kitchen.

1 cup butter, softened
1 cup confectioners' sugar
1 egg
1 tablespoon grated orange peel
2-1/4 cups all-purpose flour
Clear edible glitter
1/4 cup milk chocolate chips, melted
Brown and green milk chocolate M&M's
Orange nonpareils

In a large mixing bowl, cream butter and confectioners' sugar. Beat in egg and orange peel. Gradually add flour; mix well. Transfer dough to a pastry bag fitted with a large round pastry tip. Pipe spiderwebs (about 4 in. high x 4 in. wide) onto foil-lined baking sheets. With a pastry brush, gently brush each web with water. Lightly sprinkle with edible glitter. Bake at 375° for 8-10 minutes or until set but not browned. Cool for 1 minute before removing from pans to wire racks to cool completely.

Fill a small resealable plastic bag with melted chocolate; cut a small hole in a corner of bag. For spiders, attach two or three M&M's on each web with melted chocolate; pipe eight spider legs around each. For spider eyes, attach nonpareils with melted chocolate. **Yield:** 1-1/2 dozen.

Witch's Caviar

(Pictured on page 237)

I like to serve this dip with triangle-shaped tortillas because they look like pointy witch hats.
— Darlene Brenden, Salem, Oregon

2 cans (4-1/4 ounces *each*) chopped ripe olives, undrained
2 cans (4 ounces *each*) chopped green chilies, undrained
2 medium tomatoes, seeded and chopped
3 green onions, chopped
2 garlic cloves, minced
1 tablespoon red wine vinegar
1 tablespoon olive oil
1/2 teaspoon pepper
Dash seasoned salt
Tortilla chips

In a bowl, combine the first nine ingredients. Cover and refrigerate overnight. Serve with tortilla chips. **Yield:** 4 cups.

Magic Potion Punch

(Pictured on page 236)

At a Halloween party, the more creepy the food, the better!
I like to tuck gummy worms into an ice ring when I make this great green punch.
—*Michelle Thomas, Bangor, Maine*

2 packages (3 ounces *each*) lime
   gelatin
1/2 cup sugar
1 cup boiling water
3 cups cold water
1 quart noncarbonated
   lemon-lime drink, chilled
1-1/2 quarts lemon-lime soda,
   chilled

Dissolve gelatin and sugar in boiling
water; add cold water. Transfer to a
punch bowl. Stir in lemon-lime drink
and soda. **Yield:** about 4 quarts.

GUMMY WORM ICE RING

TO KEEP Magic Potion Punch cold during your party, chill it with a gummy worm ice ring. Here's how:
   Fill a ring mold halfway with water. Freeze until solid. Top with gummy worms; add enough water to almost cover. Freeze until solid.
   To unmold, wrap the bottom of the ring with a hot, damp dishcloth. Turn out onto a baking sheet; place in a punch bowl.

Evil Eye Truffles

A few years ago, I hosted a Halloween bash with a variety of foods.
These were a fun addition to the table and so tasty!
—*Linda Fete, Massillon, Ohio*

1 cup chunky peanut butter
1/4 cup butter, softened
2 cups crisp rice cereal
1 cup confectioners' sugar
12 ounces white candy coating
2 tablespoons shortening
36 green *and/or* blue milk
   chocolate M&M's
1 tube red decorator icing
1 tube black decorator icing

In a large bowl, combine peanut butter and butter. Stir in cereal and confectioners' sugar until well combined. With buttered hands, form into 1-in. balls. In a microwave, melt candy coating and shortening until smooth. Dip balls into coating; allow excess to drip off. Place on a waxed paper-lined baking sheet. Before coating is cool, press an M&M into the center of each ball. Cool completely.
   Using a small round pastry tip and red icing, pipe small wavy lines on the sides of balls to resemble bloodshot eyes. Use black icing frosting and a small round pastry tip to add a dot in the center of M&M for pupil. **Yield:** 3 dozen.

Ghoulish Fingers

(Pictured at right)

We serve this fun finger food at our annual Halloween party alongside sandwich rolls and condiments.
—Marilee Davieau
Allentown, Pennsylvania

3 packages (8 ounces *each*) assorted lunch meat
1 package (3 ounces) cream cheese, softened
12 grape tomatoes, halved lengthwise

Roll up each slice of lunch meat; spread a small amount of cream cheese at seam to secure roll. Insert a tomato half at one end of each roll to resemble a fingernail; secure tomato in place with a small amount of cream cheese. Place seam side down on a platter. Cover and refrigerate until serving. **Yield:** 2 dozen.

Harvest Snack Mix

Candy corn makes this a natural snack for fall gatherings. The sweet and salty flavors are irresistible.
—Marlene Harguth, Maynard, Minnesota

2 cups pretzel sticks
1 cup mixed nuts
1/2 cup sunflower kernels
6 tablespoons butter, melted
1/2 teaspoon ground cinnamon
1/8 teaspoon ground cloves
8 cups popped popcorn
1 cup candy corn
1 cup chocolate bridge mix

In a large bowl, combine the pretzels, nuts and sunflower kernels. Combine the butter, cinnamon and cloves. Drizzle a third of butter mixture over pretzel mixture; toss to coat. Transfer to a greased 15-in. x 10-in. x 1-in. baking pan. Bake at 300° for 15 minutes.

Place popcorn in a large bowl; drizzle with remaining butter mixture and toss to coat. Stir into pretzel mixture. Bake 15 minutes longer or until heated through. Cool; transfer to a large bowl. Add candy corn and bridge mix; toss to combine. **Yield:** 3 quarts.

Licorice Caramels

(Pictured on page 237)

Fans of black licorice won't be able to stop eating these gooey caramels.
I appreciate their ease of preparation.
— Donna Higbee, Riverton, Utah

1 teaspoon plus 1 cup butter,
    divided
2 cups sugar
1-1/2 cups light corn syrup
1 can (14 ounces) sweetened
    condensed milk
1/2 teaspoon salt
2 teaspoons anise extract
1/4 teaspoon black food coloring

Line an 8-in. square pan with heavy-duty foil and grease the foil with 1 teaspoon butter; set aside. In a heavy saucepan, combine the sugar, corn syrup, milk, salt and remaining butter; bring to a boil over medium heat. Cook and stir until a candy thermometer reads 244° (firm-ball stage).

Remove from the heat; stir in extract and food coloring (keep face away from mixture as odor is very strong). Pour into prepared pan (do not scrape saucepan). Cool completely before cutting. Using foil, lift candy out of pan. Discard foil; cut into 1-in.-wide rectangles. Using finger, round tops of caramels, forming tombstones. Wrap each in waxed paper. **Yield:** about 5 dozen.

Editor's Note: We recommend that you test your candy thermometer before each use by bringing water to a boil; the thermometer should read 212°. Adjust your recipe temperature up or down based on your test.

Creepy Spiders

Cake mix gives these chocolate sandwich cookies a head start.
You can even have kids help assemble the "spiders!"
— Nella Parker, Hersey, Michigan

1 package (18-1/4 ounces)
    chocolate fudge cake mix
1/2 cup butter, melted
1 egg
1 can (16 ounces) chocolate
    frosting
Black shoestring licorice, cut
    into 1-1/2 inch pieces
1/4 cup red-hot candies

In a large mixing bowl, combine the cake mix, butter and egg (dough will be stiff). Shape into 1-in. balls. Place 2 in. apart on ungreased baking sheets. Bake at 350° for 10-12 minutes or until set. Cool for 1 minute before removing from pans to wire racks.

Spread a heaping teaspoonful of frosting over the bottom of half of the cookies. Place four licorice pieces on each side of cookies for spider legs; top with remaining cookies. For eyes, attach two red-hot candies with frosting to top edge of spider. **Yield:** about 2 dozen.

Goblin Eyeballs

(Pictured at right)

Our home economists had great vision when creating these devilish deviled eggs. Guests at your Halloween party will be "goblin" them up!

12 eggs
Red food coloring
3/4 cup mayonnaise
1 tablespoon prepared mustard
Salt and pepper to taste
12 large stuffed olives, halved widthwise

Place eggs in a single layer in a large saucepan; add enough cold water to cover eggs by 1 in. Bring to a boil over high heat. Reduce heat; cover and simmer for 15 minutes. Drain; let stand until cool enough to handle. Gently crack eggs (do not peel).

Fill a large bowl with hot water; add food coloring to tint water a dark red. Add eggs, making sure they are completely covered by water; let stand for 30 minutes. Remove eggs from water; peel (eggs should have a veined appearance).

Cut eggs in half widthwise; place yolks in a bowl. Set whites aside. Mash yolks with a fork; stir in the mayonnaise, mustard, salt and pepper. To make eggs stand better on serving plate, slice a small piece from the bottom of egg white halves. Stuff with yolk mixture. Place an olive half in the center of each to resemble an eyeball. Refrigerate until serving. **Yield:** 2 dozen.

Carnival Caramel Apples

With four kids (one child whose birthday is November 1), we celebrate Halloween in style around our house. These caramel apples are a tried-and-true favorite year after year.
—Gail Prather, Bethel, Minnesota

1/2 cup butter
2 cups packed brown sugar
1 cup corn syrup
Dash salt
1 can (14 ounces) sweetened condensed milk
1 teaspoon vanilla extract
10 to 12 Popsicle sticks
10 to 12 medium tart apples, washed and dried
1 cup salted peanuts, chopped

In a large heavy saucepan, melt butter; add the brown sugar, corn syrup and salt. Cook and stir over medium heat until mixture comes to a boil, about 10-12 minutes. Stir in milk. Cook and stir until a candy thermometer reads 248° (firm-ball stage). Remove from the heat; stir in vanilla.

Insert Popsicle sticks into apples. Dip each apple into hot caramel mixture; turn to coat. Dip end of apples into peanuts. Set on buttered waxed paper to cool. **Yield:** 10-12 apples.

Editor's Note: We recommend that you test your candy thermometer before each use by bringing water to a boil; the thermometer should read 212°. Adjust your recipe temperature up or down based on your test.

Spiderweb Dip with Bat Tortilla Chips

Every year, our daughter and her friends anticipate our annual Halloween party. Among the menu items is this taco dip with bat-shaped tortilla chips.
—Sonia Candler, Edmonton, Alberta

20 chipotle chili and pepper tortillas *or* flour tortillas (7 inches)
3/4 teaspoon garlic salt
3/4 teaspoon ground coriander
3/4 teaspoon paprika
1/4 teaspoon plus 1/8 teaspoon pepper
DIP:
1 package (8 ounces) cream cheese, softened
3/4 cup salsa

1/2 cup prepared guacamole
1 to 2 tablespoons sour cream

Cut tortillas into bat shapes with a 3-3/4-in. cookie cutter. Place tortillas on baking sheets coated with nonstick cooking spray. Spritz tortillas with nonstick cooking spray. Combine the garlic salt, coriander, paprika and pepper; sprinkle over tortillas. Bake at 350° for 5-8 minutes or until edges just begin to brown.

In a small mixing bowl, combine cream cheese and salsa. Spread into a 9-in. pie plate. Carefully spread guacamole to within 1 in. of edges. Place sour cream in a small resealable plastic bag; cut a small hole in a corner of bag. Pipe thin concentric circles an inch apart over guacamole. Beginning with the center circle, gently pull a knife through circles toward outer edge. Wipe knife clean. Repeat to complete spiderweb pattern. Serve with tortilla bats. **Yield:** about 1-1/2 cups dip and about 7 dozen chips.

Pumpkin Mummies

(Pictured at right)

FOR a mummy-themed Halloween party, ordinary jack-'o-lanterns just won't do. Instead, carve out a niche for yourself by making these frightful Pumpkin Mummies!

Purchase white pumpkins in a variety of shapes and sizes. Carefully cut a circle around the pumpkin stem, lift off the lid and remove the seeds from the lid and inside the pumpkin.

With a knife, cut two narrow horizontal openings for the eyes, one opening for the nose and one opening for the mouth. Score the outside of the pumpkin to look like wrappings of a mummy. Set a black marble in each eye opening. Set a tea light candle inside the pumpkin and light.

GAUZE-COVERED PUMPKIN MUMMY

PUMPKIN MUMMIES will make a memorable impression on the guests at your ghoulish gathering. For even more fun, wrap self-adhesive athletic wrap or self-sticking first aid gauze around the outside of the pumpkin, allowing the black marble "eyes" to peek out.

REFERENCE INDEX

*Use this index as a guide to the many helpful hints, food facts, decorating ideas
and step-by-step instructions throughout the book.*

GENERAL RECIPE INDEX

This handy index lists every recipe by food category, major ingredient and/or cooking method.

ALPHABETICAL INDEX

Refer to this index for a complete alphabetical listing of all recipes in this book.

Here's *Your* Chance To Be Published!

Send us your special-occasion recipes and you could have them featured in a future edition of this classic cookbook.

YEAR AFTER YEAR, the recipe for success at every holiday party or special-occasion celebration is an attractive assortment of flavorful food.

So we're always on the lookout for mouth-watering appetizers, entrees, side dishes, breads, desserts and more…all geared toward the special gatherings you attend or host throughout the year.

Here's how you can enter your family-favorite holiday fare for possible publication in a future *Holiday & Celebrations Cookbook*:

Print or type each recipe on one sheet of 8-1/2" x 11" paper. Please include your name, address and daytime phone number on each page. Be specific with directions, measurements and the sizes of cans, packages and pans.

Please include a few words about yourself, when you serve your dish, reactions it has received from family and friends and the origin of the recipe.

Send to "Celebrations Cookbook", 5925 Country Lane, Greendale WI 53129 or E-mail to *recipes@reimanpub.com*. Write "Celebrations Cookbook" on the subject line of all E-mail entries and *include your full name, postal address and phone number on each entry.*

Contributors whose recipes are printed will receive a complimentary copy of the book…so the more recipes you send, the better your chances of "being published"!